Sailing the Graveyard Sea

The Deathly Voyage of the *Somers*,
the U.S. Navy's Only Mutiny,
and the Trial That Gripped the Nation

Richard Snow

SCRIBNER   New York   London   Toronto   Sydney   New Delhi

For Caroline McCagg Kelly, distinguished physician, amazing chef, and the world's best stepsister

Have a care, then, have a care, lest you come to a sad end, even the end of a rope; lest, with a black-and-blue throat, you turn a dumb diver after pearl-shells; put to bed forever, and tucked in, in your own hammock, at the bottom of the sea. And there you will lie, White-Jacket, while hostile navies are playing cannon-ball billiards over your grave.

—Herman Melville

Contents

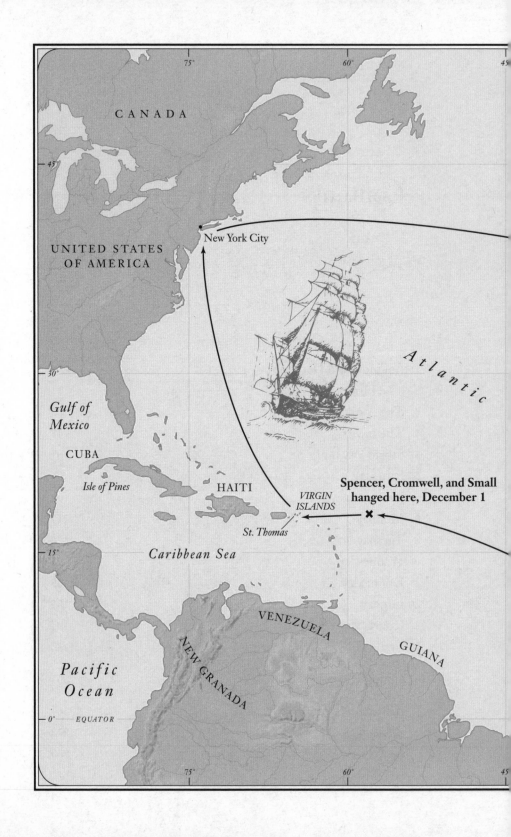

CANADA

UNITED STATES
OF AMERICA

New York City

Gulf of
Mexico

CUBA

Isle of Pines

HAITI

VIRGIN
ISLANDS

St. Thomas

Caribbean Sea

Pacific
Ocean

EQUATOR

NEW GRANADA

VENEZUELA

GUIANA

Atlantic

**Spencer, Cromwell, and Small
hanged here, December 1**

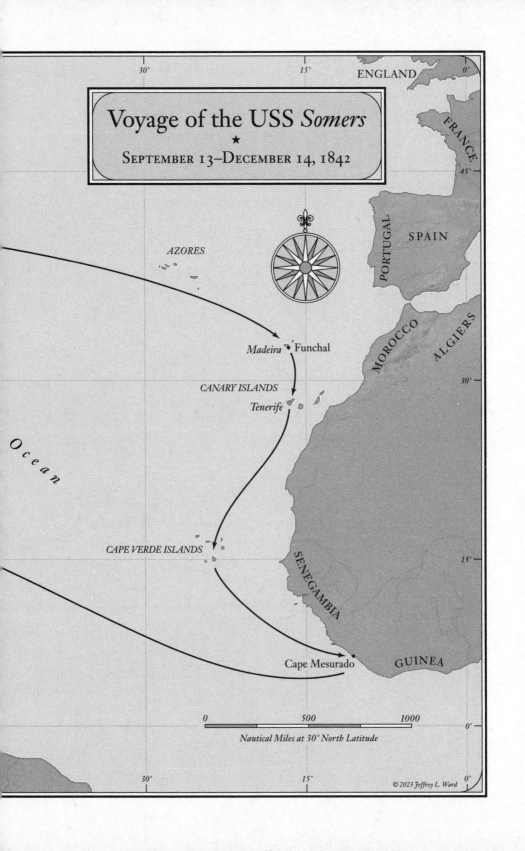

Voyage of the USS *Somers*
★
September 13–December 14, 1842

ENGLAND

FRANCE

SPAIN

PORTUGAL

MOROCCO

ALGIERS

AZORES

Madeira • Funchal

CANARY ISLANDS

Tenerife

CAPE VERDE ISLANDS

SENEGAMBIA

Cape Mesurado

GUINEA

Ocean

30°

15°

0°

45°

30°

15°

0°

30°

15°

0°

0   500   1000

Nautical Miles at 30° North Latitude

© 2023 Jeffrey L. Ward

Sailing the Graveyard Sea

1   **Boldness and Decision**

On the evening of December 14, 1842, the United States brig-of-war *Somers* sailed through the Narrows of New York Harbor. A maritime onlooker familiar with the traffic in that busiest of waterways could have sensed something unusual, even furtive, about the ship's maneuverings once she reached the Upper Bay. The brig nosed toward a fold of land far from the main anchorages and, once there, lowered a boat with a single cloaked passenger. The oarsmen rowed him to the Jersey shore, where he clambered out and disappeared into the underbrush. The boat returned to the brig, which stayed in its secluded haven for two days before setting sail to move eastward, passing more and more shipping before she dropped her hook at the Brooklyn Navy Yard.

Here the *Somers* would have attracted the attention she seemed to be avoiding, for she was a new ship, and an uncommonly handsome one—something of a thoroughbred, low and slim, with her two tall masts raked steeply aft and her bowsprit raised skyward like a poised rapier. Seeing the *Somers* among her fellow warships, a viewer from our time might have been reminded of a Ferrari parked near some Chevrolet Suburbans.

Now her captain finally came ashore to report on his newly completed cruise. Commander Alexander Slidell Mackenzie brought startling news. He had—barely—prevented a mutiny. Had it gone according to plan, he, much of his crew, and all but one of his officers would have been murdered. This would have been a bloody business: the *Somers* had aboard 120 men. Eleven of the thwarted mutineers were being held under guard as prisoners. Three had been hanged: Boatswain's Mate Samuel Cromwell, Seaman Elisha Small, and the plot's instigator, Acting Midshipman Philip Spencer. Only swift, strong, necessary action had prevented the *Somers* from becoming a pirate ship cruising the Spanish Main in the wake of the gaudy brutalities that had made its predecessors infamous two centuries earlier.

For that had been the mutineers' goal. The *New York Express* told how nearly the ship escaped disaster:

> The story we learn is, that young Spencer offered his paper or role of the conspirators to the master-at-arms to sign, who signed it, to quiet their suspicions, then immediately revealed the facts to the Commander. The moment the conspirators found out they were discovered, they met in a body, and went to the commander demanding possession of the ship, and young Spencer presented a pistol to his heart. All this was at night, and the chief part of the crew were below, when the officers on deck not knowing the extent of the conspiracy, immediately closed the hatches, and kept all confined who were below. The officers, after something of a struggle, as we understand, overpowered the conspirators, and regaining complete possession of the ship, instantly caused the ringleaders to be tried by Court Martial, and young Spencer, within ten minutes of the finding of the Court, was hung by the yard-arm, along with two of the men.

The news quickly percolated through the city. To the New York of the 1840s, a town whose life was maritime trade, pirates were far from the merry rascals one can visit today in a Disney park. Their great era had passed, but that the memory of their savagery had not faded is reflected in what the ever-excitable Horace Greeley wrote in his *New-York Tribune*:

> By the prompt and fearless decision of Captain Mackenzie, one of the most bold and daring conspiracies ever formed was frustrated and crushed. . . . The *Somers* is the swiftest vessel in the service, was fully equipped and capable of the greatest efficacy in any belligerent cause.
>
> Suppose this vessel had been converted into a Pirate Ship, sailing under the black flag which denounces [*sic*] war and death to the whole world, under the command of as desperate and determined a ruffian as Spencer and acting in conjunction with confederates of a similar character.
>
> Who can tell how many of our packet ships [which offered regular service carrying passengers and what were then called "mail packets"], would have fallen victim to her prowess—how many hundreds of worthy men would have been murdered in cold blood—how many women would have been devoted to a fate infinitely more horrible than the most cruel death that the hellish ingenuity of devils could devise?

But the seaborne world had been spared this scourge by the bravery of Mackenzie, who, the *New York Herald* said, had acted with "a boldness and decision" that "can only be paralleled . . . in the early history of the Roman Republic." The *Herald*'s rival *Courier and Enquirer* agreed: "Sufficient is known already to establish beyond a question the necessity, imperative and immediate, however dreadful, of the course pursued by commander Mackenzie, than whom, a more humane, conscientious and gallant officer does not hold a commission in the navy of the United States."

Such was the tenor of all the accounts until, on December 20, the Washington, DC, *Madisonian*—the "official organ" of President John Tyler's administration—published a letter, signed only "S," from someone who seemed to have learned a surprising amount about the affair.

"The friends of young Spencer," it begins, "who was executed, on the 1st inst. [an abbreviation of the Latin *instante mense*, "in the present month"] would have been content to abide the investigation which the laws of the country require in such cases. . . ." But many of the statements attributed to the officers of the *Somers* had been "so perverted, so exaggerated, and interspersed with so much surmise, and so much downright falsehood . . . that it is deemed an act of simple and bare justice to the memory of *the slain*, to say that an examination of the papers transmitted by Com. Mackenzie shows these facts."

How could this "S" have examined Mackenzie's account, which would not be made public for many days yet? The writer doesn't say; but here are the facts presented:

> *1st.* That acting midshipman Spencer was put in double irons on the 26th of November, and the boatswain's mate Samuel Cromwell, and seaman Elisha Small, on the day following, on a charge of intended mutiny.

> *2d.* That no disorder of a mutinous character appeared among the crew for the four succeeding days; that the vessel was going with good breezes in good weather towards the island of St. Thomas, where she actually arrived and took in supplies on some day between the 1st and 5th of December.

> *3d.* That on the 30th of November, the opinion of the officers was required by commander Mackenzie as to the disposition of the

prisoners; that they appear to have examined thirteen seamen as witnesses to prove the alleged mutiny . . . which examination was had, so far as the papers show, in the absence of the prisoners, and without giving them any opportunity to cross-examine the witness or to make any explanation or defence, or to procure any testimony on their own behalf. These officers, without even the form of a court, without even the obligation of an oath and upon this ex parte [in the interests of one side only] secret information, united in the opinion that the safety of the vessel required that the prisoners should be put to death! How far this recommendation was influenced by the acts or fears of Mr. Mackenzie does not appear.

4th. That on the 1st of December, when every thing and person on board the vessel were perfectly quiet, after four days of entire security, the three persons were, by order of Mackenzie, hung at the yard arm at mid-day.

The allegation, in some of the papers, that it was proved to have been the intention of the mutineers to execute their project on arriving at St. Thomas, is wholly destitute of any evidence. And had it been their design, it was effectually frustrated so far as these prisoners were concerned, by their confinement. At St. Thomas, any of the crew might have been left, and the power of the officers of the vessel strengthened to any extent that was necessary. . . .

The idea of the mutineers cruising off Sandy Hook to intercept the packets seems to have been thrown in for the special benefit of the merchants of New York.

The letter continued, a straightforward, rational argument by a concerned citizen—most likely a lawyer—with little in it to suggest that the correspondent had any personal connection with the ugly incident. Save for one sad hint: of Philip Spencer, the writer says,

"His age is represented in the same paper to have been over twenty. Had he lived, he would have been nineteen the 28th of January next."

And then that cryptic signature: "S."

PHILIP HONE UNDERSTOOD at once who "S" was.

Hone knew—and the nation was still small enough in 1842 for the statement not to sound absurd—everyone in public life. He himself had been briefly in it. Born the son of a German immigrant who found work in Manhattan as a carpenter, he and his brother ran an auction business so successfully that he was able to retire at the age of forty and devote the rest of his life to touring Europe and collecting books. In 1826, he became the mayor of New York, but, being a conservative Whig in the restless dawn of Jacksonian democracy, was able to serve for only a single year. (Speaking of Jackson, Hone voiced a plaint that we have heard in many eras, including our own: "That such a man should have governed this great country . . . and that the people should not only have submitted to it, but upheld and supported him in his encroachments upon their rights, and his disregard of the Constitution and the laws, will equally occasion the surprise and indignation of future generations.")

Hone's abrupt retirement from public life turned out to enrich his city more than many New York mayors have. Continuing to move in political circles as he became a genial force in social ones, he began recording his full days in a diary that he kept up until his death in 1851. Lively, trenchant, and still enjoyable, it is the single richest individual chronicle of Manhattan life in the first half of the nineteenth century.

On December 17 he had reported of the hangings, "The imminent danger of the captain and lieutenant with so large a portion of the crew in a state of insubordination, no doubt rendered this dreadful and summary exercise of power unavoidable, as an example and measure of safety. If it should so appear (as there seems to be no doubt), public opinion will support, and the government will approve, the conduct of Captain McKenzie. . . . Young Spencer was a worthless fellow."

Then, four days later, Hone read the letter signed "S" and immediately recognized its author. He was John Canfield Spencer, President Tyler's secretary of war. Midshipman Philip Spencer was his dead son.

No chance now that what had happened aboard the *Somers* would remain a simple tale of anti-piratical valor. Spencer's letter, said Hone, "will occasion some revulsion in the public mind in relation to the melancholy tragedy on board the brig 'Somers,'" as it is "one of those strong, forcible documents for which he is celebrated; fierce in style, rigid in argument, and certainly presents the subject of his son's execution in a light somewhat different from that in which it was received at first. If there exists any reasonable doubt of the absolute necessity for this exercise of power, Capt. Mackenzie may wish sincerely that he had not been born to meet such a responsibility.

"A more dangerous opponent than John C. Spencer could not be found in the United States; stern, uncompromising, obstinate in temper, determined and energetic in action, and with talents equal to any effort which his feelings may prompt, or his duty call him to execute." Hone was quite right. Cold and rebarbative though Spencer might be—the secretary spent a desolate Christmas in the company only of his grief-prostrated wife and a single friend—he was formidably capable, and a ruthless adversary.

Once published in New York, his letter broke open a far more complex story than Mackenzie had first offered. Lacking an alternative narrative, the newspapers had had no choice but to follow Greeley's lead and compete to dispense the most fulsome praise for Mackenzie's gallantry. But now that their editors had a meaty controversy to quarrel about, the national press piled on what seagirt New Yorkers saw as a local matter; it became the biggest scandal to captivate the city since the murder of a prostitute named Helen Jewett six years earlier.

James Gordon Bennett, owner of Greeley's chief competitor, the *Herald*, wrote, "Captain Mackenzie and his officers acted at the time under a species of insanity, produced by panic, lively imagination and the spirit of the age [Jacksonian ferment], all working together."

This provoked a reaction from the *Courier and Enquirer* typical of the splenetic editorial tone of the day: the *Herald*, "which at first overloaded those [*Somers*] officers with praise . . . having been *doucered* [bribed] into a little natural depravity, or having come to the opinion that something may be made out of the excitement against Capt. Mackenzie . . . is too loathsome for a moment's serious notice. . . . If rascality is ever appropriately punished . . . the scoundrel"—that's Bennett—"will be whipped out of the country . . . by the indignant detestation . . . of every man, woman, and child."

For his part, Greeley, who hours before had been comparing Mackenzie favorably to the heroes of antiquity, now found the *Courier and Enquirer*'s support for the captain and his officers "most wicked, most atrocious, and most illegal." Even worse were the paper's "inflammatory appeals to the passions of the multitude on the imaginary deeds of blood, rapine, piracy, rape, and murder, which seem to have had no other existence than in the efforts of a misguided fancy, or the struggles of a guilty conscience trying to tear itself away from its own illegal deeds."

William Seward, the governor of New York, wrote his wife, "You have read all that has transpired concerning the awful calamity that has befallen the Spencers. Was ever a blow more appalling? I, of course, knew Philip only as friends know our children. I should as soon have expected a deer to ravage a sheepfold. . . . I know that Nature has given no firmness to resist the immediate shock to the mother, but time may heal and obliterate the wound. The card which Mr. Spencer has published (or rather his communication) shows that his iron nerves were proof."

Two days later, on Christmas, Seward reported on a letter he had just received from a close friend, the agile Whig politician Thurlow Weed, who "writes from Washington that Mrs. Spencer is heart-broken, and her husband scarcely less. That article in the *Madisonian* was his. Weed says that the papers sent to Washington do not show a necessity for the execution, and that the conduct of Mackenzie, as ascertained from these papers, appears to have been cowardly and murderous."

As the story gathered momentum, the *Herald* called it "a most important affair and bids fair to produce a terrible explosion among various distinguished families and *cliques* in this state. The excitement already reminds us of the factious disputes of the noble families that flourished in Florence, Venice, Mantua, and Genoa."

Nor did that excitement fade with the waning year. It fumed and sparked on for months into 1843, as Alexander Slidell Mackenzie saw his actions aboard the *Somers* grow into a national obsession. "During the nearly four months of inquiry and trial," wrote the great naval historian Samuel Eliot Morison, "the *Somers* affair was discussed all over the country. No case of the century, prior to the assassination of President Lincoln, aroused as much interest and passion."

2 **The Pirate**

THE ISLANDS OF *the Indian Ocean, and the east and west coasts of Africa, as well as the West Indies, have been their haunts for centuries; and vessels navigating the Atlantic and Indian Oceans, are often captured by them, the passengers and crew murdered, the money and most valuable part of the cargo plundered, the vessel destroyed, thus obliterating all trace of their unhappy fate, and leaving friends and relatives to mourn their loss from the inclemencies of the elements, when they were butchered in cold blood by their fellow men, who by practically adopting the maxim that "dead men tell no tales," enable them to pursue their diabolical career with impunity. The pirate is truly fond of women and wine, and when not engaged in robbing, keeps maddened with intoxicating liquors, and passes his time in debauchery, singing old songs with choruses like*

"Drain, drain the bowl, each fearless soul,

Let the world wag as it will;

Let the heavens growl, let the devil howl,

Drain, drain the deep bowl and fill."

Thus his hours of relaxation are passed in wild extravagant frolics amongst the lofty forests of palms and spicy groves of the Torrid Zone,

and amidst the aromatic and beautiful flowering vegetable productions
of that region. He has fruits delicious to taste, and as companions, the
unsophisticated daughters of Africa and the Indies.

That passage is from the preface to *The Pirates Own Book, or*
Authentic Narratives of the Lives, Exploits, and Executions of the Most
Celebrated Sea Robbers, published in 1837 by Charles Ellms, a Boston
merchant who abandoned his trade as a stationer first to compile
almanacs, and then to write about maritime perils (*Shipwrecks and*
Disasters at Sea, 1839; *The Tragedy of the Seas,* 1841). His piracy epic
(it runs to 432 densely printed pages) was such a success that it went
through eight editions over the next twenty years, acquiring lurid
linecut illustrations along the way.

When the news of Philip Spencer's part in the *Somers* conspiracy
broke, the *Herald*'s Washington correspondent voiced a complaint as
durable as Hone's about Constitution-trampling presidents. A good
half century before the "dime novel" began to celebrate the yet-to-be
born Western gunslinger bringing his sanguinary excitements to the
yet-to-be-born Deadwood, the *Herald* was fretting about the baleful
effect that what we call the media was having on young readers with
its tales of piracy—which, although they always ended with executions and admonitions, nevertheless offered those delicious fruits
and the obliging daughters of the Indies to inflame the adolescent
imagination.

"How much of the crime of this young man," asked the *Herald*'s
correspondent, "may be attributed to the miserable trash that the
country is daily deluged with in the shape of romantic adventures
of pirates, banditti, exploits of the celebrated highwaymen, freebooters, etc."

The writer might have had a point, for Ellms's treatise on piracy
was one of Philip Spencer's favorite books. He donated a copy to
his college before leaving it. That seems to have been his most

constructive act as an undergraduate, for he was an indifferent, easily distracted student who remained a freshman for three straight years.

He was born in 1824 in Canandaigua, New York, one of seven children of John Canfield and Elizabeth Spencer, and the youngest of three brothers. His was a prosperous family, but dominated by his ill-tempered father, a successful lawyer and politician—postmaster, assistant attorney general for western New York, New York State senator, member of the US House of Representatives, secretary of war and then secretary of the treasury under Tyler—but abrasive, combative, and vituperative; one contemporary recalled with no pleasure at all the "fierce, quick-rolling eyes" set in a face radiating "an unpleasant character of sternness." His keen intelligence—he served as editor to Alexis de Tocqueville on the English edition of *Democracy in America*—was quick to dismiss those he found duller than himself, and there was an army of them. Although he usually emerged victorious from his political battles, he left few friends behind.

Spencer didn't care. His fellow New York assemblyman Erastus Root remembered chatting with him on the steps of the Albany statehouse. "Everybody is afraid of you," Root told him. "They think you are sour, proud, and crusty." He went on to advise him to lose his "confounded haughtiness." Root, being a personage of sufficient caliber to escape Spencer's disdain, received a civil answer, if not a penitent one: "Nature never made a Chesterfield of me."

The British diplomat and statesman Philip Stanhope, fourth Earl of Chesterfield, is best remembered today for his 1774 book *Letters to His Son on the Art of Becoming a Man of the World and a Gentleman*. In it, he advises making every human encounter smooth and emollient. A typical passage runs: "However frivolous a company may be, still, while you are among them, do not show them, by your inattention, that you think them so; but rather take their tone, and conform in some degree to their weakness, instead of manifesting your contempt for them."

Spencer would have scorned this suggestion. He always, said a contemporary, "expressed himself in words of burning sarcasm." Although "a man of distinguished intellectual powers—powers which placed him in the front rank of our intellectual men . . . as a class, such men are seldom popular. Their passions, even that of ambition, are tinged with severity, and lean—for this is the vice of noble minds—to a love of power. And power, in the hands of an individual, always grows irksome."

It would be difficult to imagine a parent less likely to tolerate a son's daydreaming about piracy.

Philip was sent to Canandaigua Academy—a private boys' school that had been in operation since 1791—to prepare for Geneva College (renamed Hobart in 1852). One of his classmates recalled him in the sort of terms that would often be applied to the student in later years: some kind words, and then a hint of something shadowy. He saw Philip as "a sprightly, delicate, lad who was quite a favorite with many of his schoolmates, though his queer stories and sharp tricks made him unpopular with others."

He entered Geneva College in 1838, and was not popular there. A classmate named McCullum wrote: "My class—of '42—dwindled from about twenty freshmen to seven seniors at commencement. Spencer was one of those who dropped out by the way. He was a talented young man, very quick to learn, pleasant and companionable, and to those whose kindness justified it, confiding. He seldom mingled with the students in their sports and games on the campus. . . . The ease with which he mastered the Greek and Latin was remarkable. . . . This remarkable talent proved a source of weakness to him, for it led him to neglect the proper preparations of his lessons. . . . I do not remember Spencer as a vicious or reckless or mischief-making young man. Whilst his habits were inclined to indolence, he had great self-will and firmness when the occasion called it out. While at Geneva he was operated on for strabismus and refused to be bound or held during the operation."

That is, he was walleyed. Others in his class remarked on the courage with which he submitted to an operation for it in those pre-anesthetic days, refusing the customary restraints and holding himself immobile against serious pain. But despite Philip's fortitude, the procedure was only a partial success. It improved his vision, but not his looks, and his crooked gaze must have contributed to the isolation that his schoolmates remarked on.

One of them, Paul Cooper, wrote, "My recollection is that he had a decided cast in his eyes and that otherwise he would have been thought good-looking." (The deformity is probably the reason that the only known portrait of Philip Spencer shows him in profile.) "He seemed to live very much by himself and to mingle little with the other students. If he had any intimates I do not know who they were, and my belief is that he had none." He was a poor student, recalled Cooper, but an intelligent one who squandered his potential: "Though this is often said of young fellows in college merely because they neglect their studies, I am inclined to think it was true in his case." He did have an ability—a surprising one for such a loner—that Cooper never forgot. "In one thing he excelled the whole college." Spencer was an accomplished public speaker—"he was, indeed, the best declaimer I have ever heard with the exception of one or two men whose reputation is national." His "manner must have been really remarkable or it would not have made the lasting impression that it has upon my memory. I recall it as more like that of a high bred man of the world than a boy's just growing into manhood."

But boy he remained, a boy tormented by the steady disapproval of his formidable father. One of his few friends, stopping by his room, "found him in bed, greatly depressed, yet feeling indignant toward his father on account of his severe reproof which latter, Philip told me, was that unless he turned over a new leaf and did better in the future than he had in the past, he would disown him.

"Brooding over this he had planned to leave college, go West, change his name, turn land pirate, freebooter or buccaneer on the

Mississippi River. These plans were the outgrowth of the kind of reading he had indulged in."

SPENCER'S DEATH LEFT such a residue of unwelcome fame that four decades later a Hobart professor named Charles Vail was asked by the college to look into his undergraduate performance, and came up with a few sparse facts. In February of 1840 Spencer was convicted of going into Canandaigua without permission, an enormity that led to his being "formally" sent away "to remain for a time under the care of the Rev. I.V. Van Iryen."

The cleric evidently failed to tame his charge, for the following November "Philip Spencer was a participant in the cider disturbance so-called, but does not appear to have been regarded as a leading spirit." That disturbance, says Vail, erupted when "some fourteen or fifteen students, among them Spencer, had a barrel of cider in one of the rooms and were holding a Whig merrymaking with shouting and singing. Subsequently, by a resolution, some of the participants were pronounced guilty of misconduct."

These peccadilloes seem vanishingly mild in comparison with what appears to have been the tenor of student life at Geneva in those days, at least as experienced by Andrew Dickson White when he matriculated there less than a decade later. White, who was a most serious student—he went on to cofound Cornell University—so despised the school that his autobiography does not deign to mention its name, referring merely to "a small Protestant Episcopal college in western New York."

Arriving at Geneva, White "was assigned a very unprepossessing room in a very ugly barrack. Entering my new quarters I soon discovered about me various cabalistic signs, some of them evidently made by heating large iron keys, and pressing them against the woodwork. On inquiring I found that the room had been occupied some years before by Philip Spencer. . . . The most curious relic of him at the college was preserved in the library of the [school's] Hermean Society. It was a copy of 'The Pirates Own Book': a glorification of the exploits of 'Blackbeard' and other great freebooters, profusely adorned with illustrations of their joys and triumphs. This volume bore on the fly-leaf the words, 'Presented to the Hermean Society by Philip Spencer,' and was in those days shown as a great curiosity."

Geneva, says White, "was at its lowest ebb; of discipline there was none; there were about forty students, the majority of them, sons of wealthy churchmen, showing no inclination to work and much tendency to dissipation." No discipline, according to White, because the school was hanging by a financial thread and couldn't afford to risk driving away even one of its unruly boys. "I have had to do since, as student, professor, or lecturer, with some half-dozen large universities at home and abroad, and in all of these together have not seen so much carousing and wild dissipation as I then saw in this little 'Church college' of which the especial boast was that, owing to the small number of its students, it was 'able to exercise a direct Christian influence upon every young man committed to its care.'"

He sardonically lists the manifestations of Geneva's Christian influence: "It was my privilege to behold a professor, an excellent clergyman, seeking to quell a hideous riot in a student's room, buried under a heap of carpets, mattresses, counterpanes, and blankets; to see another clerical professor forced to retire through the panel of a door under a shower of lexicons, boots, and brushes, and to see even the president himself on one occasion, obliged to leave his lecture-room by a ladder from a window, and, on another, kept at bay by a shower of beer-bottles."

Far more strenuous mischief than Philip Spencer seems to have made.

It was not the Canandaigua adventure or the cider bacchanal that caused him to leave the school in the spring of 1841; his father asked to withdraw him. "The request was made in consequence of his continued neglect of college exercises," writes Vail, "and this neglect stated in the letter of dismission; but inasmuch as a change of associating might prove favorable, it was also stated that the faculty of this college would make no objection on account of his deficient standing here, to his immediate reception at any other college." Professor Vail ends his brief account with: "I understand that Spencer was a great reader of sea stories, particularly those about pirates."

Before leaving Geneva, Spencer showed a spark of both defiance and self-mockery at the commencement exercises during his third and final year as a freshman. The school had mustered what pomp it could to put on a meager parade, a column of students led by the president and the faculty. Spencer joined at the rear, wearing a tall conical dunce cap from which fluttered a pennant that read "Patriarch of the Freshman Class."

Geneva College making no protest, Spencer was accepted by Union College in Schenectady where—again, surprisingly for one who seemed to prefer solitude—he was instrumental in founding a fraternity.

Or perhaps not so surprising: it allowed him to have a tight, exclusionary circle of chosen acquaintances, to exercise his fondness for Greek, and to devise secret rituals impenetrable to outsiders.

Spencer worked fast. Years later a fraternity brother wrote, "Leaving Hobart College on April 21, 1841, Spencer must have been directly admitted to Union College, for just one month later he banded together with our other founders to startle the college with a new secret society."

Another founder of the fraternity, James Lafayette Witherspoon, remembered that "in the year 1841, Robert H. McFaddin of Greensboro, Ala., and myself went on to Schenectady, N.Y., and entered Union College, occupying a room together in West College. Soon after entering college, we became acquainted with Philip Spencer,

Wm. F. Terhune, Samuel T. Taber and four or five other students whose names have become familiar to Chi Psi. Phil Spencer, who did not like the kind of men who composed the other secret societies then in college, conferred with us and the others above mentioned, about forming a new society composed of kindred spirits. We readily agreed to the proposition. After canvassing the matter, we decided to organize a new society, and call it Chi Psi."

Naturally, the founders thought well of themselves: "The men who founded the Chi Psi Fraternity were high-minded, whole-souled, honorable men, kind and sociable; and in our intercourse we became very much attached to one another." While Terhune—"our poet and writer," Witherspoon says—worked up the initiation ceremony, Spencer "devised the signs, grips and pass words, and made arrangements for the badge of Chi Psi to be worn by its members."

He remembered Philip Spencer as "a tall man of dark complexion, with black hair and eyes, and noble hearted and generous to a fault. He always took great delight in the initiations, grips, signs and pass words, and studied how to make them more impressive."

Decades afterward, a Chi Psi brother named Max Zinkeisen would recognize the danger lying in this standard and usually innocuous hugger-mugger as Spencer practiced it. Zinkeisen believed Tobias Smollett's 1748 picaresque *The Adventures of Roderick Random* "must have been one of Spencer's favorite sea stories" because "this novel was the prototype of sea stories in English literature" and in it "Roderick used Greek letters for ciphers, but unlike Spencer he escaped with his life to tell the world his story."

Chi Psi remains a sort of monument—the only one—to Spencer's brief life. The fraternity, just the eighth to be founded in America, flourished (its members moved into the nation's first frat house in 1846) and today is active on thirty-two campuses.

The considerable energy Spencer brought to organizing Chi Psi did not spill over into his studies at Union, where he may have felt the moral pressure of his father's reputation: John Canfield Spencer had graduated from the school with highest honors thirty-five years earlier.

Philip scarcely had time to demonstrate his indolence at Union. He entered in May, founded his fraternity, and was gone before full summer came on.

Through with trying to get Philip a college education, his father considered having him attached to a regiment of dragoons out on the western frontier; the secretary of war would have no difficulty securing a commission for the boy. But the frontier! What place could be more risky for an adolescent nurturing dreams of becoming a renegade on the fringes of civilization?

The Navy, though—surely the confinement of shipboard life would offer him little chance to run off into a career of depravity.

So in November of 1841 Philip Spencer received a letter, sent in care of his father, from Abel Upshur, secretary of the navy: "You are hereby appointed an Acting Midn [midshipman], and if your Commanding Officer shall after six months of actual service at sea, report favorably on your character, talents and qualifications, a warrant will be given to you bearing the date of this letter. . . ."

The newly minted officer was to report for duty aboard the *North Carolina*. One of the most powerful fighting ships in the world when she was launched in 1820, the three-decker was then at anchor in New York, and never going to leave. She had become a receiving ship, a floating barracks that housed sailors waiting to be assigned sea duty.

Although her oceangoing days were over, the old ship of the line was kept in taut naval trim; she was, after all, the first glimpse of the service that many future officers would get. Just before Spencer arrived, a fourteen-year-old recruit named William Harwar Parker (whose naval career would end with him in command of a Confederate ironclad) came aboard. Forty years later he wrote about his introduction to shipboard life: "I well recollect my extreme surprise at being addressed as *Mr.* by the commodore, and being recalled to my senses by the sharp *William* of my father, who accompanied me to the Navy Yard."

He went aboard the *North Carolina* "on the morning of the 28th of October. She was at anchor in the North river, off the Battery; had a full complement of officers and men, and was kept in fine order. . . . When I got upon her quarter-deck the marines were drawn up for drill, the band was playing, a large party of ladies were promenading the poop-deck, and these sights were taken in connection with unaccustomed *smells* (for this ship always had a curious odor of rum, tar, bean-soup and tobacco combined), tended to confuse me terribly."

The blend of disorienting smells remained, but the band and the martial splendor of the marines were not there to welcome Philip Spencer when he first came aboard the ship a few days later. (Parker met him then: "I remember him as a tall, pale, delicate-looking young man.")

A midshipman named William Craney had the deck when John Canfield Spencer's brother William—a Navy captain—approached and introduced his nephew, Philip. The uncle explained who the boy was, and asked if Craney would look after him and guide him through his first days in his new surroundings.

Craney was delighted. He fully understood the advantages of being able to do a favor for a high-ranking naval officer, not to mention making friends with the son of the secretary of war.

Of course, he said; Philip was welcome to visit his stateroom whenever he felt like it, and to make use of any of his books.

As the two young officers got to know one another, Spencer told Craney that after leaving Union he had gone home for a while, but "being of a wandering turn of mind, and fond of anything bordering on the dangerous and marvelous," he had made his way to Nantucket and there signed on to a whaler.

Craney was amazed: this was the hardest and most dangerous of all maritime duty, three-year voyages amid the stink and squalor of a seagoing slaughterhouse supplied by a seaman leaning out of a rowboat to spear a creature big as a church. Spencer "merely smiled at my aston-ishment" and said "he 'should like to harpoon a whale and see the blood spilt,' that he 'was not afraid of danger and liked an adventurous life.'"

To be sure, he hadn't liked his first taste of that life. He complained of being "compelled with many others to work from morning till late at night in getting them and her stores on board, being allowed thirty minutes for their meals, which were of the coarsest kind, and only five hours rest at night in a miserable forecastle in close communion with the dregs of New-York streets."

But what the hell had he been expecting? And was it even true? "In confirmation of his assertions, he showed me his hands, and they, from their horny, hardened appearance, corroborated his statement of what he had undergone at Nantucket. Having disposed of his wardrobe and replaced them by the coarse and homely garb of the whaler, he was ready, as was also the ship, in two days to sail for their cruising grounds in the South Seas."

But, Spencer went on, his father had discovered his plans; had sent word from Washington and persuaded the whaler's owners to discharge Philip in return for a thirty-dollar payment to a substitute—and so here he was aboard the *North Carolina*.

Evidently Spencer didn't think Midshipman Craney was Chi Psi material, for relations between the two quickly soured. Craney said that Philip soon began to spend his time aboard as did "some other young men in like circumstances, in occasional, and, I am sorry to say, frequent dissipation, principally at night, but not unfrequently in the face of day."

One night Craney, awakened in his berth by a noise, found Spencer rooting around in the stateroom. He wasn't looking for a book to borrow, but "trying to draw a bottle from under some place where it seems he had hidden it."

Craney told him to go away. Spencer, "who appeared to be a little intoxicated, said he would go when he chose."

When Craney again ordered him out, Spencer lunged at his berth and punched him. Craney jumped up and tried to wrestle his assailant from the cabin. "Spencer resisted and the noise brought the officers down. Spencer was ordered below."

Striking a superior officer was a most serious offense, and the next morning the *North Carolina*'s first lieutenant asked Craney if he meant to report the incident. Craney said that of course he did.

The lieutenant became grave. Look, he told Craney, as a friend I'm advising you to let the matter drop. Remember who Spencer's father is; remember that his uncle is a captain. Nobody's going to thank you for getting the Navy Department involved in an ugly squabble like this. Best to be quiet and let it blow over.

Craney kept his mouth shut.

Then, that February, Craney, under the approving eye of the ship's navigation instructor, was explaining to a group of midshipmen how a sextant worked, when Spencer burst through the knot of young officers to fetch him a clout on the side of the head so powerful, Craney said, that it knocked him backward out of his chair, tearing his coat and ripping off its epaulet.

Spencer could not have committed a more public affront. This outrage hadn't taken place in Craney's stateroom in the middle of the night, and the story spilled throughout the *North Carolina* in a matter of minutes.

Craney at once drafted a report to the Navy Department, but before it reached Washington—indeed, before it left the *North Carolina*—officialdom was trying to quash it. Now it was no mere lieutenant who was telling Craney not to make trouble, but Commodore Matthew Calbraith Perry himself, brother of the man who'd won the Battle of Lake Erie, and commandant of the New York Navy Yard.

Craney stood his ground. He could "not pass over it," he said, for it was "an offense punishable even by death if a Court Martial so ordered," and one that had been "committed in the presence of the midshipmen," and "known to the whole ship's company." Craney's "own honor" and his duty to the service demanded he press the matter.

Perry told him he was too late. Philip Spencer had already received orders transferring him to another ship, the *John Adams*, the commodore explained as he handed Craney back his report.

The infuriated Craney said he "instantly saw through this."

Spencer's uncle had written the boy's father, who had secured the transfer and persuaded Perry to sit on the charges until Spencer had left the *North Carolina*.

Craney wrote directly to the secretary of the navy, only to receive "a reply slighting the whole matter" and treating him in "a very insolent & contemptuous manner."

This account of the two midshipmen's clashes and their aftermath comes from a listener deeply sympathetic to Craney. Richard Henry Dana left Harvard in 1834 to ship out as a foremast hand (that is, a common sailor as opposed to an officer, whose realm would have been aft, at the stern of the ship), and wrote about his time at sea in the durable classic *Two Years Before the Mast*. He came ashore to practice maritime law, and tells in his journal how, in the spring of 1843, "a gentleman by the name of Craney, late a Lieut. in the U.S. Navy was introduced to me as wishing to study law in my office. After some conversation, in order to explain to me the fact of his leaving the service, he gave me the history of his unfortunate difficulty with the Department. It is a most sad story."

Very sad, as Dana concludes it:

At all events, it ended with Mr. C.'s being suspended, & Mr. S. sent upon a cruise in the *John Adams*. Mr. C remained suspended for weeks on board the *N. Carolina*. He had been insulted & openly assaulted by an inferior officer; himself & the service in his person had been disgraced, & justice & satisfaction had been refused him; and all because of the influence of S.'s powerful friends. These reflections so wore upon Mr. C., that he became ill. His pent up indignation & his wounded feelings allowed him no rest. Under the influence of those feelings he sent in his resignation, which was accepted.

After 12 or 14 years of the prime of his life spent in the service, & almost unfitted for anything else, he was thrown out upon the world. . . . Such is the story of Mr. Craney. It has made my heart ache for him. It is too strongly flavored with injustice, the triumph of wrong & the suffering of innocence not to call out sympathy & interest. . . .

Whether he has exaggerated the story, or not, I have no certain means of knowing; but I never heard a story told in a more precise, methodical & calm manner. Subsequent events as to Spencer show its probability, & Mr. C. impressed me very favorable for calmness, self respect & candor.

Not perfect candor. Never mind the extreme unlikelihood of a midshipman lecturing Matthew Perry about the duties the service demanded; the very first thing Craney told Dana was a lie: he was not a "Lieut." but one rank below, a midshipman (and thus would have no epaulet to be defiled). Nor had he been in the Navy "12 or 14 years," but fewer than 10. Those weeks of mounting anger and frustration culminating in his quitting the service were a fantasy; he resigned on February 10, 1842—the same day Spencer attacked him. And he had not told Dana that some years earlier he had been cashiered for a cornucopia of sins that included drunkenness, absence without leave, disorderly conduct, whatever "misrepresentation" was, and insulting a superior officer.

Craney, in fact, had been reinstated and reported aboard the *North Carolina* just a few weeks before Spencer's arrival. So perhaps the assault on the senior officer had not been as wholly gratuitous as Dana makes it sound. Philip Spencer, though not specifying what the cause was, both defended himself and apologized for his actions in a letter sent to Commodore Perry the next day. In it, you can perhaps catch an echo of the rhetorical fluency that impressed his Geneva classmate:

> You have informed me that Passed Midshipman Craney has made an official report of the transaction which occurred between us on Thursday the 10th inst. I would respectfully represent that the aggravation which induced the assault was of such a character that my feelings were highly excited, and laboring under the imputation of being a liar, I was led to an act of insubordination and breach of discipline which reflection has taught me was highly improper. May I respectfully request that this letter may accompany the report of . . . Midshipman Craney to the Hon. Secretary of the Navy.

Whatever the right of the matter, it went no further. As Perry had said, Spencer left the *North Carolina* for the 30-gun frigate *John Adams*, bound for duty in Brazilian waters. As for Midshipman Craney, he makes one brief, forlorn appearance in Dana's journal before dissolving into the mists of history: "Saw Mr. Craney at the hotel. He is studying law, but, I fear, is not doing very well."

Spencer's fractious nature went with him to Rio de Janeiro, where a midshipman named Robert C. Rogers saw it at work. Rogers had arrived in Brazil aboard the *Potomac*, a far more heavily armed frigate than the *John Adams*, and was temporarily bivouacked in a Rio hotel when, "one more than ordinarily sultry mid-day . . . I heard hot words in the street, a clashing and outpour of English and Portuguese expletives by no means decent or peaceful." Rogers looked down from the window of his room to see "passionate, menacing outreaches of fists, promising the catastrophe of blows." The two men trading obscenities were an American naval officer and a "brawny boatman" who had evidently been cheated out of his fare. "The contest was unequal, in so far as he who wore the buttons was tipsy, and the other was being reinforced by some chuffs [louts] who approached from the Mole." Rogers ran down into the lobby, collared his countryman, "and led the unsteady middy into the hotel. That was my introduction to Philip Spencer."

Here we have the first impressions of Spencer from a fellow sailor, but it is worth keeping in mind that Rogers published them in *United Service*, a magazine for military personnel, in 1890, when he had known for a full half century what became of the boy he'd rescued from the fight; had he truly thought him "mutinous," as he would later remark, or was that the working of years of hindsight?

They did not become friends, exactly, but "I held a certain intimacy with him." Spencer "appeared to eschew an intimacy with officers of his own grade. Mine was an unaccustomed face and he found me unprejudiced by the generally unfavorable criticisms I had heard of him." Some faint praise follows: "He was a person in his rare normal moods not without congruous and intelligent activity and observation. He had derived advantages from the generous educational opportunities a fond and accomplished father had offered him." He had "a fair acquaintance with the humanities," had kept "somewhat of his hold" on Greek and Latin, spoke fluent Spanish, and drew well. All this made him pretty good company when he chose—but it was not enough to restrain "a nature which appeared to be bereft of all conservative principle. He always impressed me as having an inbred, if not an inborn, inclination, I will not say to crime, but to the vicious at least."

In the very next sentence, however, Rogers says that inclination *was* toward crime. It did not manifest itself as "an eccentricity in the sense of the whimsical, but a vagation [an obsolete word meaning to depart from an expected course of action] so listless, indifferent, as to lead one to plunder a hen-roost or a house."

Sure, Spencer told Rogers, he'd had the usual religious upbringing of the time, but it was all just words he was supposed to memorize. They had made no real impression on him. Here Rogers makes a stinging assessment: "Indeed, it is only true when I say that a more unbalanced, vacillating, and easily-corrupted nature I have never encountered." Spencer's was a character that went beyond "mere moral infirmities" to display, "as Shakespeare has it, 'a most inherent baseness.'"

One day Rogers said to him, "Spencer, it seems to me that you are a mutinous, insubordinate sort of a fellow, constantly kicking against discipline, always in hot water. What in the devil's name induced you to enter the service?"

"I hardly know," said Spencer. "The fact is, I wasn't a model boy by any means—pretty bad, lawless if you like that better; and my father, perhaps to get rid of me—perhaps to reform me—put me in the navy. I am disposed to think it has done me harm."

"And you do not like it, then?"

"Like it! Like it! Hell, no; I hate it!"

Rogers pressed him. "What would you like, then?"

"That's hard to say," Spencer answered "lazily" and "drawlingly." "But I think I would like to own a vessel outsailing anything afloat, with a crew who would go to hell for me; going where I pleased, doing what I pleased."

"I would call that the life of a freebooter."

"Well, I can't say I'd dislike that. Would you, old fellow?"

Rogers replied huffily, "Decidedly, yes!"

Spencer's highly critical fellow midshipman found proof "of the fact that he was obsessed by just such vicious motives" when he watched him spend "many leisure moments in sketching fanciful portraits of the notorious villains of buccaneering, from Drake [not everyone would put Sir Francis in such company] to Lafitte [who had helped Andrew Jackson win the Battle of New Orleans], or of sinister-looking crafts of the rover trim; and retreats lying in remote waters where plunder could be safely hoarded, and idle days spent in dalliance with captive beauties."

And Spencer drank. "He was a dipsomaniac, brutalized by the love of liquor. . . . That vice, together with sometimes churlish and irritable ways . . . made him the most unpopular of the junior officers of the squadron, and he was generally shunned."

Shut out by his peers, when he went ashore "he rarely sought persons of his own class" and "wandered into places where gathered the odds and ends of society, in and out of *cabarets borgnes*; the reeky bagnios of the Rue Saboa, and with people who would not have paused to cut his throat, except there was no need of it, for his maudlin and promiscuous hospitality impoverished him quicker than a sheath-knife could have done."

Rogers was soon to be quit of his nettlesome acquaintance. "One day Spencer was on the Mole, the crowded point of embarcation . . . abusively, incoherently fuddled. He was unsteadily but resolutely questing an English officer, against whom he had a real or fancied grudge, and whom he vehemently threatened to shoot on sight. He was in uniform, and he was too obstreperous to escape observation." Nor did he. "He was seen by the late Admiral Wyman, who sent him to his own ship, and the facts were duly reported. Commodore Morris was the very last person in the navy to condone so gross an indecorum. The 'Potomac' was on the eve of her departure for home, and Spencer was ordered to her in disgrace."

The evening before the *Potomac* set sail, Rogers, who was to stay in Rio, went aboard to say goodbye to some friends. "When I was leaving Spencer followed me on deck, talking to me while the boat was being 'called away.' I remember well his valedictory, so passionately uttered under the glowing [Southern] Cross of that clime. He damned fleet and flag, the commodore and Wyman, rounding off with oaths and the threat to be 'even with them.'"

Spencer did not carry on in that fashion with his superiors. Now he was all contrition. He wrote a letter to Commodore Charles Morris, who commanded the American ships on the Brazilian station: "I have taken the liberty of addressing you for the purpose of giving you an exact account of my conduct on the 21st inst. . . . I had been on shore in the market boat; when there I drank considerably. When I came off I also drank with several persons, and when I went on shore for the day, by permission of the first lieutenant, I was overcome by the liquors I had drank." He begged the commodore to give him another chance, citing "my previous good conduct. This is my first offense, and I know my last." Perhaps, he concluded, "I am asking too much; but if it could be that the offence could be overlooked, I would solemnly pledge myself that the offence should never be repeated."

He also offered to resign, rather than be disgraced by a court-martial. Commodore Morris may have decided that the easiest way to deal with the son of so prominent a father was simply to duck the problem. Saying he did not have the authority to accept an officer's resignation, he put Spencer aboard the *Potomac* "to return to the U. States in that ship, there to receive the decision of the Secretary of the Navy."

Nine months after getting his commission, Spencer received a second letter from Abel Upshur. The secretary had "perused with pain the correspondence transmitted to me by Comdr. Morris" and been dismayed to learn "that one more young officer of the Navy, and one brought up as you must have been, has been guilty of the degrading and disqualifying vice of drunkenness."

Still, Upshur and the Navy he oversaw were going to be magnanimous. The letter continued: "Your frank and manly acknowledgment of your offence, your penitence for it, the fact of its being the first known to your Commander, and his interposition on your behalf have upon the whole induced me to overlook the transgression reported to me, and to put you on trial by your future conduct. If that is such as the country has a right to expect from one who wears her uniform, what has passed will be forgotten."

Whether Spencer read this with relief or with resentment that he must continue in the service he'd told Rogers he hated, we do not know. He did realize that, want the post or not, this was his final chance; if he got into trouble in the future his father would not again intervene.

Just days later, on August 13, 1842, he received his orders: "Report to Capt. M. C. Perry for duty on board the U.S. brig *Somers*." Perry, of course, would not be sailing with the brig; he was to pass Spencer along to Commander Alexander Slidell Mackenzie.

A few days later, followed by a teetering porter pushing his dunnage in a wheelbarrow, Philip Spencer stepped aboard the *Somers*, saluted the flag, and reported to the officer of the deck. After more saluting, he was directed to an auburn-haired officer whom the *Herald* described: "Captain Mackenzie in full uniform . . . is a man of fine intelligent and amiable countenance, and is apparently about forty years of age. He is tall, and thin, and his whole appearance is decidedly prepossessing . . . his entire demeanor indicative of calm but decided resolution."

Of the young man approaching him with his papers, Mackenzie wrote: "When he reported himself to me for duty at New York, about the 20th of August, I at once gave him my hand and welcomed him aboard the *Somers*."

3 The Author

THE WELCOME WAS SHORT-LIVED, for Commander Mackenzie "subsequently heard that he [Spencer] had quite recently been dismissed with disgrace from the Brazilian squadron, and compelled to resign, for drunkenness and scandalous conduct. This fact made me very desirous for his removal from the vessel." The captain enlarged on his feelings at some length, for he was a loquacious man, and one given to sermonizing: "The circumstance of Mr. Spencer being a son of a high officer of the government, by enhancing his baseness in my estimation, made me more desirous to be rid of him; on this point, I beg that I might not be misunderstood—I revere authority, I recognize in the exercise of its higher functions in this free country, the evidence of genius, intelligence, and virtue, but I have no respect for a base son of an honored father."

Like most officers of his generation, Mackenzie had first gone to sea as a boy.

Alexander Slidell was born to John and Margery Mackenzie Slidell (he would not take his Mackenzie surname until he was in his thirties) in New York City in the spring of 1803. The Slidells were prosperous,

John being a successful merchant and shipowner, as well as the first president of both the Mechanics Bank of New York and the Tradesmen's Insurance Company.

A wealthy family, and closely connected to a famous one, for Alexander's sister Jane had married Matthew Calbraith Perry on Christmas Eve of 1814. Matthew was the then-twenty-year-old brother of Oliver Hazard Perry, who had, a year earlier, overseen the building of a whole little navy from standing timber on the shores of Lake Erie and taken it out to conquer and capture a British fleet, thereby giving his young nation control of the Upper Lakes and thus what was then the American northwest.

The victory seemed something of a miracle at the time (still does, for that matter) and it dealt the American representatives a far stronger hand in the peace negotiations with England.

Small wonder, then, that Alexander was drawn to his illustrious in-law's service, and it was Oliver himself who, in March 1815, got the eleven-year-old a warrant as midshipman in the United States Navy.

Before his voice had changed, Alexander was at sea on the brig-of-war *Chippewa* for a five-month cruise and then, after six weeks at home over Christmas, headed to the Mediterranean on the frigate *Java*, under Oliver Perry.

The *Java* was helping make sure that the Dey of Algiers honored the treaty that prohibited Barbary States pirates from attacking American merchant vessels. There followed two years in the Pacific on another frigate, the *Macedonian*, and then Alexander, now in his early twenties, was dispatched to the West Indies on a much smaller ship, the sloop *Terrier*, which mounted just three guns.

That was an almost risibly small armament, but one deemed sufficient by the Navy to discourage the pirates who still infested the old Spanish Main. They were committing brutalities on a smaller scale than their famous eighteenth-century predecessors, but their attacks did not seem at all minor to those they raped, murdered, or left to burn along with the ships they'd set aflame. Like Philip Spencer, Alexander Slidell had become keenly aware of pirates, although the two men viewed them very differently.

During this tour of duty, Alexander came down with yellow fever in 1824. The violent affliction had killed Oliver Perry five years earlier; it spared Slidell, though, and he made it home from the West India station to recuperate in New York.

He was a lieutenant now, but he did not return to sea—or at least returned to it only long enough to cross the Atlantic to Europe. His naval connections and his family money had allowed him to wangle a generous two-year leave. He knew how he was going to spend his extended run ashore. He wanted to write a book.

SLIDELL HAD LANDED in France, but decided to head into Spain: "My motives for going to a country most travelers avoid were a wish to perfect myself in a language which is becoming so important in a hemisphere which it divides with our own and a strong desire to visit scenes so full of interest and attraction."

From Roussillon, in 1826, he crossed the Pyrenees and moved under mule power down through Catalonia to Valencia, then west to Castile and on to Madrid, where he settled in for a while and struck up a fortunate friendship.

Washington Irving was at that time one of the most famous writers in the Western world, at least as popular in Britain as he was in America. His English readers marveled that this high-hearted figure, a fount of civilized good humor, had sprung from a country whose coarse population battered the New World air with the jets of tobacco juice disparaged by every European visitor.

Irving the man was every bit as amiable as Irving the author. He would have befriended his young naval countryman under any circumstances. But as it happened, Alexander Slidell proved useful to him.

Irving, with trepidation, had abandoned his whimsies about Hudson Valley folklore and amusing Knickerbocker doings to take on, in dead earnest, a demanding historical project. He was in Madrid on some carelessly defined duties as an attaché to the American ministry, but his true purpose was to conduct research in fifteenth-century archives for a biography—the first in the English language—of Christopher Columbus.

Lieutenant Slidell would not have risen so relatively quickly in the undernourished United States Navy of the day had he not been a capable officer, and he was happy to decipher for Irving the mysteries of ship handling, rigging, navigation, sail setting, cargo stowage— everything that in the 1820s, as in the 1490s, made sailing vessels the most complex of all machines.

Irving found the lieutenant helpful, thanking him for correcting various charts and saying, about the consequential matter of where Columbus had first touched land, "I think you have settled the question satisfactorily." Later, he praised him in the finished biography for contributing "a very masterly paper" on the explorer's route.

He went on to offer more than gratitude. Slidell wrote up his travels under the title *A Year in Spain*, had it published in Boston in 1829, and was disappointed with the tepid response. At this point Irving stepped in. He wrote his friend from London: "I have made terrible cutting and slashing works with some parts of it, but it was necessary to do so . . . to sacrifice some of your tirades against John Bull and some of your passages applicable merely to ourselves. Some of the historical parts also would have been trite in this country, so I threw them overboard." In fact, he had rewritten much of the book, and was confident in his improvements, both as editor and tutor: "In checking over the corrected copy, you will notice a multitude of corrections which will be of service to you hereafter in point of style."

Moreover, Irving had found a most distinguished publisher, John Murray, whose authors included Jane Austen, Thomas Malthus, Sir

Walter Scott, Goethe, and Lord Byron. Irving wrote his brother, "I send a copy of Slidell's 'A Year in Spain,' which I corrected for the press and got Murray to publish in very creditable style. It will give the lieutenant a complete launch in literature."

And so it did. Slidell had resumed his maritime calling, aboard the 44-gun frigate *Brandywine*, when Irving wrote him at sea: "Your work has, upon the whole, had a triumphant launch, and has established a popular name for you in England." Irving said the same to other friends of his: *A Year in Spain* "is quite the fashionable book of the day, and spoken of in the highest terms in the highest circles. If the Lieutenant were in London at present, he would be quite a lion."

The Navy usually was leery of its officers publishing anything, unless the subject was chronometers, or perhaps gunnery, but in this case the authorities seemed proud to discover a fashionable author on one of their quarterdecks. An order issued on June 10, 1839, mandated the "books to be furnished Vessels of War when on a cruise." There, in the lofty company of Shakespeare, Plutarch, the Bible, *The American Practical Navigator*, and *Decline and Fall of the Roman Empire* was *A Year in Spain*.

It is pleasing to imagine a popular writer risen to naval command possessing the sweep of imagination of Slidell's fellow Murray client Lord Byron, blended with a sympathetic understanding of the occasional human failing. But as the stern meditation on fathers and sons with which the commander greeted Philip Spencer's arrival suggests, his was not a flexible nature.

This is evident in Slidell's second book of travels, *The American in England*. It did not do so well as *Spain*, for it is a glum narrative that can scarcely have sharpened many literary appetites with its preface: "The result of this up-hill journey is before the reader, and, however distasteful it may prove to him, his feeling of aversion can scarce exceed that with which the author now takes leave of it."

Nor was it likely to endear itself to his English readers. "His work in Spain [the author is speaking in the third person] was written with the same enthusiasm which attended the travels it described, and was truly to him a labor of love; the country, the climate, and the people, all offering themselves with new and pleasing impressions to his mind, and tinging his imagination with a romantic colouring. It was quite otherwise in England; the climate presented itself to him at the most somber season of the year. . . ." He had hoped to "describe the popular manners such as he had the opportunities to observe them in his condition as an ordinary traveler," but "these do not present, in England, the picturesque character necessary to furnish materials for amusing description." So: "Writing without enthusiasm concerning that which he saw with apathy, his work appears to himself, as it will doubtless do to the reader, a most laborious performance."

A great deal irritated Slidell on his English rambles—beginning as soon as his ship left its New York anchorage and started down the harbor, allowing him a last look "at Brooklyn, smirking in tasteless finery." Of his companions on the sixteen-day voyage, he has only this to say: "With the little interest that their society afforded, the time wore heavily enough."

He is not long ashore, in Portsmouth, home of the naval base that had sustained the town for generations, when he gets a glimpse of "the noble old *Victory*," Lord Nelson's flagship, on whose deck the admiral was shot even as he won the Battle of Trafalgar. (She's still there today, looking just as noble.) A merry scene is going on: "The beach and adjacent streets were crowded with jolly sailors" who, "some just discharged had yards of riband hanging" from them, "fluttering like the pendants from so many cruisers, and the gilded chains of one or more watches dangling from their tight-set waistbands. These rolled over the ground with a glorious swagger." But this happy show was poisoned "by the luring syrens [*sic*] that filled the streets, and ogled or frowned from the windows, furnished a true though low-lived picture of worldly interestedness. Never before did I see such teeming evidences, and not so much of the outward and visible signs of vice. . . ."

I might perhaps have been led to draw conclusions unfavourable to the chastity of England."

He is always alert to vice. In London, far from the temptations of shoreside prostitutes, he is taken to the Drury Lane Theatre and again displays a prudishness not universally shared by naval people: "From first to last the play was most plentifully interspersed with low, coarse traditional stage-jokes, execrable atrocious puns and playing upon words, and vulgar and indecent equivoques [double entendres]; while ever and anon a stout and strong-backed actor would grasp one of the lusty wenches, who, after a feigned struggle to escape, would give over her coyness and yield to his embrace, meeting him mouth to mouth, and firing round the theatre like the report of a pistol.

"What with the kisses on the stage and the kisses off it [observed between the acts, as he noted elsewhere, in "the magnificent saloons . . . set apart as the recognised resort of abandoned women"], the evidences on all sides of unbridled licentiousness, the scene was such a one as in all my wanderings I had never beheld."

This from the man whom Irving praised in an accolade for *Spain* that ran in the prominent *Quarterly Review* as "a youthful, kind, and happy spirit" with "a certain vein of humor and *bonhomie* running through it also, that gives it a peculiar zest . . . and good humor."

Nothing—with the possible exception of horror—is so perishable a commodity as humor. Much of what amused readers 150 years ago is to us either incomprehensible or unbearable. Still, it is hard to find a glint of humor anywhere in Slidell's writing. He did once create an appealing and homely simile about his lack of formal schooling: "Trained almost from infancy in a profession which rendered connected study impossible," he acquired "what little education has fallen to me in much the same discursive and vagabond manner that a chicken gets his breakfast—a kernel of information in one corner and another in the next."

This suggests both a lighthearted touch and even a bit of amusement at his own expense. It's a false dawn. Of the lighthearted touch he had little; of self-deprecation, none, ever.

Difficult as it is to prove an absence of something, Alexander Slidell's lack of humor—and, indeed, an opacity about common human feelings—is demonstrated in the extraordinary dedication with which he prefaced a subsequent book. After the disappointing response to *The American in England*, he returned to the friendly Spanish well and published *Spain Revisited*.

The prolix dedication—it runs to some eight hundred words—is to his close friend and fellow lieutenant George P. Upshur. Upshur would rise to become head of the Naval Academy, but at the time he was just another lieutenant, and by then Alexander had managed to acquire more influential friends.

He makes that clear in his dedication: "The chief advantage of the slight reputation which has fallen to my share, has been its procuring me the favor and acquaintance of some individuals, whose names might furnish a decoration to my pages, which the world would, perhaps, more highly value. . . ." In other words: You're a pretty small fish, George, but mine is so sterling a character that I'm dedicating the book to you anyway.

IT IS UNUSUAL—perhaps unique—for someone studying the career of a mid-ranking naval officer who lived two hundred years ago to have hundreds of pages of a first-person narrative from which to try to tease out clues to his character.

Alexander Slidell truly did love his service. When, at Gibraltar, he sees an American ship of the line, he remembers reading in Irving's Columbus biography that "the most stoical savage" was overwhelmed by the sight of a full-rigged vessel under sail and wonders "what would have been his wild ecstasy if, instead of the shapeless caravel of Columbus, he had first seen this ship, at least twenty times as large and a hundred times more perfect! He might not only have believed it to have come from Heaven, but that the Deity himself had deigned to visit his children." Slidell sides with Irving's savage: "I thought I had never seen any array so soul-inspiring, so imposing; and when I came . . . to look into the details of this perfect contrivance, this little world, this moving city . . . what, let me ask, did the Augustan or any other age ever produce to compare with this noble production, in which art itself is outdone, and science altogether exhausted?"

He is patriotic—there are many tributes to the flag; he is energetic and observant; he is unflaggingly moralistic. There is little from which a reader might predict the catastrophe to come when he took Philip Spencer aboard.

Yet here and there he shows a relish for violence that approaches the prurient.

During his Spanish travels, he was heading south from Tarragona in a diligence—a large, four-wheeled stagecoach—led by a mule boy and a driver. In the small hours of the morning three highwaymen stepped out of the darkness and brought the vehicle to a halt. One of them demanded that the "mayoral"—the driver—turn over his purse, which he did, saying, "Take it, cavalier, but spare my life!" Notes Slidell: "Such, however did not seem to be the robber's intention; bringing a stone from a large heap which had been collected for the repair of the road, he fell to beating the mayoral on the head with it. . . . The murderer redoubled his blows until, growing furious in the task, he laid his musket beside him, and worked with both hands upon his victim. The supplications which blows had first excited, blows at length quelled; they had gradually increased with the suffering to the most terrible shrieks, then declined into low and inarticulate moans, until a deep-drawn and agonized gasp for breath, and an occasional convulsion, alone remained to show that the vital principle had not yet departed."

This detailed account is followed by the death of Pepe, the mule boy. "The second robber . . . drew a knife from the folds of his sash, and, having opened it, he placed one of his naked legs on either side of his victim; pushing aside the jacket of the youth, he bent forward and dealt him repeated blows"—blows described with unsettling thoroughness by Slidell: "I could distinctly hear each stroke of the murderous knife, as it entered its victim; it was not a blunt sound, as of a weapon that meets with positive resistance, but a hissing noise, as if the household implement, made to part the bread of peace, performed unwillingly its task of treachery."

Although a priest in the carriage "hid his face within his trembling fingers," Slidell's "own eyes seemed spellbound, for I could not withdraw them from the cruel spectacle." He says "this moment was the unhappiest of my life," and of course he was an unwilling witness to the brutality. But at other times he sought such scenes out.

While still in France he had attended a public execution, "and the feeling of oppression and abasement, of utter disgust, with which I came from it, was such as to make me form a tacit resolution never to be present at another."

He breaks his resolution when, in Madrid, he sees "a short notice that the proper authorities would proceed to put to death two evildoers," and gives a ten-page account of their hanging. "The executioner took two of the cords which dangled from the beam [of the gallows], and having once more convinced himself that they were of equal length, he opened the nooses, and placed them about the neck of the malefactor. This done, he let himself down a single step, and seating himself firmly upon the shoulders of his victim, he grasped him tightly about his neck with his legs. He then drew powerfully upon the cords. The strangling malefactor made a convulsive but ineffectual attempt to reach upward with his pinioned arms, and then writhed his body to escape from the torture. This moment was seized upon by the executioner, who threw himself over the edge of the ladder, when both fell downward together. They had nearly turned over, when the ropes arrested their fall, and, as they tightened, they struck across the face of the executioner, and threw his hat aside among the crowd. But he clung to his prey with a resolute grasp, recovered his seat, and moved upward and downward upon the shoulders of the malefactor."

In fact, the hangman's gruesome acrobatics may have been something of a kindness, as his weight would have spared the victim a slow strangulation.

Slidell watches the next execution, and then leaves the scene with high thoughts: "I experienced a return of the same sickly feeling of disgust with mankind and myself with which I had once risen from reading of Rousseau's Confessions [!]. Surely there can be nothing in such a spectacle to promote morality, nothing to make us either better or happier: a spectacle which serves but to create despondency, and to array man in enmity with his condition."

Then, as if to ratify his creditable feelings of moral opprobrium, he takes himself to *another* execution, this one a garroting. "It was sure to be a spectacle full of horror and painful excitement; still I determined to witness it. I felt sad and melancholy, and yet, by a strange perversion, I was willing to feel more so."

And to describe it with his usual precision. "The form of it was very simple. A single upright post was planted in the ground, having attached to it an iron collar, large enough to receive the neck of the culprit but capable of being suddenly tightened to much smaller dimensions, by means of a screw, which played against the back of the post, and had a very open spiral thread. A short elbow projected at right angles from the upright post, for the criminal to sit on, the screw being attached to the post at a distance above, suited to the height of his body."

The condemned, with a friar standing by him chanting prayers, was "seated on the projecting elbow of the *garrotte*, which looked toward the east . . . and the executioner, with dextrous art, quickly and stealthily adjusts the iron collar to the neck of his victim. A hand is on either end of the powerful lever which works the tightening screw. Life has reached its extremest limit. Time is dropping his last sand; ere yet it is quite fallen, one prayer of supplication is uttered for mercy in that eternity which begins. Quick as lightning the motion is given to the fatal lever; a momentary convulsion agitates his frame, and horribly distorts his countenance, and the sinner is with his God."

That quick jump from the horribly distorted face to God is typical of the captain. He invokes religion nearly as often as he does the flag, and if the self-rebuke that accompanies his descriptions of the executions seems more perfunctory than his appetite for their details, it still suggests a spirit at odds with itself. Here is a self-righteous commander who is revolted by any breach of propriety, who reveres the Navy, who has little sense of humor, and who is fascinated by a hanging. When Philip Spencer—insolent, sullen, scornful of hierarchy—joined him aboard the *Somers*, the boy was putting himself in at least as much danger as he would have faced had his father let him become a dragoon on the frontier.

The garroting was reported in *Spain Revisited*, which appeared in 1836. That same year Alexander Slidell, again home from both Spain and the sea and now thirty-two years old, married Kate Robinson, the twenty-year-old daughter of a Manhattan banker and lawyer. "She was formerly a great belle," wrote a friend, "but is wholly free of all coquetry, a fine, a good woman."

The marriage seems to have pleased both partners; a decade into it Slidell would say his time with Kate was "most truly one of increased and increasing happiness, contentment, and enchantment."

It was also one of some material comfort, thanks to a familial whim.

Alexander Slidell's mother had come to the altar as Margery Mackenzie. Born in Scotland, she had a brother still living there, a childless bachelor who had begun to brood about the Mackenzie name dying with him. He found a solution. If his nephew Alexander would formally adopt his last name, the uncle would settle a legacy on him.

As Henry of Navarre is said to have remarked that "Paris is worth a mass" when he secured the throne of France by converting to Catholicism, so Alexander Slidell calculated that a nice home on the Hudson River was worth a surname. He agreed, the New York State Legislature enacted the change in the late 1830s, and Lieutenant Slidell ceased to exist, to be immediately recreated as Lieutenant Mackenzie and, after a promotion in 1841, Commander Mackenzie (commander was one rung below the rank of captain on the promotional ladder, but longstanding tradition called any officer in charge of a commissioned warship a captain).

The uncle kept his part of the bargain, and the freshly coined Mackenzie bought a small farm near his friend Washington Irving's home in Tarrytown.

It was there, in the spring of 1842, that he received orders to command the USS *Somers* on an unusual mission.

4 The *Somers*

In 1837 Alexander Mackenzie and his senior officer and brother-in-law Matthew Calbraith Perry collaborated on a forty-two-page article called "Thoughts on the Navy" and published it in the *Naval Magazine*, which had been founded the year before with both men on its editorial board. Neither was happy with the state of the service.

The Navy had corroded since the brave days just after the War of 1812, when national pride in America's showing at sea prompted Congress, in 1816, to put up $1 million a year—$100 million in today's money—for six years to build a fleet of twelve 44-gun frigates and nine 74-gun ships of the line. This costly goal begat the powerful *North Carolina*; its erosion saw her demoted to a floating dormitory in 1829 after less than two decades of martial life. That same year President Andrew Jackson—by no means a foe of the Navy, but an inlander if ever there was one—called for "no more ships of war than are requisite to the protection of our commerce. Our best policy would be to discontinue building ships of the first and second class."

Expensive to build, and difficult to man. While still in his early twenties chasing slavers (slave-trade ships) off the Africa coast in command of a 12-gun schooner, Matthew Perry had gone over many heads to warn the secretary of the navy that "the sources from whence we have heretofore drawn our choicest seamen are partially dried up. Unless some plan is adopted to improve the number and condition of our seafaring population, we shall find too late, that although we may have ships in abundance, yet our government in case of emergency would have to contest with insuperable difficulties in *procuring crews for them.*"

Merchant service was often easier than naval duty, and paid better. A generation earlier many young men had been drawn to the romance of the sea; now Jackson's western frontier was starting to beguile them.

And who would command those boys who did venture seaward? For generations the training of officers had been on the throw-'em-in-the-water-and-see-if-they-can-swim level. Congress had made trouble here, its members discovering that they could help an important constituent get a miscreant son out of the way by making him a fledgling midshipman. One acquaintance of Perry's felt he had to explain himself in requesting a warrant for his boy: "*I* am not one to dump my black sheep on the Navy."

Of course, young men sent to sea *did* get a real maritime education—weathering any gale would show the dullest of them a great deal about shipboard demands—but they had to learn mathematics and navigation (and, for some reason, French), and those disciplines wouldn't come to them without actual instruction. The Naval Regulations of 1802 offered the ship's chaplain as a solution, ordering the man of God to "perform the duty of a schoolmaster, and to that end he shall instruct . . . in writing, arithmetic, navigation, and in whatsoever may contribute to render them proficient." Samuel Eliot Morison didn't think highly of that program; he quotes the historian of the Naval Academy: "It was only in cases of fortunate accident that they knew anything about a subject before they were called to teach it."

The obvious answer was to establish a permanent naval academy. Although that was as clear to those in the 1820s as it would be to any reader today, the currents of the time flowed against it. Our navy had been founded on the traditions of Britain's, but the bumptious democratic spirit crackling in the land during the decades after a war in which America had broken with the hierarchal traditions of the Old World wanted nothing of the sort.

Representative Lemuel Sawyer of North Carolina spoke for thousands when he said that encouraging an officer class could only "produce degeneracy and corruption of the public morality and change our simple Republican habits." South Carolina agreed: Senator William Smith, having pointed out that Julius Caesar and Lord Nelson had done quite well without any academy, said such an institution would turn out "trifling or effeminate leaders."

The best the academy promoters could do was to open three special schools—in Boston; Norfolk, Virginia; and Philadelphia—but these were feeble. Attendance was entirely voluntary, instruction often lackadaisical, and students present only when leave permitted them to be.

That same worry about fomenting a breed of tinhorn lordlings also constricted the service. The rank of admiral did not exist in America. Captain was the top of the promotional tree. If the captain had a squadron under his command, he could call himself "commodore," but the honorific vanished as soon as the ships that conferred it dispersed.

Perry found this especially galling; it seemed to confine the entire United States Navy to an undignified adolescence, one in which promotion came only at a glacial rate, and in small increments. In "Thoughts on the Navy," he and Mackenzie wrote that the lack of higher levels to pursue imposed "a system of death-like stagnation among the officers of our Navy suited to smother hope, ambition, and every generous sentiment." They "are doomed to pass . . . their best years in subordinate drudgery, reserving the era of command for that declining age, when the broken voice, the failing vision . . . counsel retirement."

One officer calculated that a midshipman appointed in 1839 might expect to become a lieutenant in 1870.

Perry and Mackenzie were as concerned with making good sailors as they were with making capable officers. "Next to the formation of an efficient corps of officers is the creation . . . of a class of seamen, peculiarly its own." They called for an apprentice system by enlisting 3,000 boys of fourteen and older; frigates would get drafts of 150 of them, ships of the line 300. "In this way our navy would soon be manned entirely by Americans, among whom it is now not popular, owing to the existence of a harsh system which has grown out of the unlimited introduction of foreigners."

Morison writes that "on no other subject was Perry so eloquent and persistent as he was on this apprentice system." Perry was a persuasive man (he would, in the years to come, badger Japan into opening itself to foreign trade), and the article paints in the most radiant hues the advantages that would flow from Perry and Mackenzie's system:

> Those who are unacquainted with the Navy cannot understand the transition that takes place in a poor and half-clad boy, when taken from the streets and wharfs of our great cities and entered on board a man-of-war. The cleanliness, which is particularly enforced among the younger portion of the crew, by the daily muster, under the vigilant eye of the master-at-arms at seven bells, the comfortable clothing, and the sufficient food, all make an instantaneous change for the better in his physical condition. He starts up to grow and spread in a manner almost magical. His character too develops itself rapidly, as he begins to learn, and make himself useful in the duty of the ship. There is, perhaps, no pleasure which the benevolent officer experiences in a man-of-war greater than that which he feels in watching the growth and daily improvement, in appearance, character and usefulness of an active lad, aspiring to the dignity of an able seaman, with an ambition unsurpassed by any thing that we see in the loftier walks of life.

His campaign gained followers, and in 1837 Congress (knocking a year off the proposed minimum age) called for the recruitment of apprentices between thirteen and eighteen to serve, at seven dollars a month, until they reached their majority.

Perry had also asked for the "establishment of a school-ship." Not only did he get one, but it was a stunner: a fine new brig-of-war, the *Somers*. And his coauthor and brother-in-law, Alexander Slidell Mackenzie, would command it.

MACKENZIE'S NEW BRIG was named for Richard Somers, who in 1804, during the First Barbary War, took a fire ship manned by eleven volunteers into Tripoli's harbor against a pirate fleet anchored beneath the city walls. A fire ship was just that: a vessel stuffed with explosives and set ablaze, then aimed at a floating enemy. When a burning ship got in among the complexities of tarred rope and wooden spars and stored gunpowder that composed its targets, it could work terrible damage. But such a mission was about the most dangerous tactic nineteenth-century sea warfare had to offer, and Captain Somers died alongside his volunteers when his ship exploded prematurely.

James Fenimore Cooper, who'd served as a midshipman in his youth and was as comfortable writing about the high seas as he was about the forests of the New World, published a biography of Somers, saying that one of the gunboats on Lake Erie bore his name: "Perry had a schooner which was thus designated under his orders on the memorable 10th of September, 1813; and a beautiful little brig has lately been put into the water on the seaboard, which is called the *Somers*. In short, his name has passed into a watchword in the American Navy." (And so it has; to date six American warships have been christened the USS *Somers*.)

The "little brig" *was* beautiful. Designed by Samuel Humphreys, the Navy's chief constructor, with the help of Matthew Perry, and built in the Brooklyn Navy Yard, she represented the culmination of millennia of maritime evolution. The *Somers* was among the very last of our warships to rely on the wind alone; she had none of the auxiliary power that was already the snake in the garden for seamen who would have to accommodate themselves to the greasy, hissing, alien machinery visited on them by steam power.

As handsome below the waterline as above—naval terminology nicely spoke of her "wineglass-shaped cross-section and sharp ends"— she was made for speed, and looked it. She was among the fastest vessels possessed by any navy at the time. Built under the daring spur of progress, she was also, in some ways, too advanced, and her handlers would discover that she was over-rigged, that she might put out a greater spread of canvas than could easily be managed. She also carried an unfortunate weight of metal. Designed for a dozen 32-pounder guns, she was equipped with ten, which was still heavy armament for a ship of her size.

The "little brig" was also *little*. Only 100 feet from stem to stern and 25 feet at her waist's thickest, she'd been designed for a comple- ment of 90 men. But once all her schoolboys had come aboard, she would set sail with 120.

Many members of this young crew were handpicked by the *Somers*'s officers, but the recruitment of those who hadn't been was a shabby, semi-criminal process that had been in place for decades.

Not long after the *Somers* was fitting out, a boy named Charles Nordhoff determined to go to sea, and did. He'd had enough of salt water by 1854 when, just twenty-three years old, he realized that he preferred the land, and journalism. It was a wise choice; by the time he'd been an editor on *Harper's Weekly*, the Washington correspon- dent for the *New York Herald*, and the managing editor of the *New York Evening Post*, he was one of the most famous newspapermen in America. He had also published a best-seller about his youthful seafaring. *Man-of-War Life* remains in print today, and—along with

Herman Melville's *White-Jacket*—gives us the best picture we have of the lot of the ordinary seaman in the days when the *Somers* was freshly launched. Both Nordhoff and Melville can represent for us the ordeal undergone by those boys who, not smiled upon by the brig's officers, came aboard the *Somers* as strangers both to the ship and to the sea.

"Being a regular bookworm," wrote Nordhoff, "I went to school until I was thirteen. Then, by my own choice, I became apprenticed to a printer. Within six months, I was so weak and puny my friends began to fear I had consumption, and so I cast about for some means to recruit my health." He thought a sailor's life would do the trick, and in 1843 he took a steamer from Wheeling, Virginia, to Baltimore to find a berth for himself. Nothing doing. The first captain he spoke to drove him off with: "You young scamp! You think I carry runaway boys? Don't let me see you on a ship again!" Having read of Quaker kindness, he went to Philadelphia, and there found work—but only as an office boy.

He did, however, manage to attach himself to a Captain Elliott who encouraged him thus: "Boy, if I had a dozen sons, I would see them all in their graves rather than to sea." Nordhoff wouldn't give up, and plagued the man until Elliott scribbled on a piece of paper, "Officer of the Naval Rendezvous [recruiting station] will ship the bearer—a boy—Com C. Elliott." Nordhoff thanked him; the captain said, "Go to the devil!" But "instead I went to the Rendezvous." Nordhoff had already made himself such a nuisance there that the shipping officer turned his back on him. The boy waved the paper and it worked a remarkable transformation on the man. "He looked at it then me, then it again. Then politely asked me to take a seat. 'This alters the case, my lad' said he, in the tone of a gentleman (one I had not heard before), 'So your father is acquainted with Commodore Elliott.'"

Nordhoff agreed with this completely mistaken supposition, and discovered he "possessed the magic signet before which all doors fly open, all difficulties vanish. The Articles of Agreement were read over to me in a monotonous drawl, and I was asked, if, of my own free will, I proposed to sign them." He did; a small bell tinkled and a door opened on a naval doctor who gave him a cursory examination, dashed off a note in pencil, and handed it to Nordhoff. "This I rendered up to the man of the drawl, who then asked if I was fully aware of all the responsibilities I was about to take upon myself." The man guided Nordhoff's hand as he signed his name to a document in which he swore "to submit to the rules and regulations laid down for the government of seamen and the United States Navy."

"Now," said the drawler, "you belong to Uncle Sam."

Nordhoff "was shipped on that day, as a 'First-Class Boy' . . . at wages of eight dollars per month, and would immediately receive three months' advance, with which to be fitted out. That is, each non-commissioned officer, seaman, landsman, or boy, receives, on entering the United States Navy, money to defray all the expenses of uniform, clothing, bedding, etc., all of which items are to meet Navy regulations."

The young recruit was briefly taken out of Uncle Sam's arms and embraced by those of a crimp. Every large seaport was home to a population of crimps. One sailor who passed through their hands put them in the same category as "pimps and grave-robbers." They lived off the advance wages and bounties paid to newly enlisted seamen. The crimp would approach his mark, talk up the pleasures of maritime life, get him to sign shipping articles, invite him aboard a receiving ship "just to look her over," and, once there, hand the signed papers to a counterpart on the ship. With the documents came a bill for $36 for nautical dress that was said to be the newcomer's necessary clothing. Also, there would be a $4 fee to the crimp for vouching for his new friend's character and $1 for a "shipping bowl," a dire concoction of rum, sugar, and egg that had helped persuade the man to venture onto the ship. And once aboard, there he stayed; as soon as the dubious certificate had changed hands, he could not leave.

THE *SOMERS* | 55

This started a cycle that the recruit would find hard to break. He had to borrow money from the purser to replace his flimsy new clothes with proper ones, and thereafter (as a close counterpart to the shoreside sharecropper) would be in perpetual debt to the ship's store.

Pursers received a modest salary of $480 a year, but this was dramatically enhanced by their ability to make a profit of up to 50 percent on the goods they sold to the crew. Since the purser sold everything from tea and sugar to entire outfits, with never the shadow of a competitor, he always did well for himself, and sometimes astonishingly well. A frigate's purser came ashore from one cruise with $58,040. As this was the equivalent of just under $1.2 million in today's purchasing power, his sea voyage had set him up for life.

Nordhoff's crimp didn't have to fuss with any paperwork—that had been taken care of—but he was responsible for getting his charge safely aboard ship and was free to swindle the neophyte with a long-standing and well-organized scheme of commercial chicanery.

"To see that all is ostensibly done fair and above board," Nordhoff explains, "the master-at-arms shall, on the rendering on board of the recruit, examine this [newly bought] clothing to see that the requisite number of pieces—the quantity is there. So far, so good. But, unfortunately for poor 'greeny [greenhorn],' the quality of the clothing is not made a matter of regulation."

Nordhoff goes on to list the mandated articles. Here is the full rig an 1840s Navy man had to live on and in all during his time in the service: "One blue cloth mustering jacket, one pair blue cloth mustering trousers, two white duck frocks (called shirts on shore) with blue collars, two pair white duck trousers, two blue flannel shirts, one pea-jacket (overcoat), two pair cotton socks, one black tarpaulin hat, one mattress and mattress cover, two blankets, one pot, pan, spoon, and knife, and one clothes bag."

All this the crimp sold Nordhoff. Here's what the buyer soon discovered:

"It is a matter of curiosity, as well as a striking instance of the pursuit of the dollar, to see how faithfully this list could be copied, without one item coming up to the desired standards." The blue jacket and trousers, "used only for mustering on special occasions, are supposed to be made of very fine cloth." Nordhoff's turned out to be "made of rusty-looking serge, described by an old salt as 'dog's hair and oakum, and three pence an armful,'" the "dog's hair" being a reference to the whimsy "that a bull mastiff could be flung 'between any two threads of it.'" The white duck frocks and trousers "were made of a yellow bagging so coarse that it would scarcely hold peas," but that didn't much matter because they all fell apart at their first washing. "Instead of the 'neat' black silk neckerchief and shining pumps (articles of which a true man-of-war's man greatly delights), green recruits are furnished with a rusty bamboo rag, and shoes made of varnished brown paper," both kerchiefs and pumps doomed to "vanish before damp salt air as mist does before a bright sun." Worst of all, perhaps, was the "neat tarpaulin hat," because sailors devoted so much affectionate attention to theirs. It should have been "hard and heavy as a brick, smooth and glossy as though made of glass (and the crowning glory of a man-of-war's costume)." Nordhoff's crimp had left his sucker with "a miserable featherweight of lacquered straw."

Thus equipped, Nordhoff was taken, as would be the crew of the *Somers*, to the "guardo," which was what every seasoned sailor called a receiving ship.

There the master-at-arms "turned out the contents of my clothes bag on deck, kicked them over with a practised foot before pronouncing them 'All right.' Now I was shown 'forw'd'"—to the crew's quarters; officers lived aft.

Nordhoff found himself among "about two dozen regular old tars. They all, but one or two, bore about them the marks of recent excesses, and smelt strongly of bad liquor." He timidly sat down "on a shot box, at a little distance, until presently one of the more sober approached, saying, 'Well, boy. Shipped, have you?'

"'Yes, sir.'

"'Better have hung yourself,' growled another."

MOST OF THE CREW of the *Somers* would probably have been spared such a greeting, as there were few "regular old tars" there to haze them. Of the 120 souls aboard, only some 30 were out of their teens; the rest were nineteen or younger, 45 of them between the ages of thirteen and sixteen.

On a ship so small, the "saplings," as they were called, had less difficulty learning their way around their new home than they would have in the relative immensities of a ship of the line. Still, their abrupt immersion into an entirely new world—a dark, cramped, cluttered world in nervous and often violent motion—was wrenching.

Even though Herman Melville had been at sea for four years—first aboard a merchantman, then in a whaler—when he joined the Navy in 1843, he initially found the frigate *United States* nearly as intimidating as Mackenzie's boys had the *Somers* during their first taste of her a year earlier. "The living on board a man-of-war," wrote Melville, "is like living in a market; where you dress on the doorsteps and sleep in the cellar."

To sleep at all took some doing. Nordhoff "had read of sailors and hammocks, but before this had no idea of the article." He discovered it to be "an oblong strip of stout canvas, having a number of strings tied to each end." As he held his "with a puzzled air," a veteran sailor—kinder than the one who had suggested he hang himself—"took me to the lower deck, and showed me a number of hooks set into the overhead beams. . . . The little strings before mentioned—the 'clews'—I found were to be used to suspend the hammock between two of the hooks, making a swinging bedstead at an altitude of about four feet above the deck. Once slung, into it I packed my rag-and-shaving mattress, and dog's-hair blankets, and the affair was now pronounced ready for my occupancy.

"'See if you can jump in,' my mentor now advised."

The mentor gave him a match tub (a low circular wooden box used to contain slow matches to fire the guns, and not usually as a stepladder). "I was told to catch onto two of the hooks overhead, give my body a swing, and alight in the hammock." He hesitated, and was assured, "It's as easy as eating soft tack with butter." Nordhoff made his leap; the hammock swaddled him for a couple of seconds before flipping over to spit him out onto the deck.

Eventually, inevitably, he mastered the technique.

So would the apprentices on the *Somers*, although they didn't have that luxurious four feet of empty air between them and the planking below.

Their bedroom was on the berth deck (on the diminutive *Somers* this was one of just two habitable decks, the other being the spar deck—the open topside of the ship). Fifty by seventeen feet, and with some of that stingy footage taken up by the forward end of the galley, the chamber's forty-eight-inch headroom forced all but its smallest inhabitants to scuttle about in a crouch.

One hundred apprentices had to sling their hammocks in three tiers, the lowest a few inches off the deck. Each was allowed a space eighteen inches across for his hammock, which he struggled into by the dim shine of fo'c'sle lamps that burned a funereal blue in the close air. At first, nights were a muttering bedlam, the rows of bundles with their homesick, seasick occupants bumping against one another with the sway of the ship, noises of crying and retching and the curses of those awakened by them, the constant scrabbling of the rats that had been stowaways on every ship since long before Phoenician times.

Snores, swearing, and rats aside, the ship was never quiet, not by night and certainly not by day. The ruckus from the pens holding chickens and pigs that would eventually feed the officers was at least familiar to boys who had recently quit the farm, but so much was strange and alarming. The newcomer, wrote Melville, "is half stunned with the unaccustomed sounds ringing in his ears; which ears seem to him like belfries full of tocsins. On the gun-deck, a thousand scythed chariots seem to be passing; he hears . . . the clash of cutlasses and curses. The Boatswain's mates whistle round him, like hawks screaming in a gale, and the strange noises under decks, are like volcanic rumblings in a mountain. He dodges sudden sounds, as a raw recruit falling bombs."

As the apprentices squirmed toward sleep in their hammocks on the evening of September 11, they had more to discomfit them than noises. The day had been unseasonably close and muggy—like mid-August rather than mid-September—and heat still lay thick in the berth deck. If the clammy humidity didn't keep them awake, anxiety well might have. Soon these recruits would have to learn the ways of an alien civilization, hard-edged and unforgiving, one with its own language and ancient customs, and fanged with a hundred perils.

The *Somers* would sail in the morning.

THEY WERE AWAKENED—those who had slept at all—with "Turn out, there!" "Rouse a bit!" "Show a leg or a purser's stocking!" All this, as Nordhoff put it, "a most horrid din . . . being roared and reroared from half a dozen hoarse throats on different parts of the main deck."

A sharp, brief rain had settled the heat, and the apprentices stumbled out into a sparkling early autumn day. The sea was calm, but its motions so unfamiliar that many of the boys thought they were in a storm. On his first day at sea, Nordhoff "heard different sounds: twenty poor fellows groaning as they leant over the bows 'to cast up their accounts.'"

The recruits who escaped seasickness were either frightened by incomprehensible orders, or entirely ignored, and did their best to keep out of the way of men rushing to pursue tasks so endless and various that, Melville says, it "would require a German commentator to chronicle." He gives a swarm of throwaway examples: "We say nothing here of Boatswain's mates, Gunner's mates, Carpenter's mates, Sail-maker's mates, Armorer's mates, Master-at-Arms, Ship's corporals, Cockswains, Quarter-masters, Quarter-gunners, Captains of the Forecastle, Captains of the Fore-top, Captains of the Main-top, Captains of the Mizen-top, Captains of the After-Guard, Captains of the Main-Hold, Captains of the Fore-Hold, Captains of the Head, Coopers, Painters, Tinkers, Commodore's Steward, Captain's Steward, Ward-Room Steward, Steerage Steward, Commodore's cook, Captain's cook, Officers' cook, cooks of the range, Mess-cooks, hammock-boys, messenger boys, cot-boys, loblolly-boys, and numberless others, whose functions are fixed and peculiar."

"Fixed" is the telling word here. Though all seemed a windblown, tumbling chaos to the recruit, any US warship was a wonder of rigid organization, with everyone aboard assigned a post to which he automatically jumped when called, there to do a job that never varied. Each seaman, says Melville, "knows his own special place and is infallibly found there. He sees nothing else, attends to nothing else, and will stay there until grim death or an epaulette orders him away."

It was the job of Captain Mackenzie and every other officer aboard the *Somers* to see that the scores of bewildered adolescents in their charge coalesced into a trained crew who would perform their tasks with something like the mechanical precision the ship's chronometers brought to telling the time of day.

The training began with the fundamentals. As on any naval vessel, the entire crew was divided into two watches—starboard and larboard (port)—which in turn were broken into "divisions": forecastlemen, foretopmen, maintopmen, mizzentopmen, afterguard, and waisters. In the early days of training, it would be the warrant officers and the non-commissioned officers who pummeled and harassed the apprentices into their places. Nordhoff introduced the warrant officers to his readers: "boatswain, the gunner, the sailmaker, and carpenter. The boatswain (pronounced bosun) is the chief sailor. He has charge of the rigging of the vessel, and is responsible to the first lieutenant that all aloft is kept in good order. He is easily distinguished by his silver whistle, his rattan cane (the terror of little boys), his stentorian voice, and the Bardolphian [crimson, from the sun, or drink, or general rage] hue of his features."

The gunner especially irritated Nordhoff: "His principal occupation in time of peace is growling about his guns," while the gunner's mates "assist their chief in his self-imposed task of growling at everybody and everything."

The sailmaker had charge of all the canvas aboard, from mainsail to hammocks to the cots in the sick bay. The carpenter was his counterpart. All these men save the gunner went aloft every morning at sea to check that all was well with sails, masts, and rigging, and report to the first lieutenant.

"First among the petty officers is the master-at-arms, head of the police force of the ship," noted Nordhoff. He looked after any prisoners and was "lord of the berth deck, and the terror of cooks." On most American warships his authority was backed up by a contingent of marines. Their "place is not at all enviable: compelled to live and labour among the crew, yet having a principal duty to spy out and bring to punishment all offenders against the laws of the vessel." As such, they were the butt of constant hostile raillery from the rest of the crew, who called them "sojers"—"the most stinging epithet a sailor can direct at anybody." An ancient seafaring rubric holds: "A messmate before a shipmate, a shipmate before a stranger, a stranger before a dog, but a dog before a soldier."

As it happened, these despised creatures were absent from the *Somers*; there simply wasn't enough room for them. The complement of marines aboard stood at one: Orderly Sergeant Michael Garty, the master-at-arms. This might have pleased the older sailors, but it is hard not to see those vacant posts as a bad omen. Had there been even a small marine presence on the brig, its cruise might have ended very differently.

Despite Nordhoff's crabbing about the gunner's growls, he was an important figure. Melville writes, "As the specific object for which a man-of-war is built and put into commission is to fight and fire off cannon, it is, of course, deemed indispensable that the crew should be duly instructed in the art and mystery involved. Hence these 'general quarters,' which is a mustering of all hands to their stations at the guns . . . and a sort of sham-fight with an imaginary foe." That's what "general quarters" meant in the 1840s, and what it means today.

Although the guns on the *Somers*—like those on every warship— looked as inert and timeless as the granite outcroppings of a cliff, they required as much attention as a greenhouse full of orchids. Gun drill began early on the *Somers*, and there was plenty of it. Nordhoff writes, "Taking one gun crew at a time, the lieutenants of divisions, aided by warrant and petty officers and 'old hands,' began in making all familiar with their duties, while the guns themselves, rough and rusty, were thoroughly cleaned and rubbed bright with brick and canvas, and covered with a mixture of lampblack, beeswax, and turpentine, this latter preventing rust and making the surfaces smooth and bright as a looking-glass. The various accoutrements of the guns, rammers, sponges, priming wires, monkey-tails, caps, and cutlasses were also cleaned and brightened."

Once brought to a proper gloss, the guns were run in and out, fired (in imagination at first), swiveled, reloaded, and on and on. Melville found that "in warm weather this pastime at the guns is exceedingly unpleasant, to say the least, and throws a quiet man into a violent passion and perspiration. For one, I ever abominated it."

The gun Melville attended was, like all those aboard the *Somers*, a carronade; and "for the benefit of a Quaker reader here and there," he explains that "the carronade is a gun comparatively short and light for its calibre. A carronade throwing a thirty-two-pound shot weighs considerably less than a long-gun throwing a twenty-four-pound shot." Still the piece was just a hundred pounds shy of a ton, which was more than enough to bring out the sweat on its young servers.

Despite the elegant chronometers that gave exactitude both to the ship's day and to its position on the globe, Nordhoff wrote that "on board ship, we do not ask 'What o'clock?' but rather 'How many bells?'" Even the slowest of the apprentices had quickly to pick up a new kind of timekeeping, which, Nordhoff explained, "is reckoned by bells. The twenty-four hours are arranged in five watches of four hours each, and two of two hours each, which are called the dog-watches. At the end of the first half-hour on a watch, the ship's bell is struck one time, at the end of the second half-hour two times, and so on, until it is eight bells, which marks the expiration of four hours, or a complete watch, when the series recommences."

With their working lives thus musically segmented, and their early fear of having to climb a mast perhaps beginning to fade (but not their fear of the master-at-arms or the boatswain), their first heavy travails at the 32-pounders mitigated some by the inherent interest the guns held, having stowed the anchors for the voyage ahead, the apprentices settled into the unvarying routines of shipboard life: "Breakfast at eight," wrote Nordhoff, "quarters at nine, dinner at twelve, supper at five, quarters at six—these were the landmarks announcing the passing of the days."

A few days out came what Nordhoff called "the grand overhaul of clothing." This could take a full week—an excruciating one—as the wares of the crimp were exposed, one owner at a time, in all their squalor. The master-at-arms on the guardo, indifferently acquiescent when shown the stuff with which the boys had equipped themselves, had been replaced by a fierce perfectionist who swore at the shoddy blankets spread out by one recruit, kicked aside the already wilting shoes of another, and in the end sent perhaps two-thirds of the crew off to the purser to acquire honest goods, along with a hefty load of debt. Poor Nordhoff "found that of all I had paid $24 for in Philadelphia, I could not use a single article. I had to purchase an entire new outfit, costing six months' pay." In the final accounting, he owed the Navy nine months' worth of his salary.

Along with the crimps' trash, the crew left behind the initial strangeness of their ship. They were learning to sleep amid incessant hubbub, and they were getting regularly fed at their assigned seats in the mess. "It is one of the few privileges left to the crew of a man-of-war," said Nordhoff, "that messes shall be composed of individuals voluntarily associating with one another. No one can remain on a mess not willing to receive him, and changing messes is only allowed every three months." With an almost entirely green crew, the *Somers*'s petty officers would have had to take a greater role than usual in getting these little eating clubs established.

The food was not elegant—Nordhoff's first meal aboard ship was sea bread, raw salt pork, cold boiled potatoes, and vinegar—but it was as good a diet as many crewmen had known in their shore-bound days, and it was surprisingly well supervised. The mess cooks were also responsible for the state of their equipment, which, noted Nordhoff, was kept "in an extraordinary state of cleanliness." At seven bells each day the master-at-arms would pass down rows of pans, having "on his hands for the occasion white cotton gloves, and should he in rubbing those on the inside of any tins . . . get them soiled with grease or dirt, woe betide the unfortunate cook, whose organ of tidiness has lacked development." Once the pots and pans passed inspection, the cook brought a sample of the forthcoming meal to the officer of the deck, and only after he approved it would the crew be fed.

So the ship's cook had a job as demanding as that of most officers, and his position, said Nordhoff, "is generally held by a coloured man, they having been proved by experience to be the handiest or best suited for the place. The office was in olden times one of some dignity, and our old black cook used to relate with great glee, that when he was a boy in the British Navy, the ship's cook was privileged to wear a sword."

Next to the cook's productions and the daily grog ration (forbidden to the apprentices aboard the *Somers*), what many sailors most enjoyed was live firing: the great concussions, the bright stabs of muzzle-flame, the inspiriting prickle of powder smoke billowing along the deck past the crouched, reloading gunners.

And what every hand hated was Sunday muster. It began with a welter of shouted orders: "Hear this! Fore and aft! White frocks! Blue jackets and trousers! Black hats and shoes! To muster!" First, Nordhoff recounted, "there is a general groan, then forthwith a general ransacking of clothing bags for mustering clothes with a great anxiety to make a good appearance. 'Tie my neckerchief!', 'Turn down my collar!', 'Help me on with my jacket!', and an infinity of similar requests and questions."

At nine the drum beat to quarters for the preliminary muster; an hour later a tinny squeal from all the "calls"—pipes—brandished by the boatswains' mates sent every hand to assemble on deck with "the officers ranged in two rows along the weather side of the quarterdeck, behind them the boatswain and petty officers, also ranged in order, the captain . . . with pencil and paper in hand, ready to note down deficiencies."

Quiet now. The captain's clerk read the Articles of War. They are harsh. Melville complained that "of some twenty offences—made penal—that a seaman may commit, and which are specified in this code, thirteen are punishable by death." The crew listened to a somber litany. Sleeping on watch: *Shall suffer death*; disobeying a superior officer: *Shall suffer death*; striking a superior officer: *Shall suffer death*. . . . Some of the articles do conclude *Shall suffer death, or such punishment as a court-martial shall adjudge*, but this gave Melville no comfort, for didn't it suggest "a penalty still more serious? Perhaps it means, '*death, or worse punishment.*'" He concludes his thoughts on the Articles with a burst of wild, poetic warning: "Have a care, then, have a care, lest you come to a sad end, even the end of a rope; lest, with a black-and-blue throat, you turn a dumb diver after pearl-shells; put to bed forever, and tucked in, in your own hammock, at the bottom of the sea. And there you will lie, White-Jacket, while hostile navies are playing cannon-ball billiards over your grave."

Once they'd absorbed these multiple reminders of their mortality, every man answered, "Here, sir," as the purser's clerk called his name. Then he took off his hat and walked slowly down the line of officers, while every one of them from boy midshipman to first lieutenant subjected him to the most minute scrutiny. "If anything will try nerves," says Nordhoff, "it is this. I never knew anyone, even to the oldest man-of-war's man who had mustered hundreds of times, that could hear 'all hands called to muster' without a shudder. To feel hundreds of eyes looking at you, noting every peculiarity of form, dress, walk, and carriage. To be conscious that the least impropriety will elicit a grin from hundreds of faces; to know, in addition, that any real shortcoming will be noted and made subject of after punishment, and that a speck of dirt, a badly-arranged collar, an ill-fitting jacket or trousers, or an improper walk, may call forth instant public rebuke. . . ."

There was more to it than mere humiliation before your peers. During his Sunday-muster gauntlet Nordhoff had the last of his crimp's clothes discovered, snatched from him, and confiscated, but ordinary naval discipline went considerably further than putting a sailor out of pocket. Of that white-glove inspection of the mess pans, Nordhoff says, "Every mark on the gloves is scored upon the back of the delinquent scullion."

That's not a figure of speech. Those telltale gloves—and a thousand other indicators of naval malfeasance—brought on the lash.

"All hands witness punishment!" It was always administered before the entire ship's complement. Nordhoff saw his first flogging on his ship's first Saturday at sea. The felons were guilty of the timeless seagoing outrage of drunkenness. "Some of our tars, whose love of bad liquor set astir every bit of ingenuity they possessed, found means to smuggle on board quantities of a liquid compounded of turpentine, water, and a dash of country liquor. This being sold as 'rum,' but smelling like . . . faugh! I will not attempt to describe it. With a 'skin' . . . [a cow's bladder filled with] this, three or four would get gloriously fuddled at night, to wake next morning in the brig. Here they were retained in safe keeping until the vessel could get to sea as, generally, there was no flogging in harbor."

Nordhoff describes how a heavy deck grating had been canted upright at the gangway. The officers—all with sidearms, all in dress uniform—began to assemble around it. The prisoners were led out of the brig. The ship's surgeon was on hand, in a lukewarm effort to make sure the victim survived. The captain called, "Thomas Brown. You were drunk, sir. Master-at-arms, strip him." The pertinent Article of War was read aloud. "Seize him up!"

"Thomas Brown is walked forward onto the grating, to which his feet are securely fastened by lashings, his wrists being lashed above his head to the hammock rail." The prisoner stood, face toward the wooden grid, back naked before the audience. The boatswain took from a green cloth bag a thick, stiff, foot-long cylinder of rope. This was the handle of the cat-o'-nine-tails. Nine eighteen-inch lengths of braided hemp dangled from it. "A few moments of dread silence intervene, during which the chief boatswain's mate nervously runs his fingers through the cat's lashes."

"Boatswain's mate," said the captain, "do your duty." The mate reached far back behind him and swung the cat against Brown's back. Melville said the whip always made a "cutting, wiry sound" as it tore into flesh; Nordhoff said it met the back with a "*thug!*"

"One," said the master-at-arms. The victim hadn't moved. There were eleven blows to come: the captain could send as many crewmen as he chose to the grating at any time, but he could not condemn a sailor to more than twelve lashes without first convening a court-martial.

Thug! "Now the flesh on Brown's back quivers and creeps, the injured muscles contract, and the stripes assume a bright red tinge."

Thug! "The stripes turn a dark purple, and the grating shakes convulsively with the reluctant start wrung from the strong man in agony."

Thug! "Blood! O God, I could look no more." There were twenty men whipped that long morning, but Nordhoff never again looked. "Many more times was I compelled to hear the sharp whistle of the cat as it swung through the air, and the dull sound of the blow as it met the quivering flesh, but never more did I *see* a man flogged."

In less than a decade Congress would abolish flogging. Some captains already hated the practice. Part of the *Somers*'s mission was to carry dispatches to the sloop-of-war *Vandalia* on the Africa station, a ship whose master, Captain Ramsay, forbade all corporal punishment.

But the *Somers* had a flogging captain, as his charges were already beginning to learn.

THE *SOMERS*, LIKE ANY OTHER populous, close-knit community, always simmered with gossip. Much of it was far-fetched, but some was right on the mark. Well before she set sail on September 12, word had spread below decks about Captain Mackenzie's enthusiasm for the lash.

The brig's September departure was not, strictly speaking, her maiden voyage; in July Mackenzie had taken her on a shakedown cruise from New York to Puerto Rico and back. A brief trip, but long enough for the ship to have lost an apprentice overboard, a misfortune the captain seems to have felt he shared with the drowned boy: "I did hope to have gone through the first stages of training the crew and performed the cruise without a single accident but this has been denied me."

The cruise was also long enough to have given its sailors a taste of their captain's severity, and while the *Somers* was back in New York fitting out for her longer voyage, Mackenzie ordered some fifty floggings. The harshest—for attempted desertion and theft—laid on the full dozen lashes. Those were administered with the cat, but its ugly little sibling, the colt, was busy all the time. This was a lighter but by no means innocuous instrument, a three-foot-long finger-thick rope with a wooden handle—a cat-o'-one-tail, as it were, but perfectly capable of cutting into flesh.

It was reserved for the younger malefactors (the very youngest, the twelve- and thirteen-year-olds, were sometimes allowed to keep their shirts on while it did its work). During his six weeks at anchor in New York, Mackenzie put the colt to use 422 times, for crimes that ranged from spitting and throwing tea on the deck to blasphemy and "skulking."

Mackenzie may not have been aware of it, but he had already been called out in print for cruelty. In 1841 a sailor named Solomon H. Sanborn published a pamphlet entitled *An Exposition of Official Tyranny in the United States Navy*. One of the tyrants he singled out was "Alexander S. Mackenzie, better known as Lieutenant A. Slidell, the accomplished author." Sanborn reported that when Mackenzie was first lieutenant of the frigate *Independence* in 1837, a marine in the ship's company tossed some orange peels into a "spit box"—a wooden cuspidor—on the spar deck. Mackenzie gave him twelve lashes, which Solomon saw as a "cruel, unnecessary and unjust punishment." A little later, as captain of the schooner *Dolphin*, Mackenzie managed to more than triple the legal limit by meting out thirty-nine lashes to a sailor who had exhibited "mutinous conduct." Shortly after that, when he had temporary command of the sloop-of-war *Fairfield*, Sanborn said, he "was noted for his cruelty to the men for small offenses and trifling accidents."

So they were learning aboard the *Somers*. On September 15—just three days out of New York—the colt appeared: six lashes each for James Travis, Edward Anderson, and Peter Hanson, the three found guilty of skulking, a term that generally meant trying to avoid work, but was flexible enough to encompass other crimes. This started a run of bad luck for Travis. He was thirteen, popular, said to be of "good character," but before the cruise was over he would receive another thirty-three lashes.

The next day Charles Van Velsor got in a squabble with a ship-mate that earned him twelve colts (as with the cat, that was the limit allowed) for "striking Bradshaw." Next up was Richard Gilmore, another skulker: twelve blows for him, too.

Less than a week later, on the twenty-second, nine sailors were flogged, several for "disobedience" (another conveniently amorphous crime), one for skulking, one simply "by order of the Captain." The next day put twelve stripes on fourteen-year-old Dennis Manning's back; though "smart and active," Manning had been disobedient. That initial penalty evidently had little effect: before the cruise ended, he would receive 101 lashes—14 with the cat and 87 with the colt—more than anyone else aboard.

The punishments continued. Unlike lively Manning, John Finneday was "dull and stupid," so six colts for him. Colts and the cat, the cat and colts—for impertinence, for washing a jersey without permission, for dropping a knife from a yardarm, for being grimy at muster, for profanity, for misplacing a hammock, for sassing the master-at-arms . . .

Ships' logs of the era reveal a near-infinite catalog of infractions that called for flogging: smoking after 10 p.m. (12 lashes with cat); hallooing on the gun deck (8 lashes with cat); having another's shirt (8 lashes with colt); circulating false reports (12 lashes with cat); selling clothes (9 lashes with cat); throwing soapsuds in the eyes of captain of the afterguard (6 lashes with colt); smuggling cigars from ship to shore (12 lashes with cat); cursing sentry on post (12 lashes with cat); filthiness (this may have been a euphemism for homosexual activity—8 lashes with cat).

What made the prospect of punishment aboard the *Somers* more than ordinarily dismaying was who did the punishing.

Chief Boatswain's Mate Samuel Cromwell was the largest man aboard the ship, and by all accounts the fiercest. To the apprentices he was a perfect ogre, and even the officers were intimidated by him.

Once, frustrated by a wind-snarled tangle of rope and canvas, he bawled down to the deck, "God damn the jib and the lacing and the damned fool that invented it!"

This was a far more potent outburst than it might seem to modern ears. In what was a religious age, ordering the Deity to damn something was considered stronger talk than any conventional obscenity, as the speaker is putting himself on equal terms with God. Looking back on his time at sea, a sailor named Richard Gatewood said, "I profaned the name of God without any remorse of conscience. . . . I have often called on God to damn my body and my soul, yards and sails, rigging and blocks, everything below and aloft, the ship and my shipmates." By the time he was recalling this, Gatewood had repented: "O! It fills me with horror when I reflect on what I have said, and what I have done."

What's more, Cromwell had directed his profanity at First Lieutenant Guert Gansevoort—and beyond that, both men knew very well that the damned fool who'd invented the lacing was Captain Mackenzie.

A flogging offense if ever there was one, but Gansevoort merely "reproved him severely." Another time Gansevoort issued an order and Cromwell told him outright that what the officer wanted was "damned hard usage." Again, the boatswain suffered no punishment.

A Virginian in his mid-thirties, bearded and boisterous, Cromwell had a livid scar running up his forehead into his hair that may have helped give rise to the rumor that he'd once been a hand on a slaver, even on a pirate ship. Not much more is known about him. He had some education—Mackenzie would remark on his elegant handwriting—was a capable seaman, and had recently gotten married.

Cromwell's molten temper found an outlet often on the *Somers*, as it was his job to swing the lash. Purser's Steward James Wales said the boatswain struck even the youngest wrongdoers "with all his might, as though it was pleasing to him to whip them. He whipped them hard, the same as though they were men instead of boys. I have frequently heard Commander Mackenzie censure him for whipping so hard, and he has often ordered him to stop."

PHILIP SPENCER WAS NEVER sent to the grating—no officer could be—but Captain Mackenzie would probably have wanted to, for Spencer was a vexation to him from the very start.

As soon as the captain discovered that the midshipman had gotten in trouble with drink on the Brazilian station, "I earnestly desired his removal from my vessel." When Mackenzie got word "that Spencer has expressed a willingness to be transferred," he told his first lieutenant "that if he would apply to Commodore Perry to detach him from the *Somers* I would second his application." The lieutenant at once wrote the application, and the captain as quickly endorsed it. But perhaps Perry had had his fill of struggles over Midshipman Spencer and simply wanted him out of his hair. And why approve a transfer that was sure to annoy the secretary of war? He refused outright; Spencer and Mackenzie would be shipmates.

And so would Spencer and a lot of Mackenzie's friends and relatives. Two of the midshipmen were Commodore Perry's sons, and thus the captain's nephews; another midshipman, Adrian Deslonde, was related by marriage to John Slidell, Mackenzie's brother; and the rest of the midshipmen's families had given their sons over to the captain's "special care."

Spencer's bitter school years had shown that he had scant genius for making friends, and here he was living with a group of youngsters who already had tight mutual bonds. Living with them in suffocatingly close quarters, too: like the rest of the brig, the steerage that was home to the midshipmen was overcrowded. The low-ceilinged fourteen-foot-long room, only four feet wide, had been far from adequate for the five people for which it had been designed. When Spencer ducked down in and looked for a place to stow his dunnage, he was its seventh occupant.

Captain Mackenzie wrote, "The *Somers* sailed with seven in her steerage; they could not all sit together round the table. The two oldest and most useful had no locker to put their clothes in, and have slept during the cruise on the steerage-deck, the camp stools, the booms in the tops, or in the quarter boats."

In that cramped, coffin-shaped chamber, Philip Spencer was going to ride, cheek by jowl with chilly companions, to the coast of Africa.

Perhaps the destination nourished the reluctant mariner's imagination. Africa! Parrots—did they have parrots in Africa?—in any event, there would be monkeys, and those delicious fruits mentioned in *The Pirates Own Book*. And pirates, too. Spencer's favorite book had stories about the fat merchantmen snapped up off the Cape Verde Islands a century earlier, and it devoted a rousing chapter to Howell Davis, who descended on the Royal African Company's fort in the Gambia River, seized it by ruse without firing a shot, and came away with £2,000 worth of gold. Davis then joined forces with the spectacularly successful French buccaneer Olivier Levasseur, until (even *The Pirates Own Book* offered moral instruction when it could) "that dangerous enemy, strong drink, had . . . sown the seeds of discord among these affectionate bretheren." They parted ways, Davis to fall to a Portuguese bullet, Levasseur to capture a Portuguese galleon so heavy with treasure—£50,000 worth of golden guineas for every member of his crew—that they did not even bother to rob the passengers.

Other delights of Africa were suggested by a smudgy linecut showing a pirate cuddling beneath some tropical foliage with what the caption primly called "his Madagascar wife."

In his comfortless quarters, the father of Chi Psi began to turn his thoughts toward a more volatile fraternity, one bound not by secret handshakes and tag-ends of ancient Greek, but by plunder and rape and murder.

THE SOMERS WAS HEADING for Africa because of the Webster-Ashburton Treaty, which had been signed back in August. Among its happier provisions, it traded an imminent war with Britain over Maine's northern boundary (the imposing granite ramparts of Fort Knox still stand on the Penobscot River, a monument to that never-consummated conflict) in return for America's helping England suppress the slave trade.

Mackenzie was to deliver dispatches to the sloop-of-war *Vandalia*, part of the recently formed Home Squadron, a misleading name as she was far from home, patrolling for slavers along the African coast. The mission seems not to have been a crucial one—the dispatches never did get delivered—for the brig's real purpose was to turn her green crew into seamen.

The officer bearing the brunt of that responsibility was Guert Gansevoort. Although the *Somers*'s first lieutenant was second-in-command after the captain, he might have had the hardest job aboard. As Nordhoff explained, "The first lieutenant . . . has not the responsibilities as the captain, but his duties are much more laborious. He keeps no watch, but is on duty all day, a day which includes a full inspection of both vessel and crew. All reports from the minor officers are made to him. All communications to the captain pass through his hands. On occasions when 'all hands' are called—in getting 'under weigh' or coming to anchor, etc, he has charge of the deck. . . . At quarters he has charge of the quarterdeck division and, in action he manoeuvres the ship. . . ." In short, he "needs a thorough knowledge of the ship, a quick and sure judgement on the capabilities of all individuals composing the crew, and great patience and foresight." Although he is "usually a terror to all evildoers and the slovenly . . . the comfort of all on board greatly depends upon him."

On the *Somers* this protean figure was Guert Gansevoort. He was a highly capable officer, and beyond that American literature stands in his debt, for he persuaded his first cousin, Herman Melville, to go to sea.

Born near Albany in 1812 in Gansevoort, New York—that the area was named for his grandfather, a Revolutionary War veteran and canny businessman, reflects his comfortable background—he joined the Navy and was appointed midshipman in 1824. In 1831 he wrote an uncle saying, "I have enjoyed excellent health, am growing rapidly, and in ev'ry respect as happily situated as I could wish. I have lately been promoted to the situation of acting Sailing Master of this Ship." To which he added proudly, "And am perhaps the youngest person that ever held that appointment." He made lieutenant in 1837, and the posting to the *Somers* as Mackenzie's highest subordinate attests to his abilities.

He was to achieve some prominence both in the fight with Mexico and in the Civil War, so it is strange that no known photograph of him exists. Melville's sister Augusta wrote that Guert "looks very much like Herman, we all noticed it." Almost everyone did.

About what many a first lieutenant might have seen as a galling ancillary duty—running a floating schoolroom—Gansevoort wrote, on December 24, 1842, "Of those apprentices, those *children*, entrusted to the care of the Officers; for whose safety we were responsible,—to God, to their country, & to their *parents*; to many of whom, before we sailed; I had pledged myself, to extend parental care & advice . . ."

If the language seems strained and high-flown even by the standards of the era, that is because Gansevoort was very much on the defensive when he set it down. He had already read John Spencer's letter about the hanging of his son. But there is no reason to believe that at the outset of the cruise he resented his tutorial duties, or frightened the midshipmen under him more than did any other first lieutenant of the day.

No foremast hand hated to see a midshipman taken to task. Although mere children in the breeding-ground of officers, midshipmen outranked every ordinary seaman and, if they chose, could vent upon him the least appealing impulses of the adolescent. "At times," wrote Melville, "you will see one of these lads, not five feet high, gazing up with inflamed eye at some venerable six-footer of a forecastle-man, cursing and insulting him by every epithet deemed most scandalous and unendurable among men." The six-footer can only stand there on the deck and take it, for naval law "suspends death itself over his head should his passion discharge the slightest blow at the boy-worm that spits at his feet."

Aside from their being obnoxious, Melville felt midshipmen had too little to *do*. "These boys are sent to sea, for the purpose of making commodores; and in order to become commodores, many of them deem it indispensable forthwith to commence chewing tobacco, drinking brandy and water, and swearing at sailors. As they are placed on board a sea-going ship to go to school and learn the duty of a Lieutenant; and until qualified to act as such, have few or no special functions to attend to . . . they are generally great consumers of Macassar oil and the Balm of Columbia [hair dressings]; they thirst and rage after whiskers; and sometimes, applying their ointments, lay themselves out in the sun, to promote the fertility of their chins."

Moreover, Melville said that he had met few midshipmen who didn't enjoy the spectacle of a good flogging. "It would seem that they themselves, having so recently escaped the posterior discipline of the nursery and the infant school, are impatient to recover from those smarting reminiscences by mincing the backs of full-grown American freemen."

The midshipmen messed together in their steerage quarters—a junior replication of their superiors dining in the wardroom—where their position as lowest among the officers and lords over the seamen often led to close friendships. That didn't happen with Philip Spencer.

It's a rare teenaged boy who doesn't occasionally like to mock those in authority over him, and Spencer tried it early, saying "that if the commander should have another *S* to his initials, it would spell his character."

Dropping the recently adopted "Mackenzie," Spencer was appending the extra *S* to Alexander Slidell, so as to make the captain's initials form *ASS*.

This is about as funny as most mid-nineteenth-century jokes, but it didn't amuse Midshipman Henry Rodgers, perhaps because he was the son of Commodore John Rodgers, who, having earlier cowed the Barbary States into abandoning demands for tribute from American ships in their waters, played a leading role during the War of 1812 in the defense of Baltimore, the feat of arms enshrined in our national anthem.

Young Rodgers took offense once again at Spencer's mocking: "Shortly after leaving New York I was in conversation with some of the midshipmen in regard to the vessel and character of our commander. To some observation of mine, 'Mr. Spencer remarked that he did not know that he was that kind of a man. He thought he was a damned old granny.'"

Spencer was not fool enough to insult Captain Mackenzie to his face, but practiced an exaggerated politesse that gave off a whiff of mockery. In any event, nothing he tried won him friends among the *Somers*'s midshipmen. The captain had made up his mind about Philip Spencer, and did not conceal his feelings from the rest of the officers. Matthew C. Perry, Jr., the brig's acting master, said he had "a slight recollection" that even before the voyage began the captain had suggested they have little as possible to do with their caustic shipmate.

Whatever initial overtures Spencer may have made to his steerage companions, he soon abandoned them and began to court members of the crew. Mackenzie said that he "was in the habit of associating but little with the other officers, but that he was continually intimate with the crew. He was often in the habit of joking with them and smiling whenever he met them, with a smile never known but on such occasions." Midshipman Rodgers had no more use for such promiscuous fraternization than did his captain: he noticed Spencer chatting with the sailors "when he was on duty during his watch—laughing and talking with them in a more familiar manner than became an officer or a gentleman."

Part of Spencer's search for new friends involved bribery. There was a good amount of brandy aboard the *Somers* as a result of the accidental largess of the ship's victualers, who had sent twice the requested number of bottles. This so irked Mackenzie that he actually complained to the secretary of the navy about it, telling Abel Upshur that he had only allowed the liquor for medicinal purposes, as a specific against malaria, even though "the drinking of brandy is even more dreadful than malaria."

Few sailors embraced this theory, and Spencer began to win them over with smuggled brandy. Although Mackenzie allowed his officers to drink, the crew was forbidden any alcohol. The timeless tradition, inherited from the Royal Navy, of a regular rum ration for the crew had been codified by the American Navy in 1794: every seaman was to get "one half-pint of distilled spirits" every day (if he didn't want it, three cents was added to his wages). But aboard the *Somers* Captain Mackenzie forbade liquor altogether for the apprentices and foremast hands.

Spencer, however, made an arrangement with Henry Waltham, the wardroom steward, to get a regular supply of brandy, which of course was well received by the crewmen he shared it with.

Sometimes he would toss a bright scatter of coins on the deck and laugh along with the men who scrambled after them. And he entertained them with a bizarre talent: Mackenzie said that "he was in the habit of amusing the crew by making music with his jaw. He had a faculty of throwing his jaw out of joint, and by the contact of the bones playing with accuracy and elegance a variety of airs."

Mackenzie also disapproved of tobacco, and was aware that Spencer was distributing this, too. The midshipman was an enthusiastic smoker himself, but hardly on the scale of what he drew from the purser. In a month and a half he acquired ten pounds of tobacco and seven hundred cigars.

As Spencer pursued his campaign of ingratiation with the crew, he began to center his attentions on Cromwell and Elisha Small. The thirty-year-old Small was indeed small—he was the shortest man aboard, and must have looked like a ventriloquist's dummy next to the massive Cromwell. But he was a competent hand, and was serving as quartermaster when Spencer came aboard the brig. That didn't last long; drink got him demoted to seaman for "carelessness and neglect of duty." This had happened before. In 1840, far from his native Maine, he had represented a Salem shipping firm on the African coast, then quit in favor of a good post as second mate on a brig out of Boston. Dismissed for drunkenness, he'd found himself aboard the *Somers*, and penniless.

Spencer had befriended him even before they weighed anchor by lending him money. In return, Small captured the midshipman's fancy with his yarns. He said he had served aboard a slaver, furtively rushing his human cargo—it had been illegal since 1808—westward across the Atlantic.

Both Cromwell and Small realized that their benefactor liked stories of seagoing crime, and were happy to supply them—true or false—in return for drink and tobacco. The informal arrangement had a calming effect on Cromwell, and before the *Somers* reached its first port of call, Madeira, the apprentices had all noticed that he was being easier on them.

Purser's Steward James Wales said, "Just previous to our arrival at Madeira, I noticed a sudden change in his manner toward the boys: he then 'made free' with them, and let them talk and play with him and pull him about."

Wales "noticed" this. He didn't miss much.

The purser's steward held an amorphous rank in the company of a man-of-war: higher than the deckhands, lower than the midshipmen. But if he was interested at all, he could know at least as much as any officer about what went on aboard. He was, said Herman Melville, "the right-hand man and confidential deputy and clerk of the Purser, who intrusts to him all his accounts with the crew, while, in most cases, he himself, snug and comfortable in his state-room, glances over a file of newspapers instead of overhauling his ledgers." It was Wales who saw Spencer acquire his seven hundred cigars, and, as the vessel's postmaster, he had constant close dealings with his shipmates.

The *Somers* was apparently his first encounter with seagoing life. He had been a typesetter and an accountant for some New England newspapers, and there is no record of how he came to be in New York and shipping out with Captain Mackenzie on that previous shakedown cruise to Puerto Rico.

He was fat, and the hands instantly tagged him with the nickname "Whales," but this and his nebulous rank were the least of his concerns. As soon as he went ashore in Puerto Rico, he tried to work some sort of financial swindle, and got caught at it. This naturally outraged Mackenzie with his rigid standards of probity, and he said that as soon as they returned to New York, Wales would be put ashore.

He wasn't, and nobody knows why. But Wales understood that this uncharacteristic reprieve had put him in the captain's debt. He set about doing what he could to please Mackenzie, and very early in the cruise he came to understand that the captain had no use for Philip Spencer. Wales began to pay close attention to the midshipman.

5   Storm Warnings

UNAWARE OF WALES'S SCRUTINY, Spencer became increasingly indiscreet about his piratical fantasies.

In early October the lookout spotted a sail. Captain Mackenzie altered course to hail the vessel. She turned out to be a fellow American. No excitement there, but Acting Midshipman Tillotson remembered that "when we were bearing down on the brig *America*," Spencer "said he should like to have a launch full of armed men and take possession of her."

Soon after that he struck up a foolhardy conversation with Orderly Sergeant Garty. The master-at-arms was the chief legal enforcer aboard the *Somers*, and he was greatly surprised by what Spencer said. As Garty remembered it later, he opened with, "She's a fine craft, the *Somers*, Sergeant."

"She is that, sir," said Garty.

So far, so good. Then: "All the same, I think I could take her with six men."

Despite having no contingent of marines to back him up, and although he was in poor health, the twenty-eight-year-old Garty wasn't about to take this from a cocky teenager. "Take her with six men! Indeed, no, sir; nor with three times six."

"But I could. First, I'd secure the captain and officers. Then, I'd turn out the crew. When they saw me with my men, armed and ready, I've not a doubt they'd surrender."

"Have you not? You and six men against all of us? Why, sir, we'd rush you and throw you overboard. You could shoot down no more than a half dozen at the most. It's a very poor crew you think us if you think you could take it with six men."

Garty saw Spencer's boast as idle speculation, but he remembered it when the midshipman later told him that before long he would have a ship of his own. And then he blithely told Gansevoort the same thing.

Spencer got more satisfaction from his talks with Cromwell and Small. On the same subject, Garty overheard him, this time asking how the boatswain would like to sail with him. "Cromwell said he would like it very well. Mr. Spencer said it might make an alteration in him to command but that Cromwell might not take notice of that."

It was all but impossible *not* to overhear conversations in the claustrophobic confines of the *Somers*. Spencer was heard asking Cromwell what sort of pirate ship the brig would make. A fine one, Cromwell said, which was true: she was heavily enough gunned to take on any merchantman, and fast enough to outrun any stronger vessel.

Spencer's chatter wasn't entirely random. In cultivating Small and Cromwell, he knew that he was taking into his confidence the only two foremast hands aboard who understood navigation, who knew how to find their way about the pathless ocean.

But what did these seasoned sailors make of this boy and his mutinous fantasies? Could they for a moment have believed that he would be able to organize a rebellion, seize the ship, and then serve as her master? They more likely thought: What harm talking about becoming buccaneers in this peculiar boarding school where you'd be supported by fifteen-year-olds leaping alongside you onto decks

defended by real seamen? And why cut off a conversation that produced drink and cigars?

Perhaps Cromwell let his true feelings show in a moment of irritated amusement. Spencer had come to him with a ludicrous—and
pointless—plan to disguise the brig after he took command and sneak
into New York Harbor. How best, he wanted to know, to camouflage
one of the most distinctive-looking ships in the Navy? Easy, said
Cromwell: "By shipping the bowsprit aft." The bowsprit is the great
spar fixed to the stem of a sailing ship; Cromwell's proposal was like
suggesting a man disguise himself by moving his nose to the back of
his head. Clearly, this was a dismissive joke.

On October 5, 3,800 miles out of New York, the *Somers* dropped
her hook in the port of Funchal, capital of Madeira. The four-island
archipelago off the northwest coast of Africa is not officially tropical,
but it would have chimed with the tropics Philip Spencer had visited
in *The Pirates Own Book:* a steep volcanic landscape—Funchal's streets
rise four thousand feet above the harbor—brilliant green with the
lemon and orange trees that sweetened the air in competition with
the various nautical reeks of the *Somers*, and the vineyards that still
produce a famous wine.

A crate of this inconvenienced Captain Mackenzie—a gift from
the United States vice-consul at Funchal for his friend Commodore
Nicholson back in the States—and of course nobody in the crew
got to sample it, or any of the other pleasures Madeira had to offer,
during a quick stop to take on water and provisions. "There was a good
deal of work to be done," said the attentive Wales, and "Cromwell
was grumbling about the amount of duty required. I heard him say
that 'it was damned hard usage'; he said that to the crew. He did not
appear to drive on the duty, and assist in carrying out my orders as
he had done before. He would repeat my orders and then stand on
the forecastle without making any attempt to see them executed: he
would do nothing more than repeat what I said to him."

Nor did his mood improve as they raised anchor, bound for the Canaries three hundred miles to the southeast. "When getting under way from Madeira," Wales reported, "Commander Mackenzie came forward and desired to know why some rigging had not been attended to, and told Cromwell, as he was chief boatswain mate, that he ought to have attended to it. Commander Mackenzie went aft, and Cromwell further forward. Cromwell said, after he had got forward, he did not care a damn whether the rigging was attended to or not; he said the commander was anxious to get too much work out of the crew, there was no necessity for getting under way that night." He ended by "wishing the brig and the commander were further in hell than they were out."

Cromwell would get his wish; a kind of hell *was* coming to the commander and the brig. The boatswain's defiance in Funchal's harbor may have been the first light gusts of the psychic gale that was soon to burst upon the *Somers*.

THE TROUBLE SEEMS TO HAVE STARTED—or at least to have become more apparent—soon after the brig left Madeira.

Before that morale had been fine: "I never saw better," remembered Charles Van Velsor, captain of the foretop. Wales said, "Between New York and Madeira it was very good indeed; but after we left Madeira for Santa Cruz it could be seen that dissatisfaction was arising, and it continued to increase." Lieutenant Gansevoort agreed: "After leaving there the crew was very slack; and I had to frequently drive them to their work. They would frequently disobey small orders, such as putting clothes away. . . . Before, if I told them to put away an article of clothing they would do it readily; after that they paid no attention to it." He described this "change in the manner of the ship's company" as one "which is easily observed by one who understands the character of seamen on board of a vessel."

Lieutenant Matthew C. Perry, acting master of the ship, didn't find the new mood so easy to understand. Discipline on board had been good, he said, during the nearly four thousand miles they'd covered before reaching Madeira, "after which time . . . it was not so good. The elder portion of the crew were surly and morose in their manner. Orders had to be repeated several times before they were obeyed. There was a marked difference in their manner—though it is not easy to describe it."

Nor does it show in the log's record of punishments. Captain Mackenzie kept up his energetic flogging program. Between leaving Funchal and November 26, the day of Spencer's arrest, boys were whipped for theft, for dirtiness, for laziness, for "not cleaning a battle-axe," for swearing, for not wearing a white hat. But no single offender went to the gratings for insubordination, let alone mutinous conduct.

There is no doubt, however, that Philip Spencer was becoming more mulish, surly, and outspoken about his captain. So was Cromwell. Once Gansevoort came upon the boatswain's mate "sitting near the forecastle. I called to him two or three times, to order him to pipe the bags [hammocks] down. He got up very lazily with a pipe in his mouth. His manner was disrespectful, and he merely ordered the bags piped down, leaving his own bag remain[ing] on deck." Gansevoort said that now "such incidents were continually occurring."

The weather might have accounted for at least some of them. By now the *Somers* had chased the *Vandalia* to Tenerife in the Canaries, and the fragrant breezes of Madeira were a distant, taunting memory. Here the fierce breath of Africa moved slow and scalding through the rigging, and everyone who could slept topside despite the drizzle of melting tar from the ropes and yards overhead.

The fuming days only grew hotter as Mackenzie carried the still-undelivered dispatches down to Liberia, anchoring on November 10 at the colony's capital of Monrovia. Here the captain gave the crew a day's shore leave. One of what Herman Melville believed were the far-too-few duties given midshipmen was having charge of the ship's boats as they rowed to shore and back. The *Somers* lowered two cutters, one under Spencer's command. Purser's Steward Wales got aboard it, and afterward had a lot to say about the brief voyage:

"I heard Commander Mackenzie observe to Mr. Spencer that he was not in uniform; Mr. Spencer went over the side muttering. I could not understand what it was and after we had got some twenty or thirty yards from the brig the commander hailed the boat, and asked if we had the American ensign in the boat. Mr. Spencer replied 'that we had not got it,' and then in a low voice remarked, not loud enough for the commander to hear him, 'That he be Goddamned if he was going back for it either, the damned old humbug go to hell.'"

Wales wasn't the only one who kept an eye on Spencer during their brief run ashore. Oliver Perry (brother of the *Somers*'s acting master) reported that the midshipman managed to find and visit an Italian slave dealer. "I heard Mr. Spencer say he had derived a [good] deal of information from him."

Perhaps Spencer had sought out the slave trader because Mackenzie had finally given up chasing the *Vandalia*, and the *Somers* was about to head for the Virgin Islands on the first leg of her fifty-five-hundred-mile voyage home. To get there, she would be following in the wake of three centuries of slavers making for the New World.

Here was a career nearly as violent as the pirate's, its dark attractions enhanced in recent years by having become illegal. Cromwell had told Spencer that, like Small, he too had served aboard a slaver, so this could make the pair more valuable to the evolving brigand.

If Spencer was daydreaming about being master of a slave ship, his surroundings would have helped nourish the fantasy: the lean little *Somers* looked like one. So thought the captain of a British warship who spotted her in mid-November and gave chase.

Soon after sighting the strange sail, Lieutenant Gansevoort called through his speaking trumpet ordering Garty and the gunner's mate to load the small arms: powder and ball went down the barrels of twenty-three muskets and twenty-eight pistols, all flintlocks.

As the unknown vessel drew nearer and resolved itself into a man-of-war, Captain Mackenzie beat to quarters. The drumroll called the apprentices to their fighting stations through a confusion of guns being cast loose and run in, the heavy rumble of their carriages on the deck, round shot being rammed home, and above the general din the squalling of youngsters who might soon be in their first battle. And then . . . nothing but deflated silence when the Briton recognized the suspicious-looking foreigner as an ally and stood away.

Cromwell thought the flurry of activity was the funniest thing he'd ever seen. He went into an ecstasy of noisy derision. "A damned sight of humbug about nothing," he yelled at a shaken Midshipman Hayes. "I've been on a vessel where shot were fired and not half as much noise about it."

For his part, Spencer regaled anyone who would listen with details of how *he* would have handled the encounter, bringing it off far more creditably than the captain had.

He was becoming ever more incontinent about his ambitions. One night he asked William Neville if he'd like to sail with him once he had his own ship. An odd choice, Neville, as he was a favorite of Mackenzie's, an apprentice whom the captain had raised to seaman. Then the midshipman was back with the master-at-arms, grousing about the *Somers*. Garty asked if he didn't think he might be happier in the Army. "He told me that his father told him he would get him a lieutenant's commission in the Dragoons; that he thought he wouldn't like it, and he thought he was not going to be long in the Navy. He said he was going to have a vessel of his own shortly."

He became more flagrantly insolent about the commander of his current vessel. When Mackenzie called him away from a working party in his charge, Wales saw, but did not hear, the discussion. He got the gist of it, though, when an infuriated Spencer stamped back forward.

"Whatever is the matter?" Wales asked.

"God damn him!" Spencer shouted. "I'd like to catch him on that roundhouse some of these dark nights and plunge him overboard, it will be a pleasing task to me. I'll be God damned if I don't do it."

So the obstreperous midshipman continued taunting his superiors. What did they think of it? At first they seemed to take it no more seriously than Cromwell did Spencer's chattering about piracy. They had got used to their vexing midshipman. He was lax in his duties, often lapsed into stretches of torpor, made light of regulations. He wasn't much use, and he could be an irritant; his chummy behavior with the crew was a matter of perpetual reproach; his musical jaw grew tiresome. But the voyage wouldn't last forever, and the disaffected adolescent would not be a perpetual fixture in their lives. Captain Mackenzie, who was fully aware of Spencer's shortcomings, seems to have held a resigned and mature attitude toward him. As he later wrote, "Perhaps I had reproved him less frequently than others for slight deviations from duty. I had little hope of essentially serving one who had been so great an enemy to himself."

Then came the evening of Friday, November 25. The brief rich flourish of the tropical sunset had brought on a mild night, with a full moon liquefying in the calm sea and the brig being borne gently homeward by the trades. "The tranced ship indolently rolls," wrote Melville of that breeze beloved by every sailor. "The drowsy trade winds blow; everything resolves you into languor."

But Purser's Steward Wales was not about to be resolved into languor.

As he told it two months later, Wales had been forward, leaning against the bitts—pairs of stout posts sturdy enough to hold the heaviest lines—when Spencer approached him. After a few commonplaces about the weather, the midshipman asked him to come up onto the booms. This was a pile of miscellaneous spars, stowed on the deck amidships. The crew was forbidden to go there. Spencer, typically flouting the rule, clambered up, telling Wales "that he had something of great importance to communicate to me."

Once the two were uncomfortably perched in what privacy the woodpile offered, Spencer asked the purser's steward three abrupt questions: "Did I fear death? Was I afraid of a dead person, and dare I kill a person?"

Wales "was much surprised at these remarks, and paused some time to see if Mr. Spencer was in earnest, and I found him very serious in what he was saying—very much in earnest; his whole mind seemed to be wrapped up in what he was saying to me."

"I told him I was not particularly anxious about dying quite yet— that I had no cause to fear a dead man—that, should a man abuse me or insult me, I could muster sufficient courage to kill him, if necessary."

Spencer said he knew all that: he'd never doubted Wales's courage. But could he keep a secret?

Wales said he could.

Would he?

Yes.

First he was directed to take an oath, "the purport of which was, that I should never communicate that conversation to any one, so help me God."

Wales raised his hand for God to witness. Spencer "then went on to state that he was leagued with about twenty of the ship's company, to murder all the officers, take the brig, and commence pirating."

The plan had already gelled. Spencer had it in his neckerchief— here, feel. "I felt of the back part of his neck-handkerchief, and it made a noise as though there was paper inside." On it the midshipman had "the stations of the men all drawn up."

The mutiny would begin "some night when he had the mid-watch; some of those concerned with him would get in a scuffle on the forecastle. Mr. Spencer would then cause them to be brought to the mast; he would then call Mr. Rodgers, the officer of the deck, to pretend to settle the matter." Once Rodgers "had got to the gangway, they were to seize him and pitch him overboard; they would then have the vessel to themselves."

Spencer "would proceed to station his men at the hatches, to prevent anyone coming on deck" and "furnish his men with arms; this done he was to proceed to the cabin and murder the commander with the least noise possible; this done, he would go with some of his men to the ward-room, and murder the ward-room and steerage officers." No great difficulty, as "the officers had no arms, with the exception of the first lieutenant, and all the arms he had was an old cutlass, which he [Spencer] should secure before the affray commenced."

Then Spencer would dash outside to "have the two after guns slewed around to rake the deck." Covered by the cannon, "he would then have the whole crew called on deck, and would select from among them such as would suit his purposes, the remainder he should cause to be thrown overboard." The drowning crewmen would be followed over the side by the launch and the booms and some coils of rigging, as these "only tended to lumber up the deck." Any equipment the *Somers* might need in the future could easily be got from the ships Spencer would be seizing.

"This done, the brig was to proceed to Cape St. Antonio or the Isle of Pines [the second-largest Cuban island, a famous haunt of pirates mentioned in Robert Louis Stevenson's *Treasure Island*], or one of these places," where they would pick up a confederate of Spencer's "who was familiar with their intended business, and who was willing and ready to join them."

Once everything was nicely squared away, "they were to commence cruising for prizes—and whenever they would take a vessel, they would murder all hands, as dead men told no tales." All the male hands, that is: "Should there happen to be females on board, he would have them taken to the brig, for the use of the officers and men, using them as long as they saw fit; after that, to make [a]way with them."

And suddenly Small was there. He didn't get up in the booms, but stood on the rail, and began speaking with Spencer in Spanish—a piratical language if ever there was one.

"Small looked very much surprised" until Spencer said to him, "Oh, you need not be under any apprehension or fear on his [Wales's] account, as I have sounded him pretty well, and find he is one of us." Small said "he was very glad to hear it."

Wales seems never to have doubted this fantastic tale. The familiar ship must have at once taken on an alien and threatening cast to him: the chinks of smoky, sallow light showing here and there along the dark clutter of the deck, and the occasional passing figure, colorless in the moonlight, who might be yet another assassin.

Small thought that Spencer was making too much noise, and cautioned him, saying that "a number of little pictures [pitchers] with big ears" were about, "alluding to the small boys."

At that point an order called Small away; Spencer told him that he had the midwatch, and they'd make further plans then.

He turned back to Wales and "made overtures to me, saying if I would join them he would give me the post of third officer on board." When Wales didn't reply, Spencer "went on to state that the commander had a large amount of money on board, that and what the purser had, he said, would make a pretty little sum to commence with."

Then he asked Wales what he thought of "the project."

"I thought it prudent to dissemble as much as possible in order to gather further intelligence of their movements; I told him I liked the plan, and was favorably disposed toward it."

Eager to get away, Wales invented some pressing duties. He got down off the booms; Spencer followed him with a warning: "If I breathed a syllable of that which he had communicated to me, that I would be murdered, if he did not do it some of those concerned with him would; go where I might my life would not be worth a straw."

Spencer went below.

Why, of all possible recruits, had he revealed his plot in every garish detail to Wales? Did he find "Whales" a comic figure, someone it might be fun to throw a scare into? Or had he made the calculation that because the purser's assistant was still in disgrace with Mackenzie for the swindle he'd attempted in Puerto Rico, he was nursing a resentment strong enough to make him a murderer?

But perhaps Spencer spilled his story out of sheer exuberance, carried away by the picturesque setting: this conference culminating in its blood oath, up in the off-limits secrecy of the booms while the moon showed the loom of the guns along the deck of the rakish, well-gunned little brig he would command.

HEADSTRONG AND VOLUBLE though he was, Spencer would probably have left him alone had he known that Wales wanted not retribution, but only to reinstate himself with the captain. In any event, Spencer's choice of confidant was a mortal mistake.

With Spencer gone, Wales lingered on the deck for a cautious fifteen minutes before heading aft to tell Captain Mackenzie. But the captain was hard to get at; his quarters were entirely private, reached by a hatch and companionway that led to them alone.

As Wales approached, "I saw Small watching me very closely." This scared him. "I did not deem it prudent to go into the cabin at that time, though I watched for an opportunity so to do, but I was clearly watched by Small wherever I went."

He decided it was safer to tell Gansevoort about Spencer's plot. "I then went on the berth-deck, and went aft to the steerage door with the intention of making it known to the lieutenant."

But Spencer had slung his hammock at the front of the steerage, and Spencer was in it. He "wanted to know 'why in the devil I was cruising about there at that time of night, and why did I not turn in.'"

Wales feigned some errand in the nearby purser's storeroom, then hung about the deck for an hour. When he felt free to move unobserved, the wardroom lights were out, the officers asleep.

"Then thought I would let the matter rest till morning, turned in, and endeavored to sleep, but I could not do it."

He was in his hammock, twitching and wide-eyed, when eight bells struck, and November 25 turned into Saturday, November 26.

6 Saturday

WALES WAS UP AND ABOUT at daybreak, but believed himself being "dogged" by Small and Cromwell. Frightened of getting spotted by them, and especially by Spencer, he abandoned his plan of approaching the senior officers, and instead went to his immediate boss, the purser, Horace Heiskell.

"I was sitting in the wardroom," Heiskell said, "as near as I can recollect, about eight o'clock. Mr. Wales took a seat beside me, and in a low tone of voice told me that Mr. Spencer had, in the evening previous, revealed to him a plan he had formed for taking the vessel out of the hands of the officers, and murdering them and turning pirates; that he was to be made third officer on board; and requested me to make the matter known immediately to Lieutenant Gansevoort, that it might get to the ears of the commander."

Heiskell at once went and brought the first lieutenant, telling Wales "to follow Mr. Gansevoort below, and open my store-room door, which nearly closed the entrance into the ward-room; he did so; the object was to prevent Mr. Spencer or any one from seeing Mr.

Gansevoort and myself in conversation." In this improvised cranny of privacy, Heiskell half-whispered Wales's shocking tale.

As soon as he'd taken in the story, Gansevoort hurried topside and went directly to the captain's cabin. Like every space aboard the ship, it was a dollhouse room: an eight-foot-long wedge just two feet wide at its entrance and eight at its back.

"On Saturday, the 26th of November," wrote Mackenzie a month later, "Lieutenant G. Gansevoort came into the cabin, and informed me that a conspiracy existed on board of the brig, to capture her, murder the commander, the officers, and most of the crew and to convert her into a pirate, and that Acting-Midshipman Philip Spencer was at the head of it. . . . It was his object to carry the vessel to the Isle of Pines where one of his associates, who had been in the business before, had friends; to select such of the female passengers as were suitable, and after they had used them sufficiently to dispose of them. Mr. Spencer also stated that he had the written plan of the project in the back of his cravat, which he would show to Mr. Wales in the morning, after which they separated with terrible threats, on the part of Mr. Spencer, of instant death to Mr. Wales, from himself or his accomplices, should Mr. Wales utter one word of what passed."

By the time of his writing, the captain had details that Wales had left out of his account. "As one of the inducements to her capture, he stated that a box, containing wine of a rare value, brought off with much care at Madeira, as a present from I. H. Burden, Esq., United States vice-consul at Funchal, to Commodore J. B. Nicholson, contained money or treasure to a large amount [it didn't]."

Captain Mackenzie received the news, Gansevoort said, "with great coolness—said that the vessel was in good discipline, and expressed his doubts as to the truth of the report." No mention of the surly lassitude that seemed to have settled over the ship; indeed, as the captain thought about his brig-full of schoolboys, his first impulse was to laugh. The scheme "seemed to me so monstrous, so improbable, that I could not forbear treating it with ridicule. I was under the impression that Mr. Spencer had been reading some piratical stories, and had amused himself with Mr. Wales."

That would be his last mirthful moment for a long time.

He immediately began to fret. "Still I felt this was joking on a very improper theme, and determined to notice it hereafter. I also considered that duty required me to be on my guard, lest there should be a shadow of reality in this project."

Mackenzie ordered Gansevoort "to watch Mr. Spencer narrowly, without seeming to do so."

Playing the spy on a vessel as small and crowded as the *Somers* was not easy, and as the ship's bells rang the day forward, Spencer became aware that wherever he went, there was the first lieutenant watching him.

Gansevoort saw him in the wardroom with Richard Leecock, the ship's surgeon, examining a map of the West Indies. Spencer asked Leecock about the Isle of Pines. The surgeon, who doubtless knew of his interests, "informed him that it was a place much frequented by pirates and dryly asked him if he had any acquaintances there."

Spencer, reported Gansevoort, had spent much of "the day rather sullenly in one corner of the steerage, as was his custom, engaged in examining a small piece of paper and writing on it with his pencil." Then he found "relaxation in working with a penknife at the tail of a devil-fish, one of the joints of which he had formed into a sliding ring for his cravat." This unappealing bit of haberdashery completed, he went up into the rigging.

"About dinner time," said Gansevoort, "I missed Mr. Spencer from the deck. This was about two o'clock. I discovered he was in the fore-top, and immediately went up to see what he was about."

Nothing.

"He was sitting on the lee side of the top, with his chin resting on his breast—apparently in deep thought. He did not observe me till I had got into the top and was standing erect. He raised his head, and as soon as he discovered me he got up and evinced some confusion." As he well might have, guilty or not, at having the second-in-command materialize beside him on his windy perch.

Spencer asked some questions about the rigging. Gansevoort thought these were merely attempts at deflection, "but I answered in my usual manner. I think he asked how the lower shrouds answered (which were fitted differently from any I had known) and something about the top-mast stays."

The eccentric shrouds explained, Gansevoort said, "As I came through the steerage, I saw dinner was ready."

Spencer said he didn't want any.

Gansevoort left him there and returned to the deck. An hour later Spencer was still in the foretop, having an apprentice named Benjamin Green tattooing his arm, not with the Jolly Roger but with "some love-devices."

"The crew were employed in slinging clean hammocks," said Gansevoort. "I hailed the top and ordered Green to come out. Mr. Spencer put his head over the top-rail, and from his manner I thought he wished Green to remain, though he asked no question.

"I repeated the order, and then ordered Spencer to send Green and other men that might be in the top on deck. Green came down immediately but no others—Spencer remained in the top. I had not ordered him to come out. I saw no others in the top. I ordered Green to sling his hammock. He answered that he had done so already."

All this was humdrum workaday ship business, seemingly far too insignificant to report, but those moments were fraught for Gansevoort by what came immediately after.

"I was engaged in mustering the men for the purpose of having the hammocks stowed. When I got abreast of the Jacob's ladder [which gave easier access to the tops] on the starboard side forward, I observed Mr. Spencer sitting on the ladder."

He did not utter one of his insolences; he didn't say anything at all. But in the contagion of fear that was beginning to stir on the ship, a single glance proved eloquent.

"I turned my eye toward him," said Gansevoort, "and immediately caught his eye, which he kept staring upon me for more than a minute, with the most infernal expression I have ever seen upon a human face. It satisfied me at once of the man's guilt."

After Gansevoort made his report on Spencer's day to the captain, Mackenzie wrote that he "endeavored to review the conduct of Mr. Spencer throughout the cruise. . . . I had observed that he had very little intercourse with the officers, that he was exceedingly intimate with the crew; I had noticed the interchange of a passing joke, as individuals passed by him, a smile never seen but on such occasions, a strange flashing of the eye. These various recollections, added to what had been revealed to me, determined me to make sure at once of his person." The captain had been planning to send Wales back to learn more about Spencer's scheme. But now he believed "enough was already known."

He summoned his first lieutenant, and asked him about Spencer. Still shaken by that demonic glare, Gansevoort "told him that I thought something should be done, in order to secure him." Mackenzie replied "that we would keep a sharp look out—that he did not wish to do anything hastily; and that by evening quarters he would decide what to do."

This gave the captain only a few minutes for reflection, as Gansevoort said that "it was just before the drum beat to quarters." Mackenzie "asked me what I would do if I were in his situation as Commander of the vessel. I told him that I would bring that young man aft and iron and keep him on the quarter deck."

Not the usual place to confine a shipboard prisoner, but there was no space in the crammed brig that could serve as a jail cell.

"He told me that was the course he intended to pursue; and that he was very glad to find that I agreed with him."

Then the drum and fife began the urgent clatter of their evening duet, and the crew thronged the deck and took their stations.

Which Mackenzie rearranged. He was going to make something of a production of this. "I ordered through my clerk, O. H. Perry, doing the duty also of midshipman and aid, all the officers to lay aft on the quarterdeck, excepting the midshipmen stationed on the forecastle. The master was ordered to take the wheel, and those of the crew stationed abaft sent to the mainmast."

The captain walked up to his suspect and said, "I learn, Mr. Spencer, that you aspire to command of the *Somers*?"

With what Mackenzie described as "a deferential, but unmoved and gently smiling expression," the midshipman replied, "Oh, no, sir."

"Did you not tell Mr. Wales, sir, that you had a project to kill the commander, the officers, and a considerable portion of the crew, of this vessel, and turn her into a pirate?"

"I may have told him so, sir, but it was a joke."

"You admit, then, that you told him so?"

"Yes, sir; but in joke."

"This, sir, is joking on a forbidden subject—this joke may cost you your life."

He paused, then said, "Be pleased to remove your neck handkerchief."

Spencer did, and shook it out. Nothing there.

Mackenzie asked what he had done with the paper outlining his plot that he had told Wales about.

"It is a paper outlining my day's work, and I have destroyed it."

"It is a singular place to keep a day's work in."

"It is a convenient one."

This last might read like a sharp retort, but the captain said it was delivered "with an air of deference and blandness."

Mackenzie was through with his questions. "You must have been aware that you could only have compassed your designs by passing over my dead body, and after that, all the bodies of my officers; you have given yourself, sir, a great deal to do; it will be necessary to confine you, sir."

He turned to Gansevoort. "Arrest Mr. Spencer, and put him in double irons."

"I laid my hand upon his sword," said Gansevoort, "disarmed him, and ordered him to come out from among the officers."

Spencer stepped forward and Gansevoort told the armorer to bring the irons. The midshipman rolled up his sleeves "and was first put in hand-irons."

When Gansevoort had him shackled, "I asked him if he had arms concealed about him."

Spencer showed his first flash of resentment. "He said he had not, but perhaps I had better overhaul him, as he supposed I would not believe any thing he said."

The lieutenant's search yielded up "some scraps of paper and part of an old pipe."

Once Spencer's legs got their set of irons, he was taken all the way aft—half-carried, as the weight of metal made it impossible for him to walk unaided—and set on a campstool next to the port-side arms chest. This was a six-foot-long wooden locker that held the muskets; its twin sat close across on the starboard side.

With Spencer immobilized, Mackenzie told Gansevoort to stand by him and "if Mr. Spencer attempted to make his escape or to communicate with any of the crew, to blow out his brains."

This stark order was tempered, Mackenzie wrote later, in a spate of nineteenth-century treacle, by directing Gansevoort to "see that the prisoner had every comfort which his safe-keeping would admit of. In confiding this task to Lieutenant Gansevoort, his kindness and humanity gave me the assurance that it would be zealously attended to." Despite being ready to put a bullet in Spencer's head the moment he opened his mouth, the lieutenant "attended to all his wants, covered him with his own grego [a waterproof coat] when squalls of rain were passing over, and ministered in every way to his comfort with the tenderness of a woman."

For all this concern, Mackenzie was in a state of angry alarm that could not be dispelled by Spencer's heavy iron lacing. Gansevoort said, "The Commander ordered me to arm the officers of the deck with pistols." Cutlasses, too, and "the rounds of both decks made frequently, to see that the crew were in their hammocks, and no suspicious collections of individuals about the decks."

He also wanted Spencer's locker searched.

The *Somers* sailed on through the dusk, Spencer on his campstool, the tender Gansevoort standing by ready to enfold him in his grego or shoot him dead, until eight bells put an end to the troubled day.

7 Sunday

PHILIP SPENCER HAD BEEN CALM throughout his arrest and shackling; not so Elisha Small. Whatever his part in Spencer's plans, Small
knew very well that everyone had seen him spending hours gossiping
and joking with the midshipman. All those cigars, all that brandy that
had come his way now seemed especially threatening. If an *officer* could
be clapped in chains and kept on the deck, how much more heavily
the weight of discipline might fall on an ordinary seaman. From the
moment Spencer was taken, Small was terrified.

He'd gone at once to Richard Leecock's quarters. The ship's surgeon said, "Small presented himself to me to go on the [sick] list,
complaining of nausea and vomiting. I put him on the list and gave
him some medicine."

But Small's ailment was beyond the reach of a ship's doctor. "The
same day Mr. Wales's evidence on Mr. Spencer's case came to my
knowledge, implicating also Small."

That was something to be sick about, and Leecock made a different
diagnosis. "The next morning Small again presented himself, when I
saw the sick, and still complained of vomiting. From his appearance,

tone of voice, and the quivering of his hand when I felt his pulse, I perceived he was laboring under manifest fear and anxiety.

"I then made some inquiries of persons on deck as to whether he had been seen to vomit or throw up his food. Nobody having seen him do so, and believing he was feigning sickness, I refused to keep him on the list longer and discharged him. I do not think the disorder he complained of would have produced such an effect, but I heard of his being concerned with Mr. Spencer, and I thought his tone and manner betrayed more anxiety than sickness."

Small would have felt sicker still had he known what was going on in the steerage.

There, Gansevoort and Midshipman Henry Rodgers were following Mackenzie's order to search Spencer's locker. They first found some letters—from Spencer's father, his mother, and somebody named Eliza—and went on to a razor case. It was empty—no razor—save for three sheets of paper. One bore the names George A. Brest, Frederick Wells, and Edward Roberts. Nobody aboard the *Somers*, and whatever those men may have meant to Spencer was never discovered. But it was a very different story with the other two papers: "Writing in Greek characters," said Rodgers. "This was a list of his accomplices, headed certain, doubtful, and those to be retained on board *nolens volens* [willing or not]." The list was accompanied by "three explanatory paragraphs," written in Greek. Did anyone aboard read Greek? Rodgers did. "These the first lieutenant took, and I shortly afterward deciphered them for the Commander."

They read:

Those marked ✕ will probably be induced to join before the project is carried into execution. The remainder of the doubtful will probably join when the thing is done; if not, they must be forced. If any not marked down wish to join after it is done, we will pick out the best and dispose of the rest.

The list of names had many misspellings, some deliberate (*u*'s for *w*'s and *y*'s) but none wholly incomprehensible:

Sertain		*To be kept nolens volens*
P Spencer		Sibleu
E Andreus		Stremel
D M'Kenlu		Skoll
Uhales		Van Brunl
Smith		
Uillmore		
Gazelu		
Blakuell		
Doubtful		
Uillson ✕		Rodman
M'Kee ✕		Chlark
Uarno		Chnenles
Green		Cheleun
Gedneu		Selsor
Van Velsor		Chornen
Sulliuan		Dikenson
Godphrey		The Dokter
Gallia ✕		Garrebranlz
Houard ✕		Uallham
Ueel		M'Chee
Arm chest		M'Chenlu
		Spenker
Chabin	{	Small
		Uillson
Uard room		Spenker
		Spenker
Steerage	{	Small
		Uillson

The papers could scarcely have been more incriminating. They had to be the plan for a mutiny (although in the years to come the brothers of Chi Psi would loyally maintain that their author was merely outlining a companionable waterborne counterpart to his fraternity).

But they were puzzling, too.

Spencer had told Wales "he was leagued with about twenty of the ship's company." His list of those he was certain of contains only four names, one of them Wales's, and another is E. Andreus. There was no Andrews aboard the *Somers*. Small appears with those who are going to attack the cabin and the steerage, but not among the conspirators Spencer was sure of. That leaves him with a single sound ally, D. M'Kenlu. Daniel McKinley had spent too long ashore back in Santa Cruz, and gotten the full twelve cats "for breaking liberty." Perhaps that had made Spencer approach him—if he had approached him. Yet even if McKinley was ablaze with desire to start murdering officers, the list itself suggests that the mutiny could very well boil down to just two men against the whole ship.

As Mackenzie tried to figure out the roster's meaning, it evidently never occurred to him to question its author, and he never did.

THE CAPTAIN HAD, HOWEVER, persuaded himself that during the night one of the crew had managed to defy orders and have a conversation with Spencer. He didn't explain how this could be possible with Gansevoort standing guard, and Gansevoort never mentioned it.

Mackenzie was starting to see grim portents wherever he looked. He noted:

"Being Sunday, the crew were inspected at quarters at ten o'clock. I took my station abaft, with the intention of particularly observing Cromwell and Small."

Why Cromwell? He was full of abusive bluster but his name wasn't anywhere on Spencer's roster. At any event, Mackenzie found what he was seeking.

"The third of the master's division, to which they both belonged, always mustered at morning quarters upon the after-part of the quarter-deck, in continuation of the lines formed by the crews of the guns. The persons of both were faultlessly clean; they were determined that their appearance in this respect should provoke no reproof."

As had Gansevoort, Mackenzie read a great deal into squints, glances, and stares, and now he discerned plenty of ocular guilt.

"Cromwell stood up to his full stature, his muscles braced, his battle-axe grasped resolutely, his cheek pale, but his eye fixed, as if indifferently, on the other side. He had a determined and dangerous air.

"Small made a very different figure. His appearance was ghastly, he shifted his weight from side to side, and his battle-axe passed from one hand to the other; his eye wandered irresolutely, but never toward mine."

Despite his worry and suspicions, this was Sunday, and inviolable naval routine demanded prayer. "After quarters the church was rigged. The crew mustered up with their prayer books, and took their seats before five bells, or half past ten, the usual time of divine services." Mackenzie kept them waiting until the proper hour, and once he'd started, "the crew were unusually attentive, and the responses more than commonly audible."

This surprised the captain, although it shouldn't have.

Most of the crew didn't yet know what was going on—in fact, nobody aboard did—but they had seen the officers patrolling with cutlasses and loaded pistols, and there, just a few yards away, was Spencer huddled in his irons. This was no time to be slovenly or frivolous in the presence of the captain and the Almighty.

During the afternoon the wind dropped, and Mackenzie ordered all sail set. Five rows of yardarms blossomed with mainsail, topsail, topgallant sail, and skysail. As the upward progression suggests, the sky-sails were the highest, doing their work a hundred feet above the deck.

It was heavy work, and delicate. The wind pushed hard and the top-masts and topgallant masts were slender. Sailors stood by the braces, lines running from the yards to the deck that could swing them and spill wind if the topmasts began to complain.

The *Somers* was cutting along at seven knots—a good clip, given the light airs—and she was a superb sight, carrying the "towering clouds of canvas" cherished by nineteenth-century maritime writers, the image of a ship that enlivened a century of wall calendars.

But not for long.

"I had always been very particular to have no strain on the light braces leading forward," wrote Mackenzie, "as the tendency of such a strain was to carry away the light yards and masts. While Ward M. Gagely, one of the best and most skillful of our apprentices, was yet on the main-royal-yard, after setting the main-skysail, a sudden jerk of the weather-main-royal-brace . . . carried the top-gallant-mast away in the sheave-hole, sending forward the royal-mast, with royal-skysail, royal studdingsail, main-top-gallant staysail, and the head of the gaff-topsail."

This was as bad as it sounds. The elegant geometry of the lines and the carefully monitored curves of the sails had exploded into a flailing incoherence of splintered wood and shredded cloth.

Mackenzie's first thought was for his valuable midshipman. "Gagely was on the royal-yard. I scarcely dared to look on the booms or in the larboard gangway, where he should have fallen."

He hadn't. "For a minute I was in intense agony; in the next I saw the shadow of the boy through the top-gallant-sail, rising rapidly toward the top-gallant-yard, which still remained at the mast-head. Presently he rose to view, descended on the afterside of the topmast-cap, and began to examine with coolness to see what was first to be done to clear the wreck."

He added, "I did not dream at the time that the carrying away of this mast was the work of treachery." Still, treachery lay heavily on his mind. "I knew it was an occasion of this sort, [such as] the loss of a boy overboard, or an accident to a spar, creating confusion and interrupting the regularity of duty, which was likely to be taken advantage of by the conspirators."

He made sure, in directing the repair work, that as many as possible of the crew were busy, and that order was maintained throughout. "The greatest pains were therefore taken to prevent all confusion: the first lieutenant took the deck; everything connected with the wreck was sent down from aloft, the rigging unrove and coiled down, sails bent [fastened] afresh to the yards, the spare top-gallant-mast got out and scraped and slushed [greased], and the fid-hole cut, everyone employed, and everything made to go on with undeviating regularity."

But it didn't. "To my astonishment, all those who were most conspicuously named in the programme of Mr. Spencer, no matter in what part of the vessel they might be stationed, mustered at the main-top-masthead."

"Whether animated by some new-born zeal in the service of their country, or collected there for the purpose of conspiring, it was not easy to decide." This is acerbic irony: Mackenzie had decided with no difficulty at all why those men gathered together. "The coincidence confirmed the existence of a dangerous conspiracy. . . ."

Spencer's behavior ratified the captain's conclusion, once again with that self-betraying gaze. "The eye of Mr. Spencer travelled perpetually to the masthead, and cast thither many of those strange and stealthy glances which I had heretofore noticed."

But where else would he have been looking? Chained and fixed as firmly as a hitching post, he was watching half the ship's top-hamper flapping away ten stories above his head, ready to pelt him with a shrapnel of whipping lines and wooden daggers.

Among those who had further inflamed Mackenzie's suspicions by gathering at the masthead were Cromwell, Small, and Wilson. At that moment, though, he was most interested in Cromwell, and he and Gansevoort had been gathering information about him that morning.

Thomas Dickerson, the carpenter's mate, told of a squabble involving a pair of singlesticks. These were fencing foils made of wood rather than steel. (Which did not mean they were harmless; singlestick duels were preceded by no *en garde* punctilio, but rather with the opponents speaking a prayer that an enthusiast for the sport described as "beautifully terse": "God, spare our eyes!")

Dickerson said he had "carried a couple of single-sticks to store in Cromwell's store-room and told him they belonged to the First Lieutenant, and he said he did not care a damn, they should not stay there. On my leaving the store-room, he said, *'Your time's damn short.'*

"Another time he had a rule[r], which was broke, and he said that one of the carpenters had broken it. I told him they had not, it had got broken in the chest, and as I was going up the ladder he said, 'God damn you, I'll fix you!'"

Given such exchanges, it is not surprising that, when Gansevoort questioned Dickerson, he said, "That big fellow forward is more dangerous than the rest."

"I asked him whom he meant," said Gansevoort, "and he said Cromwell, the Boatswain's mate." This discussion "impressed me with the belief that it was necessary to have him confined."

The repair work went on. "The wreck being cleared," wrote Mackenzie, "supper was piped before sending up the new mast; after supper the same persons mustered again at the mast-head, and the top-gallant-mast was fidded [a fid being the bar that made the mast secure], the light yards crossed and the sails set.

"By this time it was dark, and quarters had been unavoidably dispensed with; still, I thought, under the circumstances, that it was scarcely safe to leave Cromwell at large during the night: the night was the season of danger. After consulting Lieutenant Gansevoort, I determined to arrest Cromwell."

Gansevoort, of course, agreed. "I was about to hail the top and order him to come down; but the commander told me to wait till he did come down, and then tell him that the Commander wished to see him."

The officers would be prepared for any mutinous outbreak Cromwell's arrest might trigger. Acting Master Perry was in the wardroom when Gansevoort "came below and gave me a pistol and ordered me on deck to take my station in the starboard gangway; and to shoot down any persons who should attempt a rescue, as he was going to confine Cromwell." Before long "each officer had two pistols, a cutlass and cartouch [cartridge] box."

Gansevoort was ready for Cromwell:. "As soon as he came down the Jacob's ladder I cocked my pistol and pointed it at him, and when he got on deck I told him the Captain wished to see him. When he came to the Captain he was ordered to sit down."

It hadn't gone quite as smoothly as he later reported. Gansevoort had a Colt Paterson. It was relatively new; Samuel Colt had patented this, his first revolver, less than five years earlier. Perhaps Gansevoort wasn't wholly familiar with it, or perhaps he was simply nervous, but as soon as he confronted Cromwell he jerked the trigger. An explosion, and a bright flash lit the dusk. Nobody was hurt; the bullet plowed into the deck between the two men. And the accidental shot may have made Cromwell more docile as Gansevoort led him to Mackenzie on the quarterdeck.

Mackenzie immediately asked Cromwell about "a secret conversation he had held the night before with Mr. Spencer." He apparently did not mean the phantom who had visited Spencer while he was in irons, but the conference in the booms, which was actually two nights earlier.

"It was not me, sir," said the boatswain's mate. "It was Small."

Gansevoort, standing by, listened as "the Commander told him, in effect that there were many suspicions about him, and that he considered it necessary to confine him . . . in the same way with Mr. Spencer, and taken home, where he would be tried by the laws of his country and acquitted if he was innocent; if guilty he would be punished."

No bluster from Cromwell now: "Yes, sir; but I don't know any thing about this; I assure you I don't know any thing about it."

The armorer ironed Cromwell, and he was set down by the starboard-side arms chest, across from Spencer.

The shackled midshipman took all this in, and once Cromwell was settled he called the first lieutenant over and, in what can only be seen as a spark of gallantry, told him, "Cromwell is innocent. That is the truth, Mr. Gansevoort."

AT THE MOMENT OF HIS ARREST, Cromwell had named Small, which the captain was more than ready to hear. Someone—he never said who—had told him that, when the mast began to give, Small "and another whose name I have not discovered" had leapt to the braces and administered the "sudden jerk" that brought the mast down.

So the calamity was Small's fault. But why would this man, who was already so frightened that he had twice begged the surgeon to excuse him from duty altogether, who had appeared so "ghastly" to the captain at quarters, violently—and publicly—strain at the ropes?

No matter. Gansevoort was standing beside the captain, who "then said something to me about Small, and asked if I did not think it best to confine him." As he had with Cromwell, the lieutenant offered eager agreement.

Small was brought aft and "nearly the same conversation then passed as with Cromwell. The Commander told him he would be confined as the others were, brought home and tried."

Then he asked Small, "Spencer has talked with you about the plot?"

"Yes, sir."

Gansevoort said, "Small was then confined in irons. All the officers were armed when Cromwell first came down from the rigging; and were stationed on parts of the deck ready for action in case of any attack."

They would remain fully armed for the rest of the voyage.

Despite his fumbling shot when he confronted the boatswain's mate, Gansevoort had thought through carefully how he could best use his Colt. Later, he slightly amended his account of the arrests: Mackenzie had not actually told him to blow out Spencer's brains, or those of the other captives. "The language I used was my own. The Commander's orders were *to destroy them*—to put them to death. He did not give me the order to *blow out their brains*. But I passed the order in that form because these were young Officers, and if an attempt were made to rescue the prisoners I felt the importance of putting them to death. I thought that if the shot was wasted, and the prisoners only wounded and taken forward, this might excite and drive on the mutineers to the accomplishment of their purpose. My object was to have them killed at once that those who were attempting the rescue might see and be deterred from their object. My purpose was to save shot—(as we had none to waste), and at once to destroy the dangerous persons."

Such was his state of mind when he heard some turmoil forward.

Night, the captain's "season of danger" lay fully on the *Somers* now, and the hours-long repairs were almost at an end. A new mast lay on the deck, about to be raised.

William Collins, who had been promoted from gunner's mate to boatswain's mate in Cromwell's place, was in charge. He didn't like the state of the crew: "They were slack in performing their duty. . . . I was on the quarter deck, and had to run about and act as Boatswain's

Mate, to see that the boys did not skulk. . . . When we were swaying up the topgallant mast it was getting rather dark, and the officer of the deck ordered me to keep the yard ropes manned. When I looked round I found there were only two or three on. I went forward and told them to come aft and man the mast ropes. They would not, and I told the officer of the deck they would not move for me, and that he had better send an officer forward, and he went forward himself, and they came aft stamping with their feet, all together, and alarmed the Captain and the officer."

To say the least. The officer was Gansevoort, who said, "The commander and myself were standing on the larboard side of the quarter-deck, at the after end of the trunk [a cabin on the deck above the wardroom, offering light as a clerestory does, and a couple of feet of sorely needed headroom]. We were in conversation; it was dark at this time. I heard an unusual noise—a rushing on deck, and saw a body of men in each gangway rushing aft to the quarter-deck."

This must be the mutiny!

Yelling, "God, I believe they are coming!" Gansevoort drew his Colt while Mackenzie ducked into his cabin to get his pistols. Gansevoort "jumped on the trunk, and ran forward to meet them; as I was going along I sung out to them not to come aft. I told them I would blow the first man's brains out who would put his foot on the quarter-deck."

He aimed at the tallest assailant—it was too dark to make out faces—and was about to fire when he heard a young voice shrilling: "It is me, sir; I am sending the men aft!"

This was Midshipman Rodgers, the officer of the deck urged aft by Collins. He'd ordered Oliver Browning, a newly made boatswain's mate, to get in among the crew with the mean little colt whip, and its snap and sting had started even the most laggard moving.

So that was that. Gansevoort lowered his pistol, grumbling that they "must have no such unusual movements on board the vessel," and the work recommenced.

In the hours and days ahead, though, what the officers remembered as "the rush aft" would meld with the loss of the foremast and any number of other incidents to feed the fear that was seeping through the brig.

Already Gunner's Mate Henry King "was afraid to go to sleep I had such a dread on my mind; I never unbuckled my arms from me, and slept with them from the time they were given me until our arrival in New-York."

8 Monday

Just as Mackenzie would not alter by a minute the time of divine services the day before, nor would he let the presence on the deck of three prisoners interfere with his ship's usual business. And, as so often on this ship, that business involved flogging.

Two men awaited punishment for what he called "crimes of considerable magnitude": apprentice Charles Lambert had stolen from the able Midshipman Gagely some sennit—braided hemp—for repairing a hat, and Henry Waltham, the Black steward from whom Spencer had often inveigled liquor, seems to have sneaked the prisoner a glass of brandy.

"These were vile offences," wrote Mackenzie, "and the prisoners were both punished to the extent of the law." That is, twelve cats.

The night before, in irons and awaiting his punishment, Waltham tried to exonerate himself, the captain said, by telling "Daniel M'Kinley, who had access to the ward-room as cot-boy, where three bottles of wine could be found." Most sailors would like to get their hands on a bottle of wine for purely recreational reasons, but Mackenzie saw a darker purpose here—"the object being, no doubt, to furnish the means of excitement to the conspirators, to induce them to rise, release Waltham and get possession of the vessel."

After Monday's flogging, Waltham was to get twelve more cats the next morning.

The captain had found out about the wine because Daniel McKinley had reported it to Lieutenant Gansevoort. On other ships, at other times, this confession would have been, in official eyes if not those of the deckhands, admirable. But McKinley's name was on Spencer's list, and when Gansevoort told Mackenzie what the crewman had said, the captain saw it as "an extraordinary denunciation under the circumstances, probably occasioned by his desire to relieve himself from suspicion."

Mackenzie decided it was time to tell the crew what was going on. At first the apprentices had thought Spencer was in chains because he had recently had a brief fistfight with Midshipman Egbert Thompson, who he thought had been tardy in relieving him. But that scuffle could hardly have accounted for armed officers roaming the ship at all hours, and now Cromwell and Small had joined Spencer in chains.

After the morning floggings, wrote Mackenzie, "I thought this a fit opportunity to make some impression on the crew. The number of them actually engaged in the conspiracy might not be great: that it was known to a majority of them, I had reason to believe. In general, they might be considered disaffected, and disposed on all occasions to hold back and resist the discipline of the ship; the mysterious agency that had been at work since our departure from New York, to corrupt the crew, was now disclosed."

In his anxiety, he now no longer believed that the trouble had begun at Madeira, but that it had been brewing from the moment Brooklyn dropped away astern.

With the crew mustered, he "commenced by explaining to them the general nature of the project of Mr. Spencer, studiously avoiding to excite any suspicions that I was in the possession of the names of those who were implicated. I was willing, in fact, that the worst of them should repent and hide themselves among the well-disposed portion of the crew.

"I took care to inform them that the majority of them, whatever might be their implication, were to share the fate of the officers." That is, murdered and thrown overboard. "I endeavored to divert the minds of the slightly disaffected from the picture of successful vice which Spencer had presented to them. I alluded to the circumstance that most of the crew, unlike crews in general, leaving ties of kindred to render life dear to them [slightly confusing: he meant they had families waiting at home], and expressed the hope that within three weeks we should be again among our friends. I thanked God that we had friends to follow us with solicitude and affection; for to have friends, and not to be unworthy of them, was the best guarantee that could be given for truth and fidelity."

Relying once again on his ability to read facial expressions, the captain said that his speech had various effects on its audience: "It filled many with horror at the idea of what they had escaped from: it inspired others with terror at dangers awaiting them from their connexion with the conspiracy. The thoughts of returning to that home and those friends from whom it had been intended to have cut them off forever, caused many of them to weep."

He was pleased: "I now considered the crew tranquillized and the vessel safe."

That didn't last. He soon spotted Spencer attempting "to hold intelligence with the crew"—he doesn't say how—and "I directed that all the prisoners should be turned with their faces aft."

Now the three could see only the stern of the ship and its wake spreading away through a placid sea.

Then Mackenzie lit on an additional punitive measure: "I also directed that no tobacco should be furnished them after the supply they had on their persons when confined should be exhausted."

This hit the three prisoners hard, and, said Mackenzie with petty satisfaction, "they earnestly begged to be allowed tobacco."

No, no—he ordered Gansevoort to tell Spencer that he "should have all his mess afforded," and that Small and Cromwell "should have their rations as it was allowed by the government, that everything should be supplied to them that was necessary to their health and comfort, but that tobacco was a stimulant, and [I] wished them to tranquillize their minds and remain free from excitement."

The new prohibition broke Spencer for the first time. "His spirits gave way entirely," said Mackenzie. "He remained the whole day with his face buried in the grego, and when it was for a moment raised, it was bathed in tears."

Angel of mercy Gansevoort was standing by with his "gentle and untiring attentions," and later on Spencer told the lieutenant, according to the captain, "that he was in no state at that time to speak of anything—when he felt more composed he would tell him all—he would answer any questions the commander might desire to put to him."

The commander never took him up on the offer.

WHILE THE EIGHTEEN-YEAR-OLD Spencer wept, across the quarterdeck from him Cromwell and Small watched the ever-unspooling sea and smoked the last of their tobacco.

They knew why they were there, but Cromwell in particular may have brooded over the injustice of it. Small, a lively and spirited presence, was popular with officers and men alike; not so Cromwell. But Small was on Spencer's list, and Cromwell was not, although Mackenzie had persuaded himself that the nonexistent "E. Andrews" was an alias Spencer had affixed to him. Cromwell's vile temper and growled scorn of captain and officers would have made him an appealing target. More important, though, the two men shared a dangerous ability.

As Spencer had understood, they were the only crewmen who knew enough ship handling to find their way to the Isle of Pines or anywhere else. Spencer couldn't; Boatswain's Mate Browning said that "Cromwell and Small understood navigation, and I have seen them working it," but as for the rest of the sailors, "there were none more capable of taking charge of that brig than I am of a balloon." As for Spencer, "I do not think he knew a dozen ropes aboard of her."

Meanwhile, when he wasn't ministering to Spencer, Gansevoort was questioning the crew. Although he already knew of the bad blood that existed between Dickerson and Cromwell, he nodded toward the quarterdeck and asked the carpenter's mate, "What do you think of those fellows?"

Dickerson said, "The damned fool is on the larboard and the damned scoundrel on the starboard arm-chest."

Noting that Small and Cromwell were both on the starboard side, Gansevoort "said to him, 'You mean Cromwell,' being pretty well satisfied on the same thing in my own mind."

"Yes, sir, he is the most dangerous man on board the ship."

Gansevoort moved on. "I had several conversations with King . . . I think Browning, and Anderson, Captain of the forecastle: and they all thought Cromwell was the most dangerous man concerned in the plot."

Gunner's Mate King "told me he thought there was a collection of arms in the store-room. I overhauled it but found none. I think I collected all the monkey-tails [a length of rope with a hook on it], holy-stones, marling-spikes, and such things as might be used against us."

Captain Mackenzie ended the day far from tranquilized. All about him he saw signs of peril, "dark and portentous," he said. As the swaying shadows deepened around him, he enforced another precaution: every man topside must lie down on the deck through the hours of darkness. The brig sailed into the night carrying what looked like the crew of corpses in "The Rime of the Ancient Mariner."

Earlier, during his round of interviews, Gansevoort had asked Acting Master Matthew Perry if he thought it would be safe to take more prisoners. Perry, evidently a rather cold-blooded young pragmatist, said that "the officers could not take of any more than the first three, and if they had to take any more prisoners the safety of the vessel required that the first three should be put to death."

Although he had assured Spencer, Cromwell, and Small that they would face a court-martial once the *Somers* was back home, Commander Mackenzie was beginning to think the same way.

9 Tuesday

THE TWENTY-NINTH DAWNED CLEAR, another fair, mild day with the trades pressing the brig gently along.

The first order of business was the luckless Waltham. His wounds still fresh from Monday's whipping, the steward was again lashed to the gratings and given the full dozen cats.

After he had been cut down, shuddering and bloody, Mackenzie again addressed the ship's company, "urging them to conform to the discipline of the vessel: the orders were all known, and of easy observance. I mentioned that every punishment inflicted must be known to the secretary of the navy, and that the less punishment there was, the more creditable it would be to the commander and the crew."

The reception of this second lecture disappointed the captain; it hadn't had the impact of yesterday's evocation of home and hearth. "The whole crew was far from being tranquillized: the most seriously implicated began once more to collect in knots."

He had passed a night haunted by mutinous murmurings. "Seditious words were heard through the vessel"—he did not then, nor ever, say what those words were—"and an insolent and menacing air assumed by many."

If he was on edge, so were all his officers, their suspicions now sharpened by weariness. Since the "rush aft" they had been standing watch on watch: four hours on duty, four hours off, endlessly repeated, a tiring schedule made more onerous by the weight of the arms they carried. Their reports were increasingly ominous.

"Some of the petty officers had been sounded by the first lieutenant," the captain wrote, "and found to be true to their colors: they were under the impression that the vessel was yet far from safe—that there were still many at liberty who ought to be confined—that an outbreak, having for its object the rescue of the prisoners, was seriously contemplated. . . . Several times during the night there were symptoms of an intention to strike some blow."

The only evidence for that seems to have come from Wales, who, his scurrilous dealings in Puerto Rico obviously forgotten, was on easy terms with all the officers. "In the morning," he said, "while holy-stoning the deck [that is, scrubbing it with a chunk of sandstone the size and shape of a Bible, which puts the user in a position reminiscent of prayer], I being the officer over the prisoners, I observed signs passed between Spencer, Wilson, and Mckinley; they put their hands on their chins and Cromwell, who was lying on the arm chest, rose up. I told him my orders were to shoot him down, and I should do so if he did not lie still. He lay down.

"I then went back with my pistol cocked, to the launch, where Wilson was poking about, and found that he had a number of holy-stones out and that he was taking out a hand-spike. I told him that if I saw him making any further signs I would blow his brains out."

Of course he reported this to Gansevoort, and Gansevoort to the captain; and of course both men found the incident threatening. As the day closed Captain Mackenzie "felt more anxious than I had yet done, and remained continually on deck."

Eight bells, midnight: "When the watch was called and mustered, M'Kinley, Green, and others seriously implicated, missed their muster. That they should have been asleep at all that night, was not likely. . . ." And each "had some lame excuse," which could only mean that "there was probably an agreement to meet around the officer of the deck, and commit some act of violence."

10 Wednesday

Dawn broke with the officer of the deck unmolested. At nine in the morning, Mackenzie ordered irons put on Wilson (who had "failed in his attempt to get up an outbreak in the night"), McKee ("who was to have taken the wheel, and who was entirely in the confidence of Cromwell"), and McKinley ("among the certain") who would have had to pick up familiarity with the buccaneer's trade while a waiter at the Hotel Howard, back in Manhattan.

The three new prisoners protested. From the start of the voyage, McKinley explained, he and McKee "turned in and out with one another"—meaning that they'd agreed on an arrangement in which the one coming off watch would wake the other to go on duty. And last night McKee had failed to do so. Why was that? Because of the orders to lie down on the deck all night, McKinley had fallen fast asleep and there was no McKee on hand to shake him awake, what with the petty officers preventing any crewman from moving around in the dark. A plausible excuse, but Mackenzie was in no mood to hear it: he found it "lame." And Wilson had been caught sending chin-signals to Spencer and fussing around with the holy-stones.

The armorer did his work, and Wilson got dumped on the quarterdeck between Cromwell and Small, with McKinley and McKee across the way to Spencer's right.

And then there was Green. He too had missed muster; moreover, he had recently decorated Spencer's arm with the tattooed "love device." There was an intimacy there it would be unwise to overlook. Mackenzie waffled a little, telling the sailor that overall his behavior had been good. Still, "I will put you in irons for the present." Green joined the others on the quarterdeck, to the left of Small, to whom Lieutenant Gansevoort then put some questions.

"Small, you see we have taken some more prisoners." Yes, Small had seen. "Do you know of any others that are at large from whom we may apprehend danger?"

Small told him that was "a hard thing for him to say."

Well, did he think "Cromwell was not engaged with Spencer in this plot?"

"That's a hard thing for me to say, sir." Small followed this unsatisfactory answer by explaining that the two men were "intimates together," and "he had seen Spencer give Cromwell more money than *he'd* like to give him or lend him, either."

This seeming irrelevancy exasperated Gansevoort. "That's not the thing: I want a plain answer to a plain question. Is not Cromwell deeply engaged with Mr. Spencer in this plot of Spencer's to take the vessel out of the hands of the officers?"

"If any body aboard of the brig is, *he* is, sir."

With that, Small shut up. Gansevoort let the subject drop, and went off.

Perhaps Spencer was ready to talk, as he had earlier said he would. "I went to see him about ten o'clock. He commenced by saying that he had formed this plot on board of every vessel he had been in—both in the *John Adams* and in the *Potomac*. He said he knew that it would get him into difficulty—that he had tried to break himself of it—but it was impossible: *it was a mania with him.* I think he wished me to mention it to the Commander."

That ended another oddly truncated conversation. Surely, given his bald confession, Spencer was willing to speak further. Not Gansevoort; he asked no more questions, and went away to tell the captain what little he had learned.

WITH SEVEN CAPTIVES NOW LANGUISHING on the quarterdeck, Mackenzie felt he had done all he could in that line, and it wasn't enough: "Each new arrest of prisoners seemed to bring a fresh set of conspirators forward, to occupy the first place."

Even with the "fine weather and brilliant nights there was already a disposition to make an attack and rescue the prisoners." What if a storm blew up, and the swift work it demanded proved distraction enough for the mutineers to make their move? And there were even larger considerations, which the captain expressed in a florid paragraph complete with Old Glory.

"These grave considerations, the deep sense I had of the solemn obligation I was under to protect and defend the vessel which had been intrusted to me, and the lives of the officers and crew—the seas traversed by our peaceful merchantmen, and the unarmed of all nations using the highways of the seas from the horrors which the conspirators had meditated, and above all to guard from violation the sanctity of the American flag displayed from the masthead of one of its cruisers—all impressed upon me the absolute necessity of adopting some further measures for the security of the vessel."

Usually an American warship was ruled by its captain, and not by a consensus of his underlings. "In so grave a case, however, I was desirous of having the opinion of all the officers, and was particularly anxious that no shadow of doubt should remain as to the guilt of either of the prisoners, should their execution be deemed necessary."

He wrote his officers a letter.

U.S. BRIG SOMERS
NOV. 30, 1842

GENTLEMEN: The time has arrived when I am desirous of availing myself of your council in the responsible position in which, as commander of this vessel, I find myself placed. You are aware of the circumstances which have resulted in the confinement of Midshipman Philip Spencer, Boatswain's Mate Samuel Cromwell, and Seaman E. Small, as prisoner, and I purposely abstain from entering into any details of them, necessarily ignorant of the exact extent of disaffection among a crew which has so long and system-atically and assiduously been tampered with by an officer. *Knowing that suspicions of the gravest nature attach to persons still at large, and whom the difficulty of taking care of the prisoners we already have, makes me more reluctant than I should otherwise be to apprehend, I have determined to address myself to you, and to ask your united council as to the best course to be now pursued, and I call upon you to take into deliberate and dispassionate consideration the present condition of the vessel, and the contingencies of every nature that the future may embrace, throughout the remainder of our cruise, and enlighten me with your opinion of the best course to be pursued.*

I am, very respectfully, gentlemen, your most obedient

ALEX SLIDELL MACKENZIE
Commander

To Lieutenant Guert Gansevoort, Passed-Assistant Surgeon R. W. Leacock [sic], Purser H. M Heiskill [sic], Acting-Master M. C. Perry, Midship-man Henry Rogers [sic], Midshipman Egbert Thompson, Midshipman Chas. W. Hayes.

Mackenzie had said he was simply seeking advice, but although he never used the term, the meeting he desired would have all the trappings of a court-martial: witnesses being examined by a council of officers who were to decide a life-or-death issue.

And legally speaking, the captain had no more right to convene a court-martial than he did to call a constitutional convention. The iron voice of the Articles of War was clear: A general court-martial could be ordered only by the president of the United States, the secretary of the navy, the commander of a fleet (and there were no US fleets as yet), or the head of a squadron. Twelve lashes was the greatest punishment he could inflict on a crewman; arrest and suspension from duty the limit he could impose on an officer. He certainly did not have the power to kill anybody.

Nevertheless, "on receipt of my letter," the captain wrote, "the officers immediately assembled in the wardroom, and commenced the examination of witnesses; the witnesses were duly sworn, and the testimony accurately written down: in addition to the oath, each witness signed the evidence which he had been given, after it had been read over to him. The officers passed the whole day in this occupation without interruption and without food. I remained in charge of the deck, with the three young midshipmen, on constant duty."

So Commander Mackenzie paced his quarterdeck hour after hour, guarded only by three green boys (Deslonde and Oliver Perry, who were seventeen years old, and Tillotson, who was sixteen). If ever there had been the perfect time for the mutineers to strike, this was the moment. It would have been a matter of minutes—seconds—for them to overwhelm the four and secure the eight-by-ten-foot wardroom with its seven occupants huddled around a three-by-four-foot table in a restless friction of knees and shoulders and elbows. Any attempt on the officers' part to dash topside had there been trouble on deck would have presented a spectacle like clowns tumbling from their tiny car in some future circus. But the mundane work aboard the brig continued uninterrupted.

The interrogations took all day. None of the officers involved had any legal training; there was no judge to regulate the proceedings; and though all would have shown some deference to Lieutenant Gansevoort, their simultaneous questioning made a hubbub that confused the witnesses.

Purser Heiskell had the job of writing down the testimony, which he did in pencil on a sheaf of loose pages.

By now everyone on the ship knew what the captain and his officers wanted said, and none of the witnesses would have been likely to confess to any cordial feeling toward the prisoners.

From Heiskell's transcript:

CHARLES VAN VELSOR, seaman: "A good while since Mr. Spencer said he would like to have a ship to go to the northwest coast; Cromwell and him was thick; I should think Cromwell meant to join Spencer and take this vessel. . . ."

MATHIAS GEDNEY, seaman: "Think Cromwell, when aggravated, is a resolute and desperate man; Collins told him in my hearing that he (Collins) 'was once aboard a vessel where there was a keg of gold in the hold for six months and nobody knew about it but himself,' Cromwell replied that if he had such a chance he would run off with it to the western states. . . ."

MICHAEL GARTY, master-at-arms: "Believes Spencer, Small, and Cromwell, were determined on taking this brig. . . ."

OLIVER BROWNING, seaman: "I do not believe it safe to have Cromwell, Small, and Spencer, on board. I believe that if the men were at their stations taking care of the vessel in bad weather or any other time, when they could get a chance they would try to capture the vessel, if they could get a chance—to tell you 'God Almighty's' truth, I believe some of the cooks around the galley, I think they are the main backers. . . . I believe Cromwell, Small, and Spencer ought to be made way with."

THOMAS DICKERSON, seaman: "I think if Cromwell, Small, and Spencer, were made way with, it would put a stop to it, and I think that by that means the vessel *will* be safe; have not the least doubt of the guilt of the three prisoners mentioned."

WILLIAM COLLINS, seaman: "Wishes Cromwell, Small, and Spencer, were out of the ship. . . ."

ANDREW ANDERSON, seaman: "Mr. Spencer must be at the head [of the plot], Cromwell the next. . . . I think they are safe from here to St. Thomas, but from there home I think there is a great danger, on account of the bad weather on the coast and squalls. . . ."
[Like Browning, Anderson suspects the cooks, and makes an ugly remark which, by no means extraordinary in that era, seems to be unique among all the proceedings generated by the cruise:] "I don't know about the niggers at the galley—I don't like them—Cromwell could get anything in the galley—they appeared to like Cromwell there, he would very often take his pot and get coffee there. . . ."

CHARLES ROGERS, seaman: "I think if Cromwell, Small, and Spencer, were disposed of our lives would be much safer."

CHARLES STEWART, seaman: "I think the prisoners have friends on board who would release them if they got a chance. . . ."

HENRY KING, gunner's mate: "Thinks Cromwell is the head man; thinks they have been engaged in it ever since we left New York. . . ."

PETER TYSON, seaman: "Night before Mr. Spencer was put in irons, M'Kinley and Wilson came aft, while I was lying down between 4 and 5 gun; they appeared to have been conversing before; Wilson said to M'Kinley, 'Come here, I want to tell you'; M'Kinley then said, 'He told me we have got spies on us, and had better be careful'; Wilson said, 'I defy any man to find out my business; I know my business; I have been in too many scrapes; he knows what I am, and that I never look to what is to come afterward; I don't fear nothing, and go right ahead.' I did not know what they alluded to, but when Wilson said, 'I would not mind joining them,' M'Kinley said, 'I don't know, I would rather go in a regular slaving expedition, for there you have $35 a month, and prize-money; when we get to St. Thomas we will be fitted out. . . .'"

JAMES WALES, purser's steward: [Wales recounted the conversation with Spencer on the booms.]

GEORGE WARNER, seaman: "Thinks Cromwell a desperate character, thinks Cromwell would have put Mr. Spencer to death if he could not make him of service; thinks Small a desperate character; Spencer did not enforce the orders lately on the forecastle as other officers did; Mr. Spencer has been intimate with the crew; I have seen him give cigars to Cromwell."

The officers had been peppering the witnesses with questions from the very start, but only one appears in Heiskell's minutes: "What was the reason for your saying to Green, 'The damned son of a bitch (meaning Cromwell) ought to be hung?'"

Warner's answer, as recorded by the purser: "Because I thought him guilty."

Warner never said that.

THE OFFICERS MUST HAVE RECOGNIZED that Captain Mackenzie, in his seemingly democratic decision to let each have a part in his quasi-legal exercise, was enlisting them as allies, distributing responsibility for what might follow and thus diluting his own part in it.

Only one witness ever cracked the hermetic carapace they were building over their trial, and he didn't do so until 110 years later.

In 1954 a novelist and journalist named Frederic F. Van de Water published a brisk and lively book about the *Somers* affair under the succinct title *The Captain Called It Mutiny*.

Van de Water was a freelance writer in the days when you could begin as a newspaperman and graduate to earning a good living turning out stories for the "slicks"—higher-class magazines printed on glossy paper rather than pulp—and there was enough hunger for print in the land that you might bulwark the generous fees of *Collier's* and the *Saturday Evening Post* with any number of books: Van de Water's number was well upward of thirty. His novels had the sorts of titles novels did in the 1930s and '40s—*Elmer 'n' Edwina, Death in the Dark, Hurrying Feet, Catch a Falling Star*—and he published no fewer than six collections of fond essays about his Vermont home: *We're Still in the Country, In Defense of Worms, The Circling Year,* and so forth.

An antique naval scandal might seem an odd detour in such a career, but for Van de Water it was a personal matter. Seaman Warner was his great-uncle.

George Washington Warner had a mean stepmother, and in 1838, at the age of seventeen, ran away to sea. He ended up on the *Somers*, and, eventually, in chains aboard her.

During his confinement, he had access to pen and paper, and wrote about what had happened to him with the council of officers. His is the only description we have of that proceeding.

"Before a question of one officer was answered," he said, "others would be put by other officers, thus not only confounding the person being examined but themselves.

"As an indication of the correctness of the so-called 'depositions,' I cite one instance. I was asked why I said: 'If I had my way with the damned son of a bitch, Cromwell, I would hang him,' which had no answer. The question as put was not answered by me for the reason I had no answer to make to it. I hated Cromwell, and he me."

Nothing to do with any mutiny; just intense personal dislike of the boatswain.

"The discovery was made by Purser Heiskell in making up a clean copy and he left a blank to be filled. He wanted me to fill in my answer."

Warner refused. "I answered that I had no answer to make. After some time spent to induce me to make an answer, which I did not, he said: 'Well, sign it and I will fill up the answer.' I signed and left the wardroom. He subsequently wrote in as my answer: 'Because I believe him guilty.'"

As the amateur prosecutors and jurists (each man was both) fumbled their way through the haphazard proceeding, Captain Mackenzie grew "exceedingly anxious to know the result of the investigation." Still, he must have been fairly confident of that result, as he spent part of the long afternoon drawing up a watch bill showing the stations that crewmen and officers were to take for an execution.

The captain impatiently dissolved his council at six o'clock: night was coming, and the armed patrols had to begin. As the officers paced fore and aft trying not to stumble over the sailors lying on the deck, eight bells signaled the end of the day and the month. Close to home now, with the Virgin Islands off to her west, the *Somers* dipped and lifted into December while Mackenzie "obtained, at intervals, during the midwatch, an hour or two of refreshing sleep."

11 Doomsday

THE COUNCIL RECONVENED IN THE MORNING to question a few more witnesses. No explanation was ever given for how any of the witnesses had been chosen, and these last interviews must have been merely pro forma.

After about an hour, Lieutenant Gansevoort delivered to Commander Mackenzie the council's letter written in response to his of the day before. It contained just two sentences, but the first one was colossal, bumping along over parenthetical hill and dale for more than two hundred words.

U.S. BRIG SOMERS,
Dec 1. 1842.

SIR: In answer to your letter of yesterday, requesting our counsel as to the best course to be pursued with the prisoners, Acting-Midshipman Philip Spencer, Boatswain's Mate Samuel Cromwell, and Seaman Elisha Small, we would state, that the evidence which has come to our knowledge is of such a nature as, after as dispassionate and deliberate a consideration of the case as the exigencies of the time would admit, we have come to a cool, decided, and unanimous opinion, that they have been guilty of a full and determined intention to commit a mutiny on board of this vessel of a most atrocious nature; and that the revelation of circumstances having made it necessary to confine others with them, the uncertainty as to what extent they are leagued with other still at large, the impossibility of guarding against the contingencies which 'a day or an hour may bring forth,' we are convinced that it would be impossible to carry them to the United States, and that the safety of the public property, the lives of ourselves, and of those committed to our charge, require that (giving them sufficient time to prepare) they should be put to death, in a manner best calculated as an example to make a beneficial impression upon the disaffected. This opinion we give, bearing in mind our duty to our God, our country, and to the service.

We are, sir, very respectfully, your obedient servants,

GUERT GANSEVOORT, Lieutenant,
R. W. LEECOCK, Pas'd Ass. Surg'n,
H. M. HEISKELL, Purser,
M.C. PERRY, Act'g Master,
HENRY RODGERS, Midshipman,
EGBERT THOMPSON, Midshipman,
CHAS. W. HAYES, Midshipman.

"I at once," wrote Mackenzie, "concurred in the justice of this opinion, and in the necessity of carrying its recommendation into immediate effect."

While the crew was being called to quarters, the captain went down to his cabin and put on his full-dress uniform. When he came back on deck, all blue and gold in the bright morning, McKinley briefly thought a ship had been sighted and that the captain was preparing for a visit.

Mackenzie told Gansevoort to arm the petty officers. The lieutenant said the captain "had expressed a wish that they should be armed before, but not having myself full confidence in them, I had until now discouraged it. On that morning I obeyed the order and armed the petty officers that were true; there were seven of them. The Commander ordered me, after they were armed, to report to him. He then addressed them and gave them their orders."

As Mackenzie reported those orders, they were as brusque and confident as any John Paul Jones might have issued: "My lads, you are to look at me, to obey my orders, and to see my orders obeyed. Go forward."

To Gansevoort, the captain enlarged on that considerably: he told his lieutenant that if any officer "saw an attempt made to rescue the prisoners, to blow out the brains of both the prisoners and those making the attempt; if they saw the prisoners forward of the mainmast and in communication with the crew, they were to destroy them; they were to keep a watchful eye upon the crew, and if they saw any mutinous attempt they were to use their arms upon them."

No communication; no mutinous gestures—so Mackenzie himself walked forward. "I gave orders to make immediate preparations for hanging the three principal criminals at the main-yard arms; all hands were now called to witness punishment. The after-guard and idlers [specialists who didn't have to stand watch: the carpenter, for instance, and the sailmaker] of both watches, were mustered on the quarter-deck at the whip [a length of tackle used to hoist lighter items] intended for Mr. Spencer; the forecastle men and foretopmen at that of Cromwell, to whose corruption they had been chiefly exposed; the maintopmen of both watches at that intended for Small, who for a month or more had held the situation of captain of the maintop."

First, though, the killing equipment had to be laid out on the deck: three 7-inch blocks—pulleys—which some of the crew were directed to thread with the 2¾-inch rope that had come up from the hold.

The prisoners, still facing aft, would not have seen these preparations.

Mackenzie "proceeded to execute the most painful duty that has ever devolved on an American commander—that of announcing to the criminals their fate."

Spencer first. The captain felt the occasion called for some oratory.

It was noon; the sun stood right above the mainmast, and the eighteen-year-old, who was now beginning to realize that he would not see it set, had to sit in the small pool of his own shadow and listen to this: "I informed Mr. Spencer that when he had been about to take my life, and dishonor me as an officer in the execution of my rightful duty, without cause of offence to him, on speculation; it had been his intentions to remove me suddenly from the world in the darkness of night, in my sleep, without a moment to utter one murmur of affection to my wife and children, one prayer for their welfare. His life was now forfeited to his country, and the necessities of the case, growing out of his corruption of the crew, compelled me to take it. I would not, however, imitate his intended example, as to the manner of claiming the sacrifice. If there remained to him one feeling true to nature, it should be gratified. If he had any word to send to his parents, it should be recorded and faithfully delivered. Ten minutes should be granted him for the purpose, and Midshipman E. Thompson was called to note the time, and inform me when ten minutes had passed."

Spencer began to weep. He said he "was not fit to die." Mackenzie, in what sounds like an unseemly taunt, "repeated to him his own catechism"—the one he had administered to Wales. *Do you fear death? Are you afraid of a dead person, and dare you kill a person?* The captain "begged him at least to . . . set, to the men he had corrupted and seduced, the example of dying with decorum."

This Roman exhortation, according to Mackenzie, "immediately restored him to entire self-possession."

The captain left Spencer and went over to the starboard arms chest, where Cromwell was trying to divert himself with a copy of the *Penny Magazine*.

Mackenzie spent less time with Cromwell than he had with Spencer. The captain told him he was to hang, and the big boatswain's mate dropped his magazine, struggled off the chest, fell to his knees, and cried, "God of the universe, look down upon my poor wife! I am innocent!"

Small took the news calmly.

The captain returned to Spencer who, there in chains with the shadow of death upon him, said: "As these are the last words I have to say, I trust they will be believed. Cromwell is innocent."

Although he had said the same thing several days before, this was such a departure from how Mackenzie had expected his hangings to go that—he said—he was "staggered." He hurried to Gansevoort, who reassured him that "there was not the shadow of a doubt" as to Cromwell's guilt. Still shaken, he had his lieutenant take a poll, whose outcome he reported in a curious sentence: Cromwell "was condemned by acclamation by the petty officers."

Mackenzie, still unsettled by Spencer's defense of Cromwell, set about calming himself with a move as cruel as any flogging. He told the midshipman that "Cromwell had made use of him. I told him that remarks had been made . . . not very flattering to him, and which he did not care to hear."

Of course he did. "He expressed great anxiety to hear what was said."

Mackenzie quoted the remark about "the damned fool" on the larboard and the "damned scoundrel" on the starboard arms chest. But that was nothing Cromwell had said; it had been Dickerson. He went on—and who knows where this had come from—"Another had remarked that after the vessel should have been captured by Mr. Spencer, Cromwell might allow him to live, provided he made himself useful; he would probably make him a secretary." The captain's smug and teasing conclusion: "I do not think this would have suited your temper."

Having thus done his best to batter the boy's remaining pride and spirit, Mackenzie reported seeing that infallible sign of guilt: Spencer's "countenance assumed a diabolical expression."

Mackenzie returned to Small and asked if he had any final message to send home. Still calm, Small replied, "I have nobody to care for me but my poor old mother, and I would rather that she not know how I have died."

Then he was back with Spencer.

Had he "no message to send to his friends?"

"None that they would wish to receive."

This sounds plausible. What he next reports Spencer saying does not: "Tell them I die wishing them every blessing and happiness; I deserve death for this and many other crimes—there are few crimes that I have not committed; I feel sincerely penitent, and my only fear of death is that my repentance may come too late."

Mackenzie's next question feels as stilted as Spencer's answer to his last one (even in the nineteenth century, would a naval officer use the word "obloquy" in a spoken sentence?): "I asked him if there were any one whom he had injured to whom he could yet make reparation—any one who was suffering obloquy from crimes which he had committed."

"I have wronged many persons, but chiefly my parents; this will kill my poor mother."

This apparently shocked the captain even more than the insistence on Cromwell's innocence. "I was not before aware that he had a mother." Not only is it strange for the captain to have been amazed that an eighteen-year-old might have a living mother, but stranger still because during his previous command Mackenzie had entertained Spencer's parents—father and mother both—aboard his frigate.

It took the captain a moment to absorb the mother revelation; then: "When recovered from the pain of this announcement, I asked him if it would not have been still more dreadful—" And once more he summarized the carnage that the mutineers had been planning.

"I do not know what would have become of me had I succeeded," Spencer replied.

Mackenzie repeated what he said were Cromwell's plans for his accomplice, this time upping the ante from making Spencer a secretary to murdering him.

But Spencer had lost interest in the betrayal. "I fear," he said, "this may injure my father."

Mackenzie was brusque: "Too late to think of that."

And then he said an extraordinary thing.

He had told his three captives that they were going to be court-martialed once they were back in the States. Now he said to Spencer "that had it been possible to have taken him home, as I intended to do, it was not in nature that his father should not have interfered to save him—that for those who have friends or money in America there was no punishment for the worst of crimes. . . . I on this account the less regretted the dilemma in which I was placed; it would injure his father a great deal more, if he got home alive, should he be condemned and yet escape; the best and only service he could do his father is to die."

That is: if Philip Spencer were to reach home, his father's influence would see that he escaped hanging, no matter what a court-martial might have found.

Midshipman Thompson came by and, as ordered, said the ten minutes were up.

Mackenzie ignored him, and continued his colloquy with Spencer. Now, in these final minutes of Spencer's life, he asked the midshipman nothing about the details of a plot that, he believed, was still pullulating throughout the ship. Who was involved? When was the mutiny to have taken place? Were any of the petty officers conspirators?

Nothing like that. Instead, by his own account, he wanted to preach about the ethics of the situation.

Gansevoort "went forward to my duty and left the Commander in conversation with Mr. Spencer. I was not near enough to hear the reply which Mr. Spencer made to Com. Mackenzie's remarks. When I saw them again Mr. Spencer had a Bible in his hand and the Commander was seated near him with a paper upon which he appeared to be writing. I did not hear the conversation then." Nor did anyone else aboard the brig.

The captain had sent for paper and an inkwell, and was taking notes. The ten minutes were long up; half an hour, and then an hour passed.

At one point, Spencer asked, "But have you not formed an exaggerated estimate of the extent of this conspiracy?"

"No." Spencer's "systematic efforts to corrupt the crew and prepare them for the indulgence of every evil passion; since the day before our departure from New York, had been but too successful. I knew the conspiracy was still extensive—I did not know how extensive."

This, again, would have been the time to ask. Instead, Mackenzie returned to his pilfered-liquor bugaboo.

"I recapitulated to him the arts which he used; he was startled by my telling him that he had made the wardroom steward steal brandy and had given it to the crew; he said, 'I did not make him steal it'; I told him it was brought at his request—that he knew where it came from—it was, if possible, more criminal to seduce another to commit crime than to commit crime one's self."

Spencer was not to be drawn into a discussion of the relative malignity of various crimes: "But are you not going too far—are you not fast? Does the law entirely justify you?"

This was rewarded with haughty irony. "I replied that *he* had not consulted *me* in making his arrangements." Moreover, "his opinion could not be an unprejudiced one" (did that need saying?) and "I had consulted all his brother officers, his messmates included."

Spencer asked how he was to die. "I explained it to him; he objected to it and asked to be shot." No: "I told him that I could not make any distinction between him and those he had corrupted."

Then could his face be covered? "This was readily granted, and he was asked what it should be covered with; he did not care; a handkerchief was sought for in his locker, none but a black one found, and this brought for the purpose."

The two other condemned men wanted their faces covered as well, "and frocks were taken from their bags to cover their heads."

Mackenzie says that Spencer told him, "I am a believer—do you think that repentance at this late hour can be accepted." This gave the captain a chance to discuss "the case of the penitent thief who was pardoned by our Savior upon the cross." (Rather surprisingly, he seems to have refrained from mentioning to Spencer that the other thief who was there that day was damned.)

Then—most unusually for a naval commander in such a position—Mackenzie wanted to make sure there were no hard feelings. "I asked him if I had ever done anything to him to make him seek my life, or whether the hatred he had conceived for me, and of which I had only recently become aware, was fostered for the purpose of giving him a plea for justification."

Spencer answered wearily, "It was only a fancy—perhaps there might have been something in your manner which offended me."

Mackenzie decided it was time to move things along. "The petty officers had been assigned to rank, to conduct the several prisoners to the gangway; at the break of the quarter deck is a narrow passage between the trunk and the pumpwell—Mr. Spencer and Cromwell met exactly on either side. I directed Cromwell to stop, to allow Mr. Spencer to pass first."

Neither man said a word to the other, but a moment later Spencer asked to be allowed to see Wales. When the purser's steward was brought forward, Spencer extended a hand. "Mr. Wales, I sincerely hope that you will forgive me for tampering with your fidelity."

Wales started crying, and choked out, "I do forgive you from the bottom of my heart, and I hope that God may forgive you also."

"Farewell," said Spencer.

"Farewell," said Wales.

Now at the gangway, Spencer was in front of Small. Again he held out his hand. "Small, forgive me for leading you into this trouble."

Small, unlike Wales, had only minutes to live. "No, by God! Mr. Spencer, I can't forgive you."

Spencer asked him again.

"Ah! Mr. Spencer, that is a hard thing for you to ask me; we shall soon be before the face of God, and there we shall know all about it."

"You must forgive me, Small—I can not die without your forgiveness."

Here Mackenzie, taking the role of a man of the cloth, intervened. Telling Small that this "was no time for resentment," he went on, "Don't go out of the world with any hard feelings at your heart— forgive him."

"Since you request it, sir, I forgive him." Small took "the still-extended hand of Mr. Spencer."

Mackenzie broke in. "Small, what have *I* done to you that you won't bid me goodbye?"

This question would seem to have a single, obvious answer. But Small avoided it, instead saying, "I did not know that you would bid a poor bugger like me goodbye, sir."

And then asked the captain for *his* forgiveness, which gave Mackenzie the chance to wheedle the condemned man into absolving him of any wrongdoing: "I asked him what I had ever said or done to him to make him seek my life, conscious of no injustice or provocation of any sort: I felt it was yet necessary to my comfort to receive the assurance from his own lips."

That assurance came at once: "What have you done to me, Captain Mackenzie? what have you done to me, sir?—nothing, but treat me like a man."

This was still not enough to console the captain: "I told him, in justification of the course which I was pursuing, that I had high responsibilities to fulfil . . ." As in his other such talks, this one ended with the Stars and Stripes. ". . . to the government which had entrusted me with this vessel—to the officers placed under my command—to the boys whom it was intended either to put to death, or reserve for a fate more deplorable: there was yet a higher duty to the flag of my country."

This entirely self-referential appeal seemed to move Small. "Yes, sir, and I honor you for it." He glanced up into the rigging and added, "God bless that flag."

He had more to say, this time to the whole ship: "Shipmates and topmates, take warning by my example. I never was a pirate. I never killed a man. It's for saying that I would do it that I am about to depart this life. See what a word will do. It was going in a guineaman [slaver] that brought me to this. Beware of a guineaman."

He turned to Spencer—"I am now ready to die, Mr. Spencer, are you?"—and then to the sailors holding his whip: "Now, brother topmates, give me a quick and easy death."

It was not likely to be quick or easy. At the signal, the men holding the whips were to run forward, pulling the condemned aloft. But with no trap to drop the victims suddenly, the brutal kindness of a broken neck and a fast death were not to be theirs. They would strangle slowly, and Small, being the lightest, would perhaps suffer the longest.

Lieutenant Gansevoort went to say goodbye to Cromwell, who "seized my hand, grasping it very violently. He said he was innocent, and hoped we'd find it out before six months."

Spencer spoke up. He wanted a word with Gansevoort. "You may have heard that I am a coward, and *you* may think I'm not a brave man. You can judge for yourself whether I die like a coward or a brave man." Once more he spoke with Mackenzie, asking what was the signal for the execution.

The captain said he would hoist the colors—"to give solemnity to the act." There would be two drumrolls, and on the third a gun would be fired, and the men hanged.

Spencer asked if he could give the word to fire the gun.

Mackenzie was solicitous. He dismissed the drummer. Spencer "begged that no interval might elapse between giving the word, and firing the gun."

In that transitional time for military technology, the guns on the ship had different firing mechanisms. The captain "asked if they were firing with lock and wafer, which had always proved quick and sure, but was told that they had tube and priming, and were prepared to fire with a match; some delay would have been necessary to open the arms chest, and get out a wafer. I ordered a supply of live coal to be passed from the galley, and fresh ones perpetually supplied; then assured him there would be no delay."

There was a brief one. Cromwell cried out, "Tell my wife I die an innocent man; tell Lieut. Morris [a friendly officer on an earlier voyage] I die an innocent man."

Reporting those final words, Mackenzie would give a postmortem rejoinder: "But it had been in the game of this man to appear innocent, to urge Mr. Spencer on, to furnish him with professional ideas, to bring about a catastrophe, of which Mr. Spencer was to take all the risk, and from which he, Cromwell, was to derive all the benefit. He had taken a great many precautions to appear innocent, but he had not taken enough."

Now, though, with the three condemned sitting quietly in their irons, Mackenzie got up on the trunk house, "from which my eye could take in everything," and waited for Philip Spencer to give word for the gun to fire.

Nothing happened.

The crew, too, waited, carefully arranged at the stations the captain had set down in writing before the verdict came in—the "after-guard and idlers" on the quarterdeck near Spencer; the forecastlemen and foretopmen about Cromwell; the maintopmen beside Small.

Everyone in his proper place, but the captain was still anxious. He had given "orders to cut down whoever should let go of the whip with even one hand. Or fail to haul on it when ordered." Waltham was holding one of the ropes; what if that much-flogged man should rebel? What if any of them did?

Browning, holding Spencer's whip, seemed to be talking with him through the black cloth that covered his face. He broke off and came aft to report to the captain. "Mr. Spencer says he cannot give the word; he wishes the commander to give the word himself."

Mackenzie shouted, "Fire!"

The gun spoke, Gansevoort calling, "Whip!" through its enormous voice. No one at the whips hesitated. The men trotted forward, hoisting their masked bundles up through the eddying powder smoke. Clear of the deck, clear of the rail, Spencer, Small, and Cromwell spun out over their graveyard sea, swinging in wide spirals whose cones narrowed as they neared the yardarm. Once there—"Belay!"—the lines were made fast, and the three men, dead or soon to be, dangled twenty feet up, moving only with the leisurely roll of the ship.

ALTHOUGH IT MAY HAVE taken some restraint on Captain Mackenzie's part, that connoisseur of executions was wise enough not to describe the death throes of his mutineers in a document that was to go to the secretary of the navy, and that would surely be read by Philip Spencer's father. In a rare moment of verbal economy, he wrote: "The word was accordingly given, and the execution took place." That was all.

But his literary urge soon reasserted itself. There were lessons to be drawn.

"The crew were now ordered aft, and I addressed them from the trunk on which I was standing.

"I called their attention first, to the fate of the unfortunate young man, whose ill-regulated ambition, directed to the most infamous end, had been the exciting cause of the tragedy they had just witnessed. I spoke of his honored parents, of his distinguished father, whose talents and character had raised him to one of the highest stations in the land." And there was the "social position to which this young man had been born," showered with every possible advantage and set on a path that would lead in time to a ship of his own.

Yet "after a few months' service at sea most wretchedly employed," Philip Spencer had instead "aspired to supplant me in command, which I had only reached after nearly thirty years of faithful servitude." He told his silent audience that "they might rise to command in the merchant service—to respectability, competence, and to fortune. But they must advance regularly, and step by step; every step, to be sure, must be guided by truth, honor, and fidelity."

About Cromwell: "He must have received an excellent education; his handwriting was even elegant; but he had fallen through brutish sensuality, and the greedy thirst for gold."

The captain had worked him into a parable, and called Collins up on the trunk to share it with the crew. It was the story the youngster had told the tribunal the day before, about his shipping in an Indiaman onto "which the supercargo, a Mr. Thorndyke, had brought a keg of doubloons," with Collins "alone entrusted with the secret of its being on board." He kept the secret, but when, on the *Somers*, he mentioned it the boatswain's mate, a jeering Cromwell had said that "had the case been his he would have run away with the keg."

"This tale contained all the moral that it was necessary to enforce. I told the boys, in conclusion, that they had only to choose between the morality of Cromwell and that of Collins—Cromwell at the yard-arm, and Collins piping with his call."

Not really in conclusion, though, because Small's behavior needed to be explained. He "had also been born for better things. He had enjoyed the benefits of education, was a navigator, had been an officer in a merchantman, but he could not resist the brandy which had been proffered to him, nor the prospect of dishonorable gain." Perhaps, though, his soul was not entirely forfeit: "He had, however, at least died invoking blessings on the flag of his country."

Mackenzie was done with his oration, but he wasn't satisfied. There should be something more. According to Lieutenant Gansevoort, "Previous to going to dinner the Commander asked how I thought to give three cheers." Gansevoort was all for it: "I told him I thought it would do well, as it would be easy perhaps to tell from that among those who were left who were wrong and who were right—when the men assembled aft he told them to give three cheers for the American flag, which they did, and hearty ones they were."

Mackenzie thought them better than that: "Never were three heartier cheers given. In that electric moment, I do not doubt that the patriotism of even the worst of the conspirators, for an instant broke forth."

The remaining prisoners joined in; after hours of excruciating suspense they had at last been informed that they were not to join their three shipmates on the Atlantic seabed, but would stand trial back in the States. McKinley—whom Mackenzie's ever-evolving theories of the conspiracy now placed at its head—broke down and wept.

The cheers still warming him, the captain wrote, "I felt that I once more was completely commander of the vessel that was intrusted to me, equal to do with her whatever the honor of my country might require."

Gansevoort immediately noticed "there was less sullenness than there had been before in the manner of some of the men." Wales saw this, too, sensing "a change instantly after [the hanging]. Those who had been the most surly immediately turned about."

Still, the officers kept their sidearms strapped on as the hands were piped to dinner.

While the crew shuffled below, the captain "noticed with pain, that many of the boys, as they looked at the yard-arm, indulged in laughter and derision."

Perhaps not a callous or inexplicable response. A good number of those apprentices must have believed they'd come close to dying—the absolute ruler of their current world had told them so—and felt the greatest relief that the threat had vanished, however grim the means. The pressure-cooker atmosphere aboard the brig had become steadily more intense in the six days since Spencer's arrest. The nights of armed officers prowling through the creaking murk of the berth deck, peering into hammocks inhabited by teenagers away from home for the first time; the dusk-to-dawn hours spent prostrate on the spar deck when you weren't actually pulling a rope; shipmates plucked from their messes and chained aft, in plain sight but agents of instant death should you try to speak with them . . . small wonder that hysteria should manifest itself in unusual forms on that first day of December.

WHEN DINNER WAS OVER, wrote Mackenzie, "the watch was set and the bodies lowered from the yard-arms and received by the messmates of the deceased, to be decently laid out for burial, the midshipmen assisting in person."

The armorer unshackled the still limbs, and "when all was ready the first lieutenant invited me to accompany him, to see that these duties had been duly performed." Mackenzie looked over Small and passed on, then paused at Cromwell.

"Traces of a saber cut were visible on his forehead." As they had been from the moment the boatswain's mate first boarded the *Somers*; but now, when those scars were about to disappear from sight forever, they tantalized Mackenzie. He wanted further evidence of old violence, and ordered the dead man's head shaved. "On the removal of his hair, four or five more [scars] were received. Cromwell, by his own admission, had been in a slaver, and had been an inmate of the Moro Castle at Havana. It was the general impression of the honest part of the crew, that he had already been a pirate. He[,] only[,] could answer to the description of the individual alluded to by Mr. Spencer as having been 'already in the business.'"

Mackenzie's macabre forensics were interrupted by a squall. Given the extraordinary events of the day, no one seems to have noticed the thickening air and fitful gusts that preceded the storm, and now there was a sudden tumult of scrambling up near-perpendicular decks and shinnying out on the yards to take in rain-pummeled sail.

It was soon over. The tarpaulins that had been hastily slung over the dead were removed, and Captain Mackenzie went across the still-streaming deck to Philip Spencer. He "was laid out on the starboard arm-chest, dressed in complete uniform, except for the sword, which he had forfeited the right to wear."

Naval propriety demanded a coffin for an officer, but this presented difficulties. Mackenzie was going to have planks pried up from the berth deck to fashion one, but Gansevoort produced two mess-chests that the carpenter was able to marry into a serviceable casket.

In the meantime, crewmen sewed Cromwell and Small into their hammocks, weighted them with round shot, and, following ancient practice, drove the last loop of thread through their nostrils. (This was not just some superstitious medieval holdover, but meant to offer final proof that the deceased were, in fact, deceased.)

Night had fallen; Gansevoort said the dead would be "buried by candle light—on the second day watch—and about seven I should think, when it was so dark that you could not read print."

Noted Mackenzie: "The three corpses, arranged according to rank, Mr. Spencer aft, were placed along the deck. All hands were now called to bury the dead, the procession was formed according to rank; reversed of the colors which had continued to fly, the ensign was lowered to half-mast. Before the corpses had been placed on the lee, hammock-sails were ready for lowering overboard . . . all the battle-lanterns, and the other lanterns in the vessel, were lighted and distributed among the crew. Collected, with their prayer-books, on the booms, in the gangways, and lee-quarter-boat, the service was then read, the responses audibly and devoutly made by the officers and crew, and the bodies consigned to the deep."

12 Inquiry

On the morning of January 4, 1843, Richard Henry Dana put off from the Manhattan shore to get a look at "the Court of Inquiry, appointed by the Secretary of the Navy to examine the facts connected with the recent alleged attempt at mutiny on board the U.S. Brig-of-War *Somers*."

The significant word attending the court was "Inquiry." It was just that—an attempt to establish facts. Although the proceedings had all the rituals of a full-blown trial—cross-examinations, the calling of witnesses—the court had no power to punish. Convened on December 28, at the time of Dana's visit the inquiry was in its sixth day.

Dana, friend of the ill-starred Midshipman Craney and staunch supporter of Captain Mackenzie, brought to his account the same spirited writing that had made *Two Years Before the Mast* such a success.

"We had a fine, clear, cold day, and the Brooklyn ferry-boat zigzagged us across the river, to avoid the floating ice, and a lively sleigh took us to the navy yard. The court is held on board the North

Carolina, a large ship of the line, which lies moored a few rods from the wharf."

Two sailors were helping visitors up the *North Carolina*'s tall flank, and Dana thought it "interesting to see these poor fellows attending about a ship in which a court of great personages was sitting to determine whether a commander can string them up at a yard-arm at sea for a mutiny."

He wanted to ask the pair how they felt about it, "but it would have been improper for me to touch upon the subject with them."

A marine guard stood aside to let Dana's party in, "and we found ourselves in the upper cabin, and in the midst of the grave and rather imposing assembly."

Many uniforms gave their dark-blue solemnity to a long table. "On one side of it sat the three commanders who compose the court; Mr. Mackenzie sat at one end, Mr. Perry (the witness under examination) stood at the other end; and opposite the court sat the clerk and Mr. Hoffman, the judge advocate. . . .

"Notwithstanding my desire to see Mr. Mackenzie, my eye rested for some time on the venerable president of the court, Commodore Stewart, one of the Old Ironsides' [the frigate *Constitution*] heroes, and the manager of what always seemed to me to be the best manoeuvered battle in our late war." (Under Stewart, the *Constitution* captured two British warships in a single action.) "He has a good head, and carries the appearance of a man who can command himself as well as others, and has that calm manner which usually attends one who feels that his reputation is settled. The whole court is one in which great confidence must be placed, for they have the name and appearance of possessing clear heads and right minds."

Now Dana got to examine Captain Mackenzie, and again liked what he saw. "I next carefully observed the features and expression of the party on trial; for this case is one which receives its complexion very much from the character of the chief actor. . . . It is not questioned that he acted upon the best of his deliberate judgment. How is he qualified, then, in moral and intellectual character, in forming a judgment?— becomes an important question.

"On this point his appearance is very much in his favor. He is apparently about forty years of age, and I am told that he entered the service at ten, and he says he has served thirty years. He has every mark of a calm, self-possessed, clear-minded man, entirely free from any of that dashing off-hand or assuming manner which sometimes attends the military button, I felt much confidence in him." Which is expressed in a peculiar compliment that many naval officers might not care to receive: "This confidence was increased by my being informed that he is more noted for conscientiousness, order and thoroughness, than for imagination or enthusiasm."

Satisfied with Mackenzie's character, Dana went over to his ship, which was anchored close by. "Here I must say that no one ought to form an opinion upon the issue of this conspiracy without first see-ing the *Somers*." Assuming his reader has been aboard a man-of-war, Dana says, you have doubtless "formed your notions of the state of things in the *Somers* by what you have seen before. In the ships of the line, frigates, or sloops of war which you have visited there is great appearance of protection, defence, and imposing authority connected with the after end of the ship.

"There is a poop deck, a cabin built above the main deck, with doors and windows looking forward, a marine with bayonet and loaded musket at the door, another at the gangway, and others on guard at various parts of the ship, clear, roomy decks, a plenty of officers about, and the quarters of officers furnished with arms, and well guarded."

Forget all that.

Take a look at the *Somers*, and "you would hardly believe your eyes if you were here to see, as the scene of this dreadful conspiracy, a little brig, with low bulwarks, a single narrow deck flush fore and aft, and nothing to mark the officers' quarters but a long trunk-house . . .

raised a few feet from the deck to let light and air in below, such as you may have seen in our smaller packets which ply along the seaboard."

To Dana, the entire ship might have been designed to facilitate a mutiny. "You feel as though half a dozen resolute conspirators could have swept the decks and thrown overboard all that opposed them before aid could come from below." That aid, Dana believed, would never get there. "The officers would have to come up the steps and through the small companion scuttles, at which a couple of men could easily have cut them down, or shot them as they appeared. The officers' quarters and the cabin are on the same floor with the berth deck of the crew, separated only by bulkheads, and there was not a marine on board to keep guard at the doors, in the gangways, over the spirit room, powder magazine, or arm chest."

Dana was forbidden to go below, but he imagined the hold "so occupied by stores, ammunition, ballast, and the numerous necessaries of a ship of war in actual service, to leave no place where half a dozen conspirators could be safely confined."

He did "not yet mean to give you an opinion upon which I am willing to be held, for the facts are not yet all in." But give an opinion he does, and a firm one: "In short, no one at all acquainted with nautical matters can see the *Somers* without being made feelingly aware of the defenceless situation of those few officers dealing with a crew of ninety persons, of whom some were known to be conspirators, while of the rest they hardly knew upon whom to rely for active and efficient aid in time of danger."

Finishing his account, the reader might almost believe that the crew really had mutinied. Dana thought they'd been certain to, and had it come off the officers would have shared the blame with the mutineers. "If, from any over-humanity, or a fear of the consequences of an execution to themselves professionally, or before the public, or from too much confidence in their own power, they had suffered the conspirators to prevail, and the dreadful consequences had come to our ears—not even the personal sufferings and death of these officers would have saved their memory from our reproaches."

Dana couched this lengthy report as a chatty note to his friend the novelist Catharine M. Sedgwick, but he was casting a wider net, for just two days after he wrote it the letter appeared in the January 13 edition of the *New York Evening Post*. Picked up by almost every other newspaper, it drew a sharp response from a reader of the *Boston Courier*:

I read with some regret, Mr. Editor, and not a little surprise, in a New-York paper . . . a letter from Mr. R. H. Dana, Jr. . . . There is some mystery in this affair. Mr. Dana goes to New-York,—possibly for this very purpose,—visits the *Somers*, with a friend—returns to Boston—thence, we know not why, writes a long letter to a friend in New York . . . as if he went on board for that purpose and no other . . . , and then the public are presented with a document . . . evidently intended to affect the public favorably in regard to Commander Mackenzie. . . .

Mr. Dana, while a very young man, if not while a mere boy, went out on *one voyage* from Boston, before the mast, in a merchant vessel. . . . What possible advantage could such a voyage, in such a capacity, give a very young man over any landsman, in bringing home for trial Spencer and his associates in irons? Not the slightest. The opinions he expressed are worth just as much as those of any other person and no more. . . .

A writer in one of our papers has since stated that he has ten times the means of hearing the opinions of people—especially seafaring people—that Mr. Dana has, and he finds most of the shipmasters he has conversed with, think the prisoners might have been safely brought in. . . . The letter of Mr. Dana has not, to *my* mind, much weight.

By the time of Dana's trip to Brooklyn, such opposed views were rattling through the editorial columns of every newspaper in the country. The day after his visit to the *North Carolina*, Washington's *National Intelligencer* reported: "The gaiety of the holydays, however, is but an ellipse in the discussion of the exciting subject of *the Mutiny*. . . . It is the one table-talk—the theme of the boys at the corners, of the hackmen in the street, of servants and masters, of the grave and the gay, the busy and the idle."

Declared the *New York Herald*, "There has never been any case whose examination has awakened such universal and pervading interest. It is the great topic of the day."

A New York playhouse had already mounted a show that bruised the sensibilities of the *Chicago Express*: "*U.S. Brig Somers.*—The occurrence on board this vessel has been dramatized and brought out in defiance of all good feeling and taste, at the Bowery Theatre."

LATER, THE OFFICERS AND PETTY OFFICERS all agreed that from the moment the condemned men's feet left the deck, a healing harmony settled on the *Somers*. But there was little evidence of it on the homeward voyage. The four prisoners still crouched manacled aft near the guns; the nightly patrols continued; no officer shed his sidearm; the captain's sermons and warnings continued.

Spencer, Cromwell, and Small had been hanged some five hundred miles from St. Thomas, where the brig then headed.

That had been on Thursday.

On the following Sunday, Mackenzie mustered the ship's company, read the Articles of War (and not a listener missed the frequent repetition of "punishable by death"), and went on "to draw from the past history and example of the criminals whose execution they had so recently beheld, all the useful lessons that they afforded, to win back to the paths of duty and virtue the youthful crew which they had been so instrumental in leading astray."

He brandished a Bible. It had belonged to Small, and Mackenzie had rifled through it and "found a letter to him from his aged mother, filled with affectionate endearment and pious counsel." Mrs. Small "expressed the joy with which she had learned from him that he was so happy on board the *Somers*," and was especially pleased "that no grog was served on board of her."

Mackenzie said that "Small had evidently valued his Bible, but he could not resist temptation. I urged upon the youthful sailors to cherish their Bibles with a more entire love than Small had done." And to treat their prayer books the same way, for they contained "a medicine for every ailment of the mind."

Time for more cheering. "In conclusion I told them that they could give three cheers for their country—they now should give three cheers for their God, for they would do this when they sang praises to his name (the colors were now hoisted); and above the American ensign, the only banner to which it may give place, the banner of the cross."

The crew sang the "Old Hundredth" ("Praise God from whom all blessings flow . . ."). When they'd finished, Mackenzie says, "I could not avoid contrasting the spectacle presented on that day by the *Somers*, with what it would have been had she been in pirate's hands."

And then, in a small masterpiece of self-unawareness, he added, "But on this subject I forbear to enlarge."

FIFTEEN MINUTES INTO THE NEXT DAY, December 5, the *Somers* dropped anchor at Charlotte Amalie in St. Thomas. This was the briefest of stays—just long enough to take on fresh water, bread, and a few other provisions—and while he was ashore Mackenzie wrote, hurriedly "and with a wretched pen," an account of his voyage to

Secretary of the Navy Upshur. The letter was, by his standards, a brief one, but he wanted to get it off should "the overpowering violence of the elements, collision with another vessel in the night, or other accident of this order . . . cause us never to be heard of." If this happened, "be assured, sir, that she has not been captured from her commander and her officers."

It says something of his state of mind that he believed if his school ship disappeared, Upshur would at once assume a mutiny had been the cause.

The *Somers* left St. Thomas before nightfall, heading north now, away from the balmy trades and into the jagged gray swells of the winter Atlantic.

Captain Mackenzie had been spending far more time in his cabin than he had during the days preceding the executions, but he still kept his guard up. Officers warned the crew against gathering into groups, and although they now had to stand only one watch in three—rather than the wearing watch-on-watch routine—their patrols never ceased. Less than a week after they'd quit St. Thomas the mercury had dropped thirty degrees, and everyone aboard did his best to keep out of the bitter winds—except, of course, for the prisoners on the deck.

For them, Mackenzie came up with a penological novelty: the sailmaker sewed together large canvas bags and had the four men squirm into them; even their heads were covered. The officers later asserted that these bags—supplemented with wool blankets—had made the prisoners warmer and more comfortable than anyone else aboard.

Warmer, for a while, but not more comfortable. McKinley, who got his sack just before they reached St. Thomas, said, "After a while the bag got very hot. Whoever was the officer I don't know. I told him I was smothering. I could not breathe. He came back with the orders that I could not have it untied. I turned myself round as well as I could and got my mouth to the opening of the bag and stayed so till morning." The restraint became less suffocating once they were sailing up the Eastern Seaboard, but then Wilson's bag "would get full of rain water up to my knees."

Still, the worst of Wilson's torments were nearly over. Nine days out of St. Thomas they were coasting along the Brooklyn shore, and on the frigid night of December 14 the *Somers* dropped anchor in New York Harbor.

The apprentices, who had spent a quarter of a year at sea, got the coldest of welcomes: no marine band on the pier playing "Hail, Columbia" and "Home Sweet Home" and no crowd of parents waiting to be entertained with hard-won maritime technical talk. In fact, the boys weren't allowed to leave the ship.

The sole escapee was the captain's clerk, Oliver Perry, who was rowed across the harbor on the first leg of his trip to Washington, DC, with news that the whole nation would soon know.

In the meantime, Mackenzie went to the navy yard to see the commandant, his brother-in-law, Matthew Perry. He had prepared a report "of my cruise and of some extraordinary events which have attended it," but wasn't happy with the result; it was too sketchy because north of St. Thomas the weather had "been so boisterous throughout the passage" that "during the last three days I have not had my clothes off, nor have I slept continually for an hour for the last fifteen days."

Just before calling on Perry, Mackenzie took a final swipe at his mutineers. Once more he put his armorer to work, shackling crewmen Richard Hamilton, George Warner, Charles Golderman, Charles Van Velsor, George Knevals, Eugene Sullivan, the much-punished steward Henry Waltham, and another steward, the Maltese Henry Gallia.

There is a curious postscript about these tardily corralled sailors. Thirty years later, in 1873, *Harper's New Monthly Magazine* ran a story attributed only to "An Old Stager." That is an archaic term for one who has gathered long experience on the stage of life—any sagacious old-timer. The military historian A. B. Feuer identifies him as a journalist named T. M. Parmalee.

The writer had no doubts about where the guilt in the story lay. He finds it "amazing that the perpetrator of that great crime should have been permitted to escape the severest penalty of the law. The cowardly and tyrannical exercise of authority, the illegal and atrocious hanging of his three victims, were slurred over by the government through the influence of Mackenzie's powerful connections." The court-martial, he says, "was nothing but a solemn farce."

Parmalee was in Brooklyn when the *Somers* returned from her cruise, "and made acquainted with the particulars of the affair at the time."

While the ship was still lying offshore, Mackenzie went to the yard to give his first reports on the hangings, and then called on an old friend, a Captain Elisha Peck, who had command of the receiving ship *Hudson*.

Shortly after, Peck told Parmalee about the visit. "Mackenzie gave his friend his version of the *Somers* affair, horrifying him with the statement of the mutiny and the hanging of Midshipman Spencer and two confederates in the crime. Peck naturally inquired how many of the mutineers were in irons aboard the vessel, and expressed surprise she had not been brought up to the yard. Mackenzie replied that the mutinous crew were none of them under arrest; that he had been able to subdue the insurrection; and after the execution it had not been found necessary to confine any of the men. 'What,' exclaimed Peck, 'a mutiny so extensive and formidable as to justify hanging an officer and two of his associates and nobody in irons!'"

Responding at once to Peck's incredulity, "Mackenzie returned immediately on board the *Somers*, and seizing upon the first dozen of the men upon whom he could lay his hands, clapped them in irons. This fact never came to the knowledge of the court, and it was carefully suppressed in the published accounts of the transaction."

At least the men in this panicky, haphazard culling would not have to shiver away the final hours of 1842 on the wind-scoured spar deck.

They, and their fellow prisoners, were moved to the *North Carolina*. Mackenzie had urged they be put in solitary confinement, but they had relative warmth and a roof over their heads.

IT WAS CHRISTMASTIME IN NEW YORK, and the season had already taken the form we are familiar with today. The assiduous diarist Philip Hone wrote, "There never was a more beautiful Christmas than this. . . . Broadway from the Battery to Union Place has been an animated scene of new bonnets and happy faces under them, and little gentlemen and ladies bending under the weight of toys and riding on the top of Christmas, and shops disregarding the injunction 'lead me not into temptation,' spreading their tempting treasures which are all the time connecting themselves by the invisible chains of sympathy and attraction to the coin in the pockets of passers-by. . . . When I was in Fulton Market on Saturday I wondered where mouths could be found for the turkeys, geese, ducks, and chicken which I saw there, and to-day when walking up Broadway I was tempted to exclaim: 'Where can ducks and chickens, turkeys and geese, be found to fill all these mouths.'"

Despite all this mercantile sparkle, Hone found time to wonder about the *Somers*. "Nobody, not even the near relations of the officers, was permitted to visit her." Why?

Guert's cousin Hunn Gansevoort, also a Navy man, had himself rowed across to the moored brig, only to be imperiously waved away by the officer of the deck. And there was no arguing with those carronades. He left without seeing Guert.

Almost no one was allowed off the *Somers*, either. But a few nights after the brig's arrival, Guert—"almost by stealth," said his mother, Mary—slipped ashore and visited his family in Brooklyn. Mary Gansevoort was horrified. "Guert was then in such a situation from fatigue & exposure," she wrote her brother-in-law, "that I sca[r]cely knew him—he had a violent cold; coughing constantly; very hoarse his limbs so contracted; that he walked like an infirm man of seventy; his eyes were red & swollen, & his whole face very much bloated—his back & sides were so sore, from the strap & weight of the huge and heavy ships Pistols; that he could not raise himself erect—Having imprisoned so many of the crew; they were short of hands & he poor fellow, did more than double duty—the eveg of which I speak, his first visit to us; he had not had even his coat off in four days."

Captain Mackenzie, too, got ashore and made his way to Tarrytown, where his wife, Kate, appalled by his appearance, at once asked, "What is the matter?"

Oh, it's nothing, Mackenzie told her; just some bad weather that kept me on deck a lot. He did not mention the hangings.

THE COURT OF INQUIRY CONVENED on Wednesday, December 28, 1842, barely two weeks after the *Somers* had returned.

The *New-York Tribune* published an admiring description of the venue:

> The ship *North Carolina*, on which the Court is held, lies at a few yards' distance from the wharf, in winter quarters, has on board about 900 persons, including a large number of boys at the Naval school. About 150 of these, embracing those who have parents and friends in the vicinity, were dismissed on Saturday for the holidays; and as we went on board, about 25 others were receiving their two shillings each with *liberty* till sunset, for holiday diversion.
>
> The ship is in her winter trim, with hatchways housed and every part made as comfortable as stoves and abundant fuel can possibly effect. She is kept in the neatest order, her armory is well filled and the arms burnished and well arrayed, and the strictest discipline is maintained throughout.

The court had three senior officers. Its president was Commodore Charles Stewart, whom Dana so admired; what the *Tribune* called "the second member," Alexander James Dallas, commanded the Pensacola Navy Yard, and had to sail up from Florida to take part; the "third member" was Commodore Jacob Jones, "Port Admiral, commander of all the vessels afloat in this harbor. His flag ship is the *North Carolina*."

There was a civilian among these very high-ranking Navy men, but he was no stranger to naval ways. Ogden Hoffman had served under Stephen Decatur—foremost among all post-Revolutionary sailor heroes of the young Republic—in the Barbary Wars. Decatur was disgusted that "young Hoffman should have exchanged an honorable profession for that of a lawyer."

At least he became a good one. Now US Attorney for the Southern District of New York, he was to be judge advocate—that is, the prosecuting attorney—during the inquiry. He had a reputation for such scary competence that Gansevoort's uncle had sent Guert, on Christmas Eve, what may have been the season's least merry message: "I have reflected with painful anxiety on the effect which the influence of a strong power may exert over the proceedings in the nature of an Inquiry which is about to take place. You & your Commander will be placed upon the defensive under unparalleled circumstances."

Still, Mackenzie was going into the inquiry with unusual advantages right from the outset, ones he would not have enjoyed in a civil court. Aboard the *North Carolina* he, rather than the prosecution, was allowed to make the opening statement. And he could do it in his favorite medium, writing. And he could also examine the witnesses with written questions. This cumbersome process did not merely allow him to frame his words more carefully; had he spoken, he would have left himself open to cross-examination.

Mackenzie had composed three accounts of the mutiny. The first, with the "wretched pen," at St. Thomas on December 5, had been superseded by a lengthier one drafted while a pilot was guiding the *Somers* into port nine days later.

This was the version with which young Perry had hurried to Washington. When Navy Secretary Upshur received it—and after his initial shock at what it contained had waned some—he wrote to Mackenzie saying that he wanted more details, and that, in a matter of such consequence, they shouldn't be brought him by a seventeen-year-old messenger, however renowned his name.

Mackenzie was happy to supply a fuller version. Commodore Perry had offered his brother-in-law the use of his house, and he drafted it there. On December 19 he sent it off to Washington. A midshipman—Rodgers—was again the messenger, but by this time Upshur had summoned Gansevoort to the capitol.

Gansevoort's mother was dismayed. "Mr. Upshure," she told her brother-in-law, "wrote to Mr. Mackensie, for Guert to proceed to Washin[g]ton—He was here, & had just sent a note to Mackensie, saying that he was really sick, & that I had prevailed on him to remain, & have medical attendance; which he would not do. . . . Nothing could stop him; he went; was sick one night at Phila. But got there safe—had three interviews with the Secretary [Upshur]—*very satisfactory to Guert*—but this to *your ear only*.

"Commander & Guert seem well pleased with the Officers composing the Court—God grant, that all *is, & was* right."

THE COURT OPENED ITS HEARING at 11 in the morning. "Commander ALEXANDER SLIDELL MACKENZIE of the *Somers*, appeared in full uniform," wrote the *Tribune*'s correspondent. "He is a man of medium hight [*sic*], with a fine head covered rather thinly by light auburn hair, a high forehead, and an amiable and pleasing rather than stern and commanding presence.

"After administrating the oath to the several members of the Court, the Judge Advocate read the warrant from Secretary UPSHUR, constituting the Court, and authorizing it to inquire into all the facts touching the alleged mutiny on board the *Somers*, and the conduct of Commander MACKENZIE in ordering the execution of Midshipman PHILIP SPENCER and of SAMUEL CROMWELL and ELIJAH SMALL, *and to report to the Department its opinion as to the right and propriety of these proceedings.*"

The *Tribune* goes on to say, "Some conversation then took place concerning the arrangements for conducting the inquiry."

A whole lot of conversation.

Like so many trials, this one began with hours of procedural stuttering. Judge Advocate Hoffman wanted to know if Mackenzie had "drawn up a narrative of the transaction." Yes, he had. But were the papers Judge Hoffman was holding the original document? No, he had sent that to the Navy Department. The court adjourned until the next day.

By then some mail had come in from the Navy. "A packet of papers was produced by the Judge Advocate, which had been received from the Department; but on examination they were found to have nothing to do with the case and were ordered to be sealed and returned."

Again the court was adjourned, and it wasn't until the third day that Mackenzie's full statement could be unfurled. Judge Hoffman read it aloud to the court. It took him two solid hours; the authorial flame burning hot within him, Mackenzie had written thirteen thousand words.

"Despite having been frequently interrupted, especially by the solicitude of friends," he began, "I have been forced to relinquish my first intention to confine myself entirely to a sketch of the principal occurrences.

"After leaving the Azores and Madeira in October, I proceeded . . ." Several sentences later: "On Saturday, the 25th of November,

Lieutenant G. Gansevoort came into the cabin, and informed me that a conspiracy existed on board of the brig, to capture her, murder the commander, the officers, and most of the crew, and convert her into a pirate, and that Acting-Midshipman Philip Spencer was at the head of it. . . ."

His account, florid and smooth, and full of apostrophes to the flag and the moral lessons to be drawn from the failings of the men he'd executed, is as detailed as Upshur could have wished. It's all there: a score of insolences uttered by Spencer against his fellow officers; the falling topmast and the rush aft; the "Greek letter"; the ever-darkening mood aboard the ship (although no concrete example given, only some perceived surliness among the crew); the suspicious neatness of Cromwell and Small at muster; Spencer once having "drawn a brig with a black flag" and asking "one of the midshipmen what he thought of it"; on up to "I learn, Mr. Spencer, that you aspire to the command of the *Somers*." Then the hangings, and the happy result they had on the crew.

He concluded with "the pleasing duty of adverting to the conduct of the under officers. The first Lieutenant, throughout the whole difficulty has borne himself with courage, and sustained a lofty and chivalrous part. Always armed, his pistol often cocked—only in a single incident has any accident occurred [the shot Gansevoort squeezed off at Cromwell's feet]. . . . Never since the existence of the Union has a commander been more ably and zealously seconded by a First Lieutenant."

Next came Wales, whose mysterious sin on the earlier voyage by now had come to reflect well on him. "By his coolness and presence of mind and firm integrity, [he] has rendered to the American Navy a memorable service. I had some difficulty with him in Porto Rico; and on that account he was singled out and tampered with; but he remained true to the flag of his country. A Purser's post or a handsome pecuniary recompense would be a small compensation for the services he rendered."

Sergeant Garty—"he rose from his hammock, where he had been confined by sickness, and did duty throughout the whole affair"—should be "promoted to a Second *Lieutenancy* in the Marine Corps."

The other officers deserved similar treatment, he said, but the roll ended with a request of amazing effrontery, given the forum in which it was made: that "my nephew, Mr. [Oliver] Perry . . . be placed in the situation left vacant by the death of Mr. Spencer."

With that, Mackenzie gave himself over to the court, "trusting to that consciousness of rectitude in my own bosom which has never for one moment forsaken me, or wavered in the slightest degree."

DESPITE THE THREE REVISIONS and all his writerly care, Mackenzie's report did not have the effect he wished.

Philip Hone, who had been sympathetic toward the captain, read it in the *Tribune* with growing revulsion, and wrote in his diary:

Great interest is excited by the proceedings of the court of inquiry, now sitting at the navy yard on the affair of the *Somers*. The first testimony was the production of the report sent on to the navy department by Capt. McKenzie [*sic*], immediately after his arrival in New York; and well would it have been for him if it had never seen the light. "O that mine enemy should write a book!" was the vindictive exclamation of some such person as the Secretary of War. I have learned by experience and observation, that nine-tenths of all the scrapes men get into are occasioned by writing or saying *too much*. Here is a document ten times longer than was necessary, written without consultation with any judicious friend, who, from not being immediately interested in the event, would have been better able to look at the consequences, full of public details of trifling circumstances and irrelevant conversation, and interspersed with sage reflections. . . .

Not only the character of Captain McKenzie, but that of the flag under which he sails and of the nation which he served, is deeply concerned in his making out a complete justification. There is no middle ground in this business; it was altogether right, or altogether wrong. And here, instead of a concise, manly statement of his proceeding on the discovery of the mutiny, the necessity which, in his judgment, existed for his summary exercise of power, and his regret that he had been called upon to adopt measures so painful to his feelings, we have a long rigamarole story about private letters discovered on the person of young Spencer, orders to blow out the brains of "refractory men," religious ceremonies, cheers for the American flag, and conversations with the accused, in one of which he said to Spencer that "he hung him, because if he took him to the United States he would escape punishment, for everybody got clear who had money and friends,"—a national reproach, which, even allowing it to be true, came with bad grace from an officer of the American navy. . . . In the name of all that is wonderful, why should he stigmatize himself by relating such a conversation in a document which will be carried on the wings of the wind to the most distant part of the earth?

The truth is, there is much to be seen, in this statement, of the pride of authorship. Captain McKenzie, when he was Alexander Slidell, wrote a clever book called "A Year in Spain," which gave him some reputation as an author, and he disdained to take advice in regard either to the matter or the manner of the narrative. Even in this particular regard it is a failure; it will add nothing to his literary renown.

One of the captain's own legal counselors called it "a diabolical document," hoping to "winnow Mackenzie's brain of the notion that he is a lawyer as well as a sailor and historian."

Still, Hone finished his entry about the narrative with: "The oral testimony of the officers thus far is greatly in his favor and I trust he

will stand justified before God and his country, notwithstanding his ill-judged report."

THE TESTIMONY OF THE OFFICERS AND CREW would continue to favor the captain, and perhaps they all spoke frankly and truly. But they were testifying under unusual circumstances.

Secretary Upshur had pressed on Commodore Jones that it was "of the utmost importance that the crew of the *Somers* should be kept as to prevent the possibility of any improper tampering with them." Hence the ship's state of quarantine, when even the first lieutenant had to sneak away in order to visit his family.

Mackenzie's report ended: "For myself, I only ask that in whatever proceedings it may be necessary to institute against me, as I have considered before all things honor of my country and the sanctity of its flag, my own honor may also meet with the consideration. I ask only that I may not be deprived of my command until proved unworthy of it."

Upshur granted the request. So for the two weeks during which they waited for the court of inquiry to begin, and throughout the proceedings, officers and men remained as thoroughly isolated in the navy yard as they had been off the coast of Africa, and under the same commander. Perhaps, the *Somers* being a school ship, they might have been spending their Christmas learning about American naval achievements or refining their skills with the sextant.

No: the depleted Gansevoort was back aboard the *Somers*, and he began interviewing crewmen and his fellow officers, seeking stories that would justify the captain's actions. He, of course, had a deep personal interest in the outcome of the hearing; if Mackenzie was not acquitted, he would probably be put on trial for murder, and his first lieutenant might well be named as an accessory to the crime. And other officers might be swept up, too. The captain had that letter, signed by them all, calling for the executions. That was the stick; the carrot was the multiple promotions Mackenzie was seeking for his supporters.

One by one, promising witnesses had been led either into the *Somers*'s wardroom or to the hospitable Commodore Perry's house, where they got to rehearse their parts. Some would claim that nobody had told them what to say in court; but their stories were remarkably consistent.

After Mackenzie's narrative had been heard, James Wales was sworn in. His testimony wasn't as coherent as his captain's—he tended to break the chronology and back up when he remembered some new incident—but it was detailed and comprehensive, especially when he was telling about his conversation with Spencer on the booms. Having gone over the executions, he finished up by recalling Spencer's largess: he'd given $15 to Cromwell—"a pretty good present"—and "also drew some $15 or $20 worth of tobacco and cigars during the cruise, which he distributed to the crew—the tobacco rather to the boys than the men. He gave Cromwell a bunch or two of cigars at one time, and also to Small. . . . I have seen Spencer give van Velcher [*sic*] a pound of tobacco at a time, and to others smaller amounts. I recollect no other conversation or facts that would throw any light upon the mutiny."

The transcript shows that then "the President informed Commander MACKENZIE that he had the privilege of cross-examining the witness, by questions in writing, to be approved by the Court." His very first question was a strange one:

"Did you ever hear Cromwell speak of his wife?"

"I have. Two or three days after we were out we had a heavy gale. Cromwell came down and began to speak about friends at home. He spoke of his wife in a very light manner for a man who had just been married, at least." The transcript does not quote the rest of Wales's answer verbatim, instead offering a delicate paraphrase: "The words

Philip Spencer in his midshipman's uniform. The portrait, though doubtless somewhat romanticized, was said to look like him by his brothers in the Chi Psi fraternity, which he helped found during his fleeting stay at Union College. The painting hangs in the school today.

Midshipman Spencer's nemesis, Commander Alexander Slidell Mackenzie.

3

THE U. S. BRIG-OF-WAR SOMERS.

Nathaniel Currier (still fifteen years away from his famous partnership with James Merritt Ives) published this lithograph of the *Somers*—oddly, showing only two of the three condemned hanging from the yardarm.

4

The carronade was shorter and lighter than a regular naval gun, but could be devastatingly effective at short range—hence its nickname, the "smasher." The *Somers* was designed to mount twelve of them, but they proved too heavy, and she set sail with ten.

Mackenzie confronts Spencer in an illustration from an 1889 issue of the long-lived *Cosmopolitan* magazine.

"I LEARN, MR. SPENCER, THAT YOU ASPIRE TO THE COMMAND OF THE *Somers*."

A flogging aboard a nineteenth-century man-of-war. Mackenzie applied the lash liberally throughout the cruise, with the entire ship's company assembled to witness each punishment. The difference between this scene and the many floggings aboard the *Somers* is that the contingent of marines at the upper left was absent: there was no room for them aboard the ship.

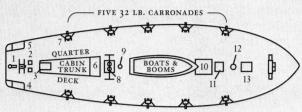

FIVE 32 LB. CARRONADES

SPAR DECK OF *SOMERS*

1. Wheel
2. Binnacles
3. Entrance to captain's cabin
4. Starboard arms chest where Spencer was chained

5. Port arms chest where Cromwell was chained
6. Entrance to steerage
7. After port gun, where Small was chained
8. Pump

9. Mainmast
10. Fore hatch
11. Galley scuttle
12. Foremast
13. Fore scuttle

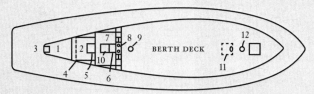

BERTH DECK OF *SOMERS*

1. Captain's cabin
2. Wardroom
3. Exit to spar deck, pantry under
4. Wardroom mess locker

5. Hatch to magazine
6. Sliding doors to steerage and wardroom
7. Steerage— midshipmen's cabin
8. Pump

9. Mainmast
10. Exit from steerage to spar deck
11. Galley stove
12. Foremast

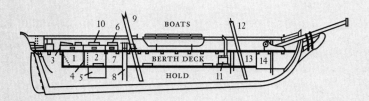

PROFILE OF *SOMERS*

1. Captain's cabin, 8' x 8' x 4'
2. Wardroom, 6' x 10'
3. Entrance to captain's cabin
4. Wardroom mess locker

5. Powder magazine
6. Sliding doors to steerage and wardroom
7. Steerage, 4' square
8. Pump
9. Mainmast

10. Exit from steerage to spar deck
11. Galley stove
12. Foremast
13, 14. Storerooms

NOTE: *Headroom of berth deck was 4'10"*

SCALE 0 5 10 15 20 25 ft.

An edifying illustration from
The Pirates Own Book, a
favorite of Philip Spencer's.

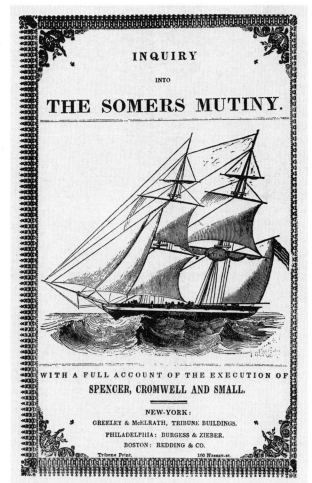

INQUIRY

INTO

THE SOMERS MUTINY.

WITH A FULL ACCOUNT OF THE EXECUTION OF
SPENCER, CROMWELL AND SMALL.

NEW-YORK:
GREELEY & McELRATH, TRIBUNE BUILDINGS.
PHILADELPHIA: BURGESS & ZIEBER.
BOSTON: REDDING & CO.
Tribune Print.   160 Nassau-st.

The title page from
the published transcript
of the Court of Inquiry.

John Spencer, Philip's stern and vengeful father, did his angry best to get Captain Mackenzie tried in a civil court rather than a protective naval one.

Commodore Matthew Calbraith Perry, commandant of the Brooklyn Navy Yard, early became aware of Midshipman Spencer as a troublemaker.

THE TRIAL.

Cosmopolitan magazine's artist imagined the council of officers in the *Somers* wardroom a half century after it convened.

James Fenimore Cooper believed the charges of a mutiny aboard the *Somers* were absurd, and said so at length in a scathing commentary.

12

13

14

Herman Melville, painted by
Asa W. Twitchell five years
after the cruise of the *Somers*.
This portrait will have to
also stand in for his cousin
Lieutenant Guert Gansevoort,
of whom, surprisingly, no
image exists. But members of
both families agreed that the
two men looked almost
uncannily alike.

Raphael Semmes, the last
captain of the *Somers*. He
survived her sinking during
the war with Mexico and
went on to command the
much-feared Confederate
commerce raider *Alabama* in
the Civil War.

he used indicated that he [Cromwell] cared nothing for her chastity while he was gone."

Hoffman didn't like this: "The Judge Advocate objected to the question and asked why Com. Mackenzie wished to ask it."

The captain said "it was merely to counteract any feeling of sympathy that might be sought to be drawn from his wife and family."

Hoffman shot back that "that purpose was already sufficiently answered."

This tart rejoinder aside, Hoffman—perhaps the foremost criminal lawyer of his day—would show strangely little prosecutorial zeal during the inquiry.

Back when he was in Congress in the 1830s, his angry eloquence had amazed John Quincy Adams, who himself was far from helpless in a debate. An opponent named Churchill C. Cambreleng, making fun of Hoffman's nautical background, said he liked to "tack and veer." Hoffman rounded on him with what Adams called "a half-hour of the most tremendous invective that ever was uttered. A shout of applause burst forth from the galleries as he closed. I told Hoffman that I had prepared for a settlement of accounts with Cambreleng myself, but that he had settled all my balances with him as well as his own. I could not call a dead man to account."

None of that flaying rhetoric would be heard aboard the *North Carolina*. Possibly Hoffman had not strayed as far from the Navy as Decatur had feared, and was softening his tongue out of reluctance to bring discredit to his former service. Whatever the reason, he often seemed to favor Mackenzie and his crew.

A few minutes after complaining about bringing Cromwell's wife into the proceedings, he actually helped the captain make a point.

Like almost every other literate person in New York, Mackenzie had by now read the "S" letter that John Spencer had composed as soon as he learned of his son's execution. The captain wanted to challenge it in court. "Commander Mackenzie said that the officers of the *Somers* had been charged . . . in an article supposed to have been written by the Secretary of War, with harshness and cruelty, and asked if there was no way of showing that this was untrue."

Commodore Stewart, the court's president, said "that no notice could be taken of it."

Mackenzie insisted that, coming as it did from a source "so high," the court *had* to take notice of it.

Stewart was firm: "It must be regarded only as a newspaper report, and that it did not come within the scope of the inquiry."

At this point, in a helpful intervention, Hoffman offered to rephrase the question in such a way as "would answer the purpose of Commander Mackenzie."

That was permitted, and to the question, "What was the conduct of Commander Mackenzie generally during the difficulty on the *Somers*?" Wales promptly replied, "He appeared to labor under no fear, was humane, and did everything he could for the comfort of the prisoners."

A generous answer, given that the last thing he did for the comfort of the prisoners was to end their earthly worries. But it wasn't good enough for Mackenzie, who said he would "waive these questions altogether, as he only wished to ask them to meet a particular case, which he was not allowed to do."

This petulance was rewarded with another rewording of the question: "During the continuance of the difficulty on board the *Somers* did you observe any conduct in the Commander exhibiting unmanly fear, a despotic temper or any quality unbecoming a commanding officer and a gentleman?"

Wales replied with such vigor that it is the only moment in the transcript where capital letters are used to signify vehemence, and the tone of a reply is reported: "(With much energy and decision.) NO! SIR, I did not."

With that staunch declaration, the court adjourned.

*   *   *

WALES WAS RECALLED THE NEXT MORNING—a Saturday, and New Year's Eve. Mackenzie wanted to know: "How soon after your interview with Mr. Spencer did you understand the mutiny was to take effect?"

"I understood that it was to be very shortly;—before our arrival at St. Thomas."

This seems to have been the first time Wales revealed that highly pertinent fact. It had apparently slipped his mind soon after he'd climbed down from the booms, only to return some weeks later.

LIEUTENANT GANSEVOORT TOOK THE STAND. Like those of Wales, his answers were thick with detail. A sinister knife was described.

"I came up and found King and Dickerson talking together. King said to me, '*Has Wilson drawn two or three knives from the store-room lately?*' I told him none that I knew of. He said, 'I heard that he had several knives in his sail-bag, and I think it would be a good plan to over-haul it; he had his bag there where Mr. Spencer is, nearly all day, and a knife hid away in the rigging,' which he thought he *intended to put in the hands of Mr. Spencer.* I over-hauled the sail-bag, and found no other knife than an African dirk, very sharp, and having the appearance of having been lately sharpened. This is the knife."

The weapon was produced: about six inches long, an inch and a half wide at the haft, sharpened on both sides, with a bone handle. If Hoffman, who knew the ways of the seafaring life, thought this hardly an unusual souvenir for a sailor to possess, he said nothing.

Gansevoort dropped that subject to describe the conversation that he had found particularly incriminating—the one where Dickerson said that Cromwell "is the most dangerous man on board the ship."

The lieutenant's testimony ended the day, and the year. The members of the court went ashore into the onset of 1843. The *Herald* that morning—having warned its readers to beware of counterfeit sixpenny pieces recently in circulation ("they have a greasy feel")—called Mackenzie's narrative "a singular mixture of folly, silliness, and blasphemy." The last apparently referred to the captain's having demanded three cheers for that jolly good fellow, God. (The "three cheers" seem to have been offered in the more suitable form of hymns, but Mackenzie's account failed to make this clear.)

If the captain happened not to see those three hurtful words the *Tribune* had attached to him, he had already begun to feel a dismaying turn in the wind. The papers were no longer putting him forward as a model of the classical virtues.

His narrative had been full of even-tempered, complacent self-justifications. He no longer felt so high above the fray, and his tone got harsher.

In the sorting-through of Philip Spencer's possessions to send home to his family, some letters from his mother had turned up, in which she called her son "a thief, a liar, and a villain." Before setting off on the *Somers*, the boy had robbed his home not only of $300 in cash but of a valuable pair of gold spectacles.

Mackenzie had the letters, and, his frequent references to his high sense of honor notwithstanding, he wanted to publish a dead man's personal mail. "I consider it due me," he wrote Secretary Upshur, "to introduce private matters into a public communication."

To persuade Upshur, he reminded him of how he had dedicated *Spain Revisited* to the secretary's brother George, despite the fact that, as he'd made clear in the dedication, he had friends far more useful to him than lowly George. Now, years later, he reverted to exactly the same tone-deafness, telling Upshur that he had bestowed that honor on his brother "when I believed him to be on his deathbed and scarcely likely to see what I had written of him, I offered in the dedication a work of public homage which I knew to be less than just and true. . . ."

If Upshur didn't enjoy being told that his brother hadn't, after all, been worthy of Mackenzie's praise, he surely would have been no happier to have an underling instruct him on how to handle the investigation. But this the captain proceeded to do: he had learned "that you passed the greater part of the day subsequent to the receipt of the dispatches from the *Somers* in conference with the Secretary of War. I will not, sir, do you the injustice to ask that when my case comes under consideration, if it be necessary to seek counsel anywhere, it will not be with the Secretary of War."

And now the shade of Samuel Cromwell was beginning to make trouble. A group of New Yorkers had come forth saying the boatswain's mate had been "an upright, good-hearted, respectable man." James Carroll (331 Water Street), Nicholas Code (56 James Street), and Joseph Murphy (325 Water Street) all spoke warmly of his amiable respect for those above him and his kindness to those below. Twenty-three Manhattanites put their names to a petition swearing they had known him well (one, since he was twenty years old); many had served with him "and always found him a good sailor and companionable man."

The papers liked this, and more vexation was coming Mackenzie's way, for the tightly buttoned-up *Somers* had received a visitor that nobody on board could shoo away: Captain Francis Gregory, commander of the *North Carolina*. When Mackenzie had asked that his prisoners be transferred to the larger ship, Gregory had come aboard to see about arranging this.

He was appalled by what he found, and wrote Commodore Jones, "From my own observations . . . I am free to say that I have never known the crew of an American man-of-war so dirty and dejected in their personal appearance as hers were at the time of her arrival here."

The logbook of the *Somers* had somehow made its way aboard the *North Carolina*, "lying," Gregory said, "in the wardroom and freely inspected by any of the officers who chose to do so." Gregory had a yeoman copy it, and reported its contents to the commodore. The floggings meted out by Mackenzie, "though not passing the bounds of the law, have been very frequent, and in the aggregate beyond all precedent within my knowledge.

"From the 3 of June last to the 10 December the log book of the *Somers* exhibits *two hundred and forty-seven punishments with cats and colts*, in which *two thousand two hundred and sixty-five lashes* were inflicted on that crew of boys!, all within a period of six months and seven days."

Captain Gregory did not keep his indignation to himself, complaining to his fellow officers and civilian visitors. Before long the New York papers were letting their readers know about the ordeal of poor young Manning, whose fourteen-year-old back had absorbed eighty-seven blows with a colt, and fourteen with a cat.

EVEN BEFORE ALL THOSE BEATINGS became public knowledge, Mackenzie was worrying about his growing reputation for harshness. When the court reconvened, on the third day of the new year, Gansevoort was to resume testifying, but first Mackenzie wanted to insert in the record a summary of mutinies in the Royal Navy that had been brought about by captains far more brutal than he'd ever been. Hoffman objected—they were not relevant to the case at hand. The objection sustained, Gansevoort took the stand.

Mackenzie had a question that he hoped would show himself in a less bloodthirsty light: "Did you distinctly recollect that the Commander [he continues to speak of himself in the third person throughout the hearing] gave orders to blow Mr. Spencer's brains out, or to put him to death, if any rescue was attempted?"

It was in response to this query that Gansevoort—who must have been coached—stressed that the captain had merely said to "destroy" the mutineers; as for the more savage-sounding "blow out their brains," "the language I used was my own."

The first lieutenant described the executions as had the earlier witnesses, but added a conversation that strains credulity.

Gansevoort: "The Commander had detailed the different men who were to take the men under the main yard, on which they were to be executed. He told me that the two of the highest rank were to take Mr. Spencer.

"Just before he had ordered me to take the men there, I applied to him for permission to take leave of Mr. Spencer. He gave me permission. I went up to Mr. Spencer, who took my hand in both of his, and begged me very earnestly to forgive him for the many injuries he had done me. He said he did not object to the sentence—he thought it was right and that his punishment was just."

At the end of Gansevoort's testimony, Mackenzie asked, "Did you see in the Commander or any of the officers of the *Somers*, during the difficulties, any traces of unmanly fear, of a despotic temper, or any qualities unbecoming an American officer?"

The response was not surprising: "I saw nothing of the kind. The conduct of the Commander throughout the whole was of the most unexceptionable character, and I consider the country fortunate in having had such a Commander. . . ."

The witnesses who followed Gansevoort—midshipmen, crewmen, the African American galley workers (whose testimony would not have been permitted in many shoreside courts)—all said the same thing: a bad situation had overtaken the *Somers*, and its captain had no choice but to pursue the course he did.

George Warner's testimony was different. He was the seaman who had written the private account of being questioned in the wardroom that his great-nephew published a century later, in which he said Purser Heiskell had supplied his answers for him.

184 | SAILING THE GRAVEYARD SEA

Warner was among Mackenzie's final draft of prisoners: he was still under arrest; still a *Somers* crew member; still under Captain Mackenzie.

He knew what was wanted of him, but he would not say that a mutiny was inevitable. "I did not believe any attempt would be made to rescue the prisoners. . . . I think if these men had been kept in confinement no attempt would have been made to rescue them."

He stuck to his story about Heiskell: "In the proceedings before the Council it is put down that I said Cromwell *ought to be hung* 'because I thought him guilty.' I did not make that answer. Mr. Heiskell put that down three or four days after, when he asked me what the answer was which I had made and I told him I did not know, and he then said he would fix it."

There had already been some questions about whether the witnesses had been told what to say.

Mackenzie asked one sailor, "Have any inducements of any sort, any promises, or any threats, been held out to you to induce you to tell what you knew about the mutiny?"

"No, sir, none."

Hoffman had picked up on this. "By anyone—your commander, or others?"

"No, sir."

"Any promises or threats?"

"No, sir."

"By anyone—officer or civilian?"

"No, sir."

"Have you been told by anyone what it was necessary for you to testify to, or to prove?"

Again, "No, sir."

Yet Warner had just testified that, perhaps worse than being told what answer to give, one had been entirely fabricated for him.

The judge advocate let this pass without a word.

Warner's testimony continued: "I might have said that 'Cromwell deserves to be hung,' but I did not think at the time they were going to hang him. I think he was the most desperate character on the ship."

"Is that a serious opinion of yours that 'Cromwell deserved to be hung'?"

Warner temporized: "If he was guilty he deserved to be hung."

"Did you think he was guilty?"

"I did think he was guilty. I had no other reasons for thinking he was guilty than those I have given. I don't know how many others were concerned in this mutiny; I cannot say how many others I thought were concerned."

Captain Mackenzie took over the interrogation. "Had you a conversation with Sergeant Garty about the officers being armed and keeping a bright look-out on the night Spencer was arrested?"

"I had a conversation with him, but I don't remember what time it was. He asked if I thought a rescue would be attempted. I told him I did not think there would; I said there might be persons on board who would like to do so, but I did not think any one would have daring enough to attempt it."

"Did Mr. Spencer ever ask you if you would like to sail with him or become his coxswain?"

"No, sir. I don't remember ever hearing him ask that question."

"Were you the Commander's coxswain?"

"Until we arrived at St. Thomas."

Here the judge advocate asked a question to which Warner answered, "I do believe the brig could have been taken to St. Thomas at any rate without the execution taking place. The day of the execution the officers and petty officers being all armed, I was satisfied we could proceed to any port in safety."

The court did not pursue this.

* * *

THE WITNESSES SPOKE, the days went by. Mackenzie tried again, and again unsuccessfully, to present his history of *truly* mean captains— Bligh of HMS *Bounty*, the ghastly Hugh Pigot of the British frigate *Hermione* (a spectacular rebellion: the mutineers murdered nine officers and turned the ship over to the Spanish).

The captain wrung out of Surgeon Leecock a lengthy tribute to his compassion:

"Was the Commander attentive to the comfort of the sick, and did he ever ask you to send for food from the Captain's table to those in delicate health?"

Oh, yes, Leecock said: "He was uniformly attentive, and I recollect his sending food from his table to the sick."

"Did the Commander, in every port, ask you to make requisitions for fresh fruit for the sick and crew?"

"I think in every port we went he desired me to make requisitions for fresh fruit and such other articles as would administer to the comforts of the sick."

"Was there any unnecessary punishment, on board the *Somers*, and was the punishment of the crew cruel or humane?"

"There was no unjust punishment, and the punishment of the crew humane."

THE INQUIRY WAS NEARLY OVER. Hoffman said he had run through all his witnesses.

On the eighteenth, and penultimate, day of the proceedings, Mackenzie "stated that he wished to lay before the Court a fuller explanation of the motives which guided him in ordering the execution of those men than was contained in his report to the Secretary of the Navy."

This was permitted. Given the copious length of the report that had opened the hearing, the idea of a "fuller" version must have made hearts sink around that long table.

But for once Mackenzie was going to be succinct. He had distilled his defense down to a few points. Hoffman read them to the court.

"First, I was influenced by the conviction of the reality of the plot disclosed by Mr. Spencer to Mr. Wales. Although I received the first communication with incredulity, yet when I reflected upon the earnest and solemn manner in which the disclosure was made, and the strong impression of the realty and imminence of the danger made upon the mind of Mr. Wales himself, my doubts vanished and my mind was filled with the most earnest solicitude to discover and adopt the proper means for arresting the horrors with which we were threatened."

He was sure that at least twenty men on the ship were part of the plot, and that his "previous knowledge of the depraved character of the crew" had "convinced me that those who had agreed to it were capable of carrying it into execution and committing any atrocity."

He spoke of "the insubordination the crew manifested after we had left the coast of Africa"; of their "gloomy and angry looks"; of "their secret conferences, broken off when an officer appeared." All these "induced me to change my original determination to bring the prisoners to the United States for trial, and to deem their immediate execution necessary."

His second reason was "the uncertainty under which we labored as to the extent of the mutiny, and the inutility and danger of attempting to ascertain, by an examination of the crew, how many were to be relied on." What followed boiled down to: no point in questioning the crew because there was no way to know whether they'd tell the truth. "Universal denial," he said, would only "have increased and justified our suspicions of guilt."

"Thirdly, by the exhaustion of the officers, and by the impossibility that they could much longer sustain the fatigue to which they were subjected; and by the fact that, from loss of rest and continual exertion, we were daily losing strength, whilst that of the mutineers, from increasing numbers, was daily becoming greater."

Fourth, if a storm came up, "it would have been easy for a few resolute men to have released the prisoners and taken possession of the vessel."

Fifth, the ship was too small to accommodate any more prisoners.

"Finally, by the conviction that by the execution of the three ring-leaders the mutineers would be deprived of the power of navigating the vessel, as no other person would be capable of taking charge of her, and that this was the only effectual method of bringing them back to their allegiance, and preserving the vessel committed to my charge."

He ended by saying that "had any doubts existed in my mind . . . they would have been removed by the unanimous opinion of the commissioned, warrant and petty officers." That support "left me no room to doubt that in pursuing this course I was doing my duty to God and to my country."

That closed the hearings for the day. The final session, on Thursday, January 19, 1843, ended in a faintly comic anticlimax. Mackenzie had one more witness, a George W. Rice, who lived at 240 Rivington Street, and whose testimony began, "I think I knew Samuel Cromwell, who went out in the *Somers*, but I am not sure." Rice had heard that a nephew of his had been transferred to the *Somers* and went to visit him, but was not allowed aboard. "Some four or five days after, as near as I can recollect, two sailors came into Westbrook's, in the Bowery, No. 42. One of them said he was Boatswain's Mate of the *Somers*. I can't recollect at what period of the year this was, or whether it was before her first or last cruise."

The court never learned what Mackenzie had hoped Rice would say, because once the witness described the sailor in Westbrook's, Acting Master Perry was able to identify the man: he was someone named Phelps, who had been a boatswain's mate on the *Somers* long before Cromwell got there. The transcript of the inquiry ends with: "The testimony of the witness, it was quite apparent, would be entirely irrelevant, and he was directed to retire."

Rice went away. Commodore Stewart declared the proceedings at an end, and ordered the court cleared. Its officers began their deliberations, which were conducted in secrecy. Their decision would be forwarded to the Navy Department.

They arrived at it in a single day, and their finding was made public on January 28 (which would have been Philip Spencer's nineteenth birthday).

A month earlier, two days before the court of inquiry convened, the *Boston Courier* ran an editorial about it: "We doubt exceedingly whether a 'satisfactory opinion' will be the result of the inquiry; we mean, an opinion satisfactory to the people. We mean no imputation on the character of the gentlemen composing the Court; they are all honorable men, and will judge as impartially [as] . . . any body of men of the same profession as the officer who committed the deed. . . . To expect an opinion unfavorable to commander Mackenzie would be to expect of human nature a degree of impartiality contrary to all experience."

The *Courier* was right. The court gave Mackenzie a complete vindication. There had been a mutiny; Spencer, Cromwell, and Small had instigated it. Commodore Stewart, the court's president, said, "Commander Mackenzie under these circumstances was not bound to risk the safety of his vessel, and jeopardize the lives of the crew, in order to secure to the guilty the forms of trial, and that the immediate execution of the prisoners was demanded by duty and justified by necessity." The court found that the captain and his officers had been "prudent, calm, and firm, and that he and they honorably performed their duty to the service and their country."

13 Court-Martial

THE COURT'S WARM ENDORSEMENT of his actions may have done away with some of Mackenzie's worries, but by no means all of them. Even before the inquiry announced its verdict, the captain had written Upshur asking for a court-martial. He wanted it not so much to save his reputation as to save his neck.

John Canfield Spencer, Philip's father, and Margaret Cromwell, Samuel's widow, were working to have him put on trial for murder. Not by the officers of a self-protecting military service, but by a jury of American citizens in a civil court.

Perhaps Cromwell had not been the boorish husband Mackenzie was eager to have Wales describe. He had, after all, once spent fifteen of Philip Spencer's dollars to buy his wife winter fuel while he was away. Whatever feelings she may have had, she was enraged by his execution.

If Hoffman was a feeble prosecutor during the inquiry, he was even less active in his role as federal district attorney.

Margaret Cromwell wanted him to prosecute Mackenzie and Gansevoort. Their crime hadn't been committed in New York, of course; it would have to be a federal matter. But a thirty-year-old Supreme Court ruling held that there was no federal common law governing any crimes.

Hoffman probably told her this. If so, she and her lawyer were able to counter with a ten-year-old act that said a murder committed on the high seas beyond land-bound jurisdiction *could* be prosecuted under federal law.

With Hoffman remaining inert, Mrs. Cromwell and her lawyer went before a federal district court and demanded that the captain and his lieutenant be arrested. Guert Gansevoort's mother was horrified: "It seemed passing strange to me," she wrote her son Stanwix, "to have Guert, *honest & upright* as he is—keeping out of the way of the officers of Justice—& the idea of his being taken up, & lodged in prison under the charge of *Murder*—was it not awful—my blood chills when I write it, as coupling with the name of one of my beloved offspring."

Mackenzie, too, was chilled. "If I am arraigned before a civil tribunal," he fretted to Upshur, "for a conscientious, though it may be esteemed by others a mistaken performance of my duty as commander of a national vessel on the high seas, though I apprehend no punishment and no dishonor, I shall still be subject to delays and vexation of every sort."

The district court case went before Judge Samuel Rossiter Betts. Judge Betts was no more helpful than Hoffman, but at least he considered the matter, and even took a swipe at the Navy. Doubtful that the doings aboard the *Somers* had constituted a mutiny, he said, "The necessity of the case must be made apparent beyond any fair ground to doubt, before any functionary, under whatever plenitude of power, can, on his own mandate, take the life of a citizen." Still, he believed that the statute Margaret Cromwell had found was not explicit enough to let a civil court interfere with the working of a military one. Betts dismissed the case.

*   *   *

SECRETARY OF THE NAVY UPSHUR was as brave as the next man, but when Midshipman Perry had delivered the astonishing news about John Spencer's son, he could not summon the nerve to tell his colleague. "At last," wrote the Washington correspondent for the *New York Herald*, "he sent for Mr. [Henry] Morris, the son-in-law and private secretary of the Secretary of War, and through him the sad intelligence was communicated."

Spencer remained at home with his stricken wife for several days. "The excellent mother of the wretched youth," wrote the *Herald*, "is quite beside herself. She was in feeble health, and this shocking event has made her quite delirious. Two physicians are constantly in attendance, and her ultimate recovery is even doubtful." Spencer returned to his office and the condolences of his colleagues—"an affecting scene," one of them said—on December 28.

John Spencer was a harsh father—he was a harsh everything—but he *was* a father, and although Mackenzie's wordy narrative had omitted Philip's death throes, there was still plenty in it to wound: the midshipman breaking down in tears, asking if the sentence wasn't too harsh, being taunted by his captain even as he looked into the abyss.

When Spencer heard that Mackenzie, at the court of inquiry, was slandering his son to bolster his case, he wrote Judge Advocate Hoffman, "Nothing of the kind can afford any excuse to Mr. M for his own conduct." Given how the commander was behaving, Spencer pressed "to be allowed an opportunity to cross-examine the witnesses and to bring other evidence on the same point."

He was turned down.

Now he joined forces with Margaret Cromwell and his son-in-law Henry Morris, and in March they succeeded in putting their case before a grand jury.

When the jurors had questions, they brought them to Judge Betts. True, he had dismissed the earlier district court case, but this one was slightly different. He asked to hear legal arguments, and Mackenzie's attorney left the navy yard to explain, over the course of several hours, why the case should remain with the service.

The prosperous Spencer was able to deploy the best courtroom lawyers. One of them, Charles O'Conor, closed his argument eloquently. Dismissing sarcastically the defense's plea for an understanding of the feelings of Commander and Mrs. Mackenzie, O'Conor said, "The relatives of those who have gone, and have feelings as well . . . have a right when *their* friends, condemned without color of law, have been deprived of life suddenly and at a distance from home, put to death, to speak also. If the counsel has a right to be excused for what he pleads, has not the father of one of the departed a privilege to appear at the threshold of the temple of justice and inquire why and wherefore his son has been slain?"

Strong, but not strong enough. In the end, Judge Betts again ruled that in this case the law gave the jurisdiction to a naval court and not a civil one.

Moreover, the court-martial had already begun. Abel Upshur kept assuring Spencer that the Navy believed in justice at sea as strongly as he did in justice on land; trust our court, he said, you won't be disappointed.

The next morning, and a few miles away, the twenty-three-year-old lawyer George Templeton Strong read about the judge's decision, and recorded it in his diary. A generation younger than Philip Hone, he was every bit as dedicated a diarist, and his entries are just as entertaining.

When he first heard of the mutiny in mid-December, he'd written, "Various opinions seem to be entertained as to Mackenzie's conduct, and no opinion can be safely formed till we know more of the facts. This much I think is pretty clear—that to justify himself, Lieut. M.

must show a case of absolute necessity, that he cannot protect himself by setting up his authority as a commanding officer, but must show that it was a matter of life and death for the officers and the well-affected part of the crew. But I think this case will turn out to have been of that character . . . because Lieut. M., from all accounts, is a man not likely to act either in a passion or in a panic, and it's not likely that he'd take this step except as a last resort."

Strong followed the inquiry closely, and several weeks later the even-handed tone is gone: "Mackenzie's court-martial is slowly progressing and they are trying to get up an indictment. (May they succeed; for if ever there was a case of cold-blooded lynching, that *Somers* tragedy was one.)"

Strong knew Betts, and didn't think much of him. But when the judge gave his final ruling, he found himself in reluctant agreement—at least on the legal issue. "Old Betts has decided that the civil courts have no jurisdiction over the *Somers* murder (we may as well call things by their right names). Confound him, I think the decision is right enough, but it's a pity that he should have accidentally gone right in this case."

As PUZZLING AS THE ABSENCE of any photograph of Guert Gansevoort is how little we know about William M. Norris—which is almost nothing.

Although for weeks he was the focus of intense national attention, we have no idea why he was chosen to be judge advocate in Mackenzie's court-martial.

It was obviously a rebuke to the toothless performance of Hoffman at the inquiry, but Norris, as a contemporary put it (in as close as there exists to a description of him), was "a young man and little known in his own profession even in Baltimore." He makes a fleeting appearance among a swarm of other Baltimore lawyers in a 1910 two-volume behemoth entitled *The Bench and Bar of Maryland*. Had he any experience in maritime law? Had he ever even prosecuted a case before? The record is silent—or, more accurately, nonexistent.

This might have seemed another advantage for Mackenzie, but it wasn't. Norris stepped out of the shadows to prove himself a shrewd and determined prosecutor, and one who believed Mackenzie's handling of the mutiny had honored neither the American flag nor the American Navy.

Norris had a steep path before him. "All the officers and crew of that brig were furnished by the department for witnesses at my selection but," he complained, "with neither have I had any opportunities of conversation." At the trial, he would have to question "these gentlemen, wholly in the dark as to their disposition and acquaintance with facts."

The court granted him some time to meet with his witnesses. He was able to receive them in considerable comfort, for he was putting up at the Astor House, the seven-year-old hotel that had already established itself as the best in the city. Its own plant generated gas for the lights, and bathrooms on each floor (unprecedented in any hostelry) were irrigated with water pumped by steam engines in the basement.

But if his quarters were satisfactory, his conversations in them were not. Midshipman Charles Hayes, for instance, "waited on me, and soon manifested an ingenuous embarrassment of manner, indicating some reluctance to communicate what he knew."

More than some. "After replying to a few trivial questions, he candidly stated to me that he did not think me entitled, except on the stand, to this information."

No better luck with Midshipman John Tillotson. Norris asked if "he had an objection to afford me, in private, his knowledge of the incidents of the last cruise of the *Somers*. He politely replied that he had."

Norris was going blind into the trial.

*   *   *

IT BEGAN, AS HAD THE INQUIRY, in the spacious *North Carolina*, but with a different cast. Now there was a jury of eleven commanders and two captains: its president, Captain John Downes, had fought the Barbary pirates under Decatur; Captain Daniel Turner had commanded the brig *Caledonia* on Lake Erie where, for one desperate stretch, his two 24-pounders were the only guns that could return the fire of three British ships (Congress gave him a medal, New York State, a sword); Captain George Read, who accepted the surrender of HMS *Guerriere* to the *Constitution* in the War of 1812. . . . All these men knew their way around a ship.

Other potential jurors turned the task down. The peppery Robert Stockton, who was busy seeing to the completion of America's first propeller-driven warship, refused outright, saying he'd already made up his mind, and if he got on the court he would do his best to send Mackenzie to the gallows.

If the makeup of the presiding officers had changed, so too had the atmosphere of the whole proceeding. This trial was held not to collect information, but to pass judgment.

The tone was set at the very beginning, on February 2, with the "Charges and specifications preferred by the Secretary of the Navy of the United States, to wit:

Charge I—Murder on board a United States vessel on the high seas.

> *In this that the said Commander Alexander Slidell Mackenzie, of the navy, commanding the United States brig Somers, being on the high seas, to wit in 17° 34' 25" north latitude, and 57° 57' 45" west longitude, from Greenwich, or thereabouts, on the first day of December, A.D. eighteen hundred and forty two, did then and there, without form of law, wilfully, deliberately, and with malice aforethought, hang and caused to be hanged*

by the neck, at the main yard-arm of aforesaid brig, until he was dead, Philip Spencer, an acting midshipman, then in the service of the United States. . . ."

That was the first, and heaviest, charge leveled against Captain Mackenzie. There were four more.

Charge II—Oppression

In this, that the said Commander Alexander Slidell Mackenzie . . . did, then and there, without a good and sufficient cause, and without form of law, oppressively kill . . . Samuel Cromwell, boatswain's mate, then in the service of the United States. . . .

Charge III—Illegal Punishment

In this, that the said Commander Alexander Slidell Mackenzie . . . did then and there exceed the limits of his authority . . . by hanging and causing to be hanged, by the neck, to the main yard-arm . . . until he was dead, Elisha Small. . . .

Charge IV—Conduct Unbecoming an Officer

In this, that the said Commander Alexander Slidell Mackenzie . . . behave[d] in an unofficer-like and unfeeling manner, by addressing taunting and unofficer-like language to Philip Spencer . . . the said Spencer then and there expecting the immediate execution of death upon him by the orders of said Commander Mackenzie.

Charge V—Cruelty and Oppression

In this, that the said Commander Alexander Slidell Mackenzie . . . between the thirteenth day of September, eighteen hundred and forty-two and the twenty-fifth day of December, of said year, did oppressively and cruelly use and maltreat the crew of said brig, and inflict upon them cruel and unnecessary punishments. . . .

Commander Mackenzie did not get to make any opening statement this time. After the swearings-in and other ponderous preliminaries, Norris opened the proceedings.

He went right to work.

The recalcitrant Midshipman Hayes was the first witness.

Having established his name and age, Norris asked, "From the time of his arrest to the time of his execution, was any investigation into Spencer's guilt of any crime against the laws of the navy, made by Commander Mackenzie, or any other officer . . . in the presence of said Spencer, so that he might confront the witnesses, so that he might cross-examine them, so that he might offer vindicatory proof, so that he might object to the reception of mere hearsay?"

"None that I know of," Hayes said.

Norris moved on to Cromwell with the same question: "From the time of his arrest to the time of his execution, was Cromwell furnished with any charge and specifications of crime?"

"Not to my knowledge."

Norris brought up the fifth charge against the captain: "To your knowledge did Commander Mackenzie oppressively and cruelly use and maltreat the crew . . . or inflict any unnecessary punishment?"

"No, sir, by no means."

Hayes was excused.

Wales took his place on the stand.

As at the inquiry, the purser's steward spoke at length—Spencer, the moonlit night on the booms, was he afraid of a dead person, and all the rest. The day closed with Wales repeating his tardily recalled memory of when the mutiny had been scheduled to break out: Spencer "said very shortly before we arrived at St. Thomas."

Wales was back on the stand the next morning, but at this session Mackenzie opened the questioning. Now on trial himself, he could no longer submit his questions in writing. First he asked Wales to finish the account of the voyage that he had begun the day before;

then, with the mutineers hanged and harmony restored to the brig, Mackenzie pursued some specifics.

"Were any of the crew present when you heard Spencer threaten that he would throw the commander overboard?"

"Yes, sir." At least half a dozen, and "the effect of the remark seemed very pleasing—they smiled; Mr. Spencer went on talking with them."

"Did you observe . . . with which of the crew he was most intimate?"

"Yes, sir, with Cromwell, Small, Wilson, McKinley, Golderman, Neville, McKee and Waltham; he was very intimate with Waltham, who was a negro. I have seen him set for an hour at a time on the bitts talking with this negro. Gallia, too, he was very intimate with; he was the cook of [for] the steerage, a Maltese; he used to lend Gallia his pipe to smoke."

Mackenzie wasn't interested in Waltham or Gallia—neither of them had a widow who was trying to put him in front of a civilian jury. He was after Cromwell.

"Do you know anything of the remarks of Cromwell about the commander's fear of exposing the boys to danger?"

Oh, yes, Wales did: just after leaving Liberia, "we were struck by a squall, and some of the little boys sprung up into the rigging to take in sail; the commander ordered some of the smallest down, told them not to go up; Cromwell remarked that the commander was too damned afraid of [for] those boys, would not suffer them to go into any danger."

Back to Spencer. Had he said anything about "the small boys"?

"Yes, sir; he said that small fry eat a large quantity of biscuit, that they were a useless article aboard a vessel, and that he should make [a]way with them."

Mackenzie stayed with his most important spectral opponent. "Did you know anything of the picture of a brig drawn by Mr. Spencer?"

"Yes, sir; he drew one once, and brought it into the wardroom; I was there. . . . She had a black flag flying at her peak." Actually, this suggests a softening of Spencer's reported plans for the captives:

pirates flew the black flag to announce that if the ship under pursuit surrendered without a fight, no harm would come to those aboard it.

Mackenzie returned to one of his favorite grievances: "Do you know anything of Mr. Spencer giving segars or tobacco to the crew?"

"Yes, sir." Wales had seen the midshipman hand out "two bunches of segars at a time." Van Velsor and Green got a pound of tobacco. And "I have seen him give tobacco and segars to the smaller boys, saying, when he gave it to them, that 'he knew it was contrary to the rules of the vessel to give it to them, but if the commander would not let them have it, he would accommodate them.'"

Mackenzie moved to a larger issue than prodigally dispensed tobacco. How did Wales think matters stood in the brig on the day of the hanging? Did he believe "that, if the execution had not taken place, a rescue would have been attempted?"

He did. "I do not think that the vessel could have been brought into port by her officers if the execution had not taken place."

Mackenzie had been stung by the charge of conduct unbecoming an officer—that he had taunted the boy he had just condemned—and he went after that before Norris got his turn.

"What was the tone, the manner, the demeanor, the appearance of Commander Mackenzie in his intercourse with Mr. Spencer, from the time it was announced to him that he was to die until the moment of his death?"

"While the commander was talking with him, I observed tears trickling down his cheeks." Not Spencer's but Mackenzie's: "It appeared a very hard duty for him to perform."

"Was the conduct of Commander Mackenzie to Mr. Spencer rude or sympathetic, disdainful or courteous?"

"Very courteous, very sympathizing: I thought he sympathized with him deeply."

*   *   *

NORRIS TOOK OVER THE QUESTIONING. He was skeptical about the conference on the booms.

"You say that Spencer did not commence the conversation with any crafty inquiries as to the state of your feelings." Had the midshipman made the least effort to discover whether Wales disliked any of the officers? Had he asked if the life of a pirate held any appeal for him?

Wales didn't answer.

So, with no preliminary sounding-out from Spencer, "you say he administered to you the oath of secrecy after asking you the catechism of your courage, and at once bluntly told you a formed scheme of his own; now, sir, had you never indulged in any mutinous conversation before?"

"No sir; not with him, nor with any one else."

Norris's succinct summary may have made the initial exchange between Wales and Spencer sound so unlikely that it caused an interruption in the proceedings, of which the transcript reveals only that "the Court was cleared to consider the advisability of a question of the Judge Advocate." It was disallowed, and Norris came up with a mischievous substitute.

"Assuming Spencer to have been in jest, what would have been your predicament, Mr. Wales, had Small, when called up from the conversation, divulged what was going on in the booms to an officer?"

"I don't know what it would have been."

But of course he did. Small could have told the officer that he had just heard Wales swear on his life that he was all in favor of seizing the *Somers*. Spencer might have been fooling around, but Small could truthfully report that Wales had pledged before God to help murder his captain. If anything like that began to play itself out, Mackenzie would surely have re-revised his newly benign view of whatever Wales had done in Puerto Rico, and the brig have returned to New York with Small a hero and Wales at the bottom of the sea.

Norris proceeded to a lengthy question that verged on sarcasm, perhaps not the wisest approach to take in front of a tableful of navy brass sitting in judgment on one of their own.

"When Mr. Spencer told you to make a scuffle some night when he had the mid-watch, run with his associates to the main-mast, call Mr. Rogers, and throw him overboard, did you tell him that it would be likely to rouse the men, and prevent him from going on with his plan—which he told you was to open the arms chest and distribute them to the men, and station the men at the hatches, and proceed in person to murder the commander, and the officers in the wardroom and steerage, and of slewing the two after guns round so as to rake the deck, and to call up the crew, to select those to be thrown overboard— considering he had but twenty associates, in a crew of one hundred and twenty men and boys?"

Here the defense had an objection, which was voiced by Mackenzie's attorney, the prominent New York lawyer John Duer. He had been a federal district court judge, and, in happier times, had worked with Philip Spencer's father. His objection was long and convoluted, but it boiled down to the contention that Norris's question wasn't a question at all: "It is a brief argument, designed to show that the plan of a mutiny, as related by the witness, was so absurd and impractical" that "it was not seriously entertained by Mr. Spencer. . . . It is not a question to the witness. . . . It is an insidious and most irregular comment on the testimony that the witness had before given."

Sustained.

Norris returned to the crucial matter of the mutiny's being scheduled to erupt before the ship reached St. Thomas. The imminence of the uprising had made Mackenzie abandon his original plan of bringing the three prisoners back to the States for trial.

Wales's formidable memory began to waver. Norris asked, "When did you first tell Mr. Spencer's plan as to the taking and use of the females from the vessels he should capture?"

"I believe I told it before the examination of the council of officers; I think I did; I won't be sure."

"If you did not tell it then, did you tell it to any one before the execution, and to whom?"

"I think I told it to Mr. Gansevoort; I think I told it then; I won't be sure."

So when the captain spoke with Cromwell after his arrest, "you believe Commander Mackenzie knew that the mutiny was to break out before the arrival at St. Thomas? What were your reasons for this belief?"

Backed into a corner, Wales admitted, "I don't know that Commander Mackenzie did know about it."

The court took over the questioning. Had Spencer's conduct been "wayward or eccentric"?

"I don't know sir; I noticed that sometimes he was rather singular, dull, stupid!" That the transcript gave this answer a rare exclamation point suggests Wales had become rattled.

He was allowed to step down, replaced on the stand by William Neville: "My age is nineteen, I rate on board the *Somers* as an ordinary seaman; I am stationed in the foretop." He was the first of the younger crew members to be questioned, but far from the last.

These youngsters must have been in a state of perpetual anxiety, knowing they'd have to speak to a panel of naval heroes about a matter that had already got three of their shipmates killed.

Neville had little to add.

The court: "You have said that you saw Mr. Spencer and Mr. Wales in conversation on the booms. . . . Do you not recollect whether it was before or after dark?"

"'Twas not dark."

"Was it your watch on deck when the conversation between Mr. Spencer and Mr. Wales took place, and when did your watch expire?"

"I think it was my watch on deck; I am not certain whether my watch expired at six or seven o'clock."

"If it was not dark, why could you not recognize the man who came up and joined Mr. Spencer and Wales?"

"I didn't take no notice; I was going below; could not be certain whether it was man or boy."

How far away had he been?

"About five foot."

Ward Gagely was no more illuminating: "I am fifteen years of age. I was on board the *Somers* as first-class boy."

Norris: "Did you hear Mr. Spencer call Mr. Wales on the booms?"

"No, sir."

"Did you hear Small tell Mr. Spencer not to speak so loud?"

"No, sir."

The exchange went on like that until it petered out.

LATE IN THE DAY, Lieutenant Gansevoort took the stand. Fed questions by Mackenzie, he began by telling how he learned of the incipient mutiny, of his subsequent trailing Spencer around the ship, and how the midshipman had seared him with "the most infernal expression I have ever beheld on a human face."

Then he said, "During the time of his [Spencer's] confinement he told me he wished to have a conversation with me. . . . I told him I was ready at the time; he said he was not in a proper state of mind then; I asked him 'if he would send for me when he was. . . .' Next morning, about ten o'clock, I asked him 'if he was ready to have the conversation'; he said he had had this plot on board of every vessel he had been in; had it in the *Potomac* and the *John Adams*; but he had never got as far with it as he had on board the *Somers*; he said he knew it would get him in trouble; he had thought it over in the steerage and had tried to break himself of it, but could not; he thought it was a mania with him."

That closed the day. The court reconvened on February 11, but not aboard the *North Carolina*. The press of spectators was so great that even a ship of the line was too small to hold them. Captain Downes, the court's president, wrote asking permission to move the proceedings. Upshur responded, "You are at liberty to alter the sittings of the court as you desire," and Gansevoort resumed his testimony surrounded by the brick walls of the navy yard chapel rather than the wooden planking of the *North Carolina*.

Norris spent a day questioning the witness about the behavior of the crew: sullen and obstinate, Gansevoort maintained.

February 12 was a Sunday, and the court got the sabbath off. On Monday, Norris asked Gansevoort, "When did you first suppose it would be necessary to execute Mr. Spencer, Cromwell, and Small?"

"When we made more prisoners than we had the force to take care of, and I was more fully convinced after the examination in the ward-room before the council of officers."

What about the day spent spying on Spencer? "How was he occupied until he went aloft to the foretop?"

"I did observe him before that; he was about in different parts of the vessel; I think I saw him in the steerage; once before that I saw him on the forecastle. After I saw him on the Jacob's ladder, I think he had a watch. I am not positive."

"Was Mr. Spencer . . . till the time of his arrest, engaged in the usual duties of an officer of his station?"

"I believe that he was engaged in the usual duties of his station, except when in the foretop having India ink pricked into his arm, and his menacing look on the Jacob's ladder."

"Was he on duty when he was in the foretop?"

"No, sir."

"Was it an unusual thing for Mr. Spencer to be in the foretop?"

"I think I have seen him there before."

"Have you seen other young officers in the foretop when not on duty?"

"Yes, sir, I have."

Norris did not have to pursue that further; he had made his point that a midshipman hanging out in the foretop was hardly sinister.

He turned to the uprising's timing: "When did you first hear the mutiny was to break out before the arrival of the *Somers* at St. Thomas?"

"I don't recollect that I did hear it."

"Did Wales swear before the council of officers that Mr. Spencer had told him that the mutiny was to break out before you reached St. Thomas?"

"The evidence will show; I am not positive." But Gansevoort had been there throughout the council; why would he need to review the evidence?

The lieutenant's memory also became sketchy a little later, when Norris asked: "When Mr. Spencer told you he would have a conversation with you, did he tell you he would answer any questions you would put to him?"

"I don't recollect at this time."

"Did he not tell you that his object in proposing the conversation with you was to tell you everything?"

"I don't recollect that he did."

"Did you not tell Commander Mackenzie and other officers, that Mr. Spencer told you he would answer every question you would put to him?"

"I don't recollect that I did; I told Commander Mackenzie this conversation with Mr. Spencer."

Did Mackenzie "advise you to hold the interview with Mr. Spencer and hear what he had to say?"

"Yes, sir, I believe he did."

"Did Commander Mackenzie advise you to put free and full inquiries to Mr. Spencer as to his scheme?"

"I don't recollect, but my impression is he told me to find out all I could about it. It is impossible to recollect all the conversations that took place between the commander and myself during that affair."

This testiness didn't slow Norris down.

"Did you ask Mr. Spencer anything as to the paper found in his locker?"

"I don't recollect that I did."

"Did you ask him how far the conspiracy had gone, in those same interviews?"

"I don't recollect that I did."

Norris kept pressing: "Did you ask him the names and number of his accomplices?"

"I don't recollect. I had frequent interviews with Mr. Spencer."

"Did you not ask him how far the conspiracy had gone?"

"I don't recollect."

"You say he told you he had had this plot in the *John Adams* and the *Potomac*, but it had not gone so far as in the *Somers*. Did you not then ask him how far it *had* gone?"

"I don't recollect asking him how far he had got. . . ."

Perhaps feeling this must sound as feeble to Norris and the court as it looks on the page nearly two centuries later, he fumbled his way forward: "He did not show much of a disposition to communicate at any time; I wished to choose a time when he was disposed to talk, and his mind was in a state to do so. I may have then had a reason for not asking questions, which I do not recollect now. . . ."

Norris kept on probing this unfathomable lack of curiosity in one whose own throat had been scheduled for cutting.

"If you made none of these inquiries of Mr. Spencer, what did you do in pursuance of the commander's instructions to find out from Mr. Spencer what you could as to the mutiny?"

Gansevoort gave a particularly weak answer: "I inquired among the crew."

And the Greek list; had Spencer said anything about its "containing the names of those he conjectured would join him, or as containing the names of those who had?"

"I don't recollect."

Nor did the lieutenant's opacity lift as Norris brought the conversation closer to the executions: "Did the commander tell you that Cromwell had on his knees protested his innocence, and that Spencer begged that he might be believed, and that he [Mackenzie] was staggered by it?"

"I don't recollect; I am under the impression that he did tell me something of that nature; what the words were I don't recollect."

Gansevoort failed to recollect several more shipboard conversations before Norris led him to another matter, one possibly more dangerous for Mackenzie and (as Gansevoort was frightened he might be named) his accomplice.

"Did you on the 28th [of November], and at what time of day, advise with Mr. Perry, the master, as to whether Cromwell, Small, and Mr. Spencer should not be put to death, if you had to take more prisoners, and what was his conclusion?"

"I don't recollect as to the day; I think I spoke to the doctor, Mr. Perry, and Mr. Rodgers, and I think their conclusion was that they should be disposed of."

This interested the court: "Was that before the council of officers was held?"

"Yes, sir."

Gansevoort may not at first have understood the full implications of the question—that the captain had already decided to hang the three prisoners *before* seeking his officers' advice.

Norris got it, and jumped in: "Was it a day before the holding of the council of officers?"

Gansevoort caught on, and tried to repair any damage. "I don't think it was more than a day; I am not positive of the time."

And here came another problem for Gansevoort: "The log-book under the date of the 28th of November: there was a vessel reported on that date three points to the larboard bow? Was there any endeavor to hail or overhaul her? Was there any consultation about placing any of your prisoners aboard her between you and Commander Mackenzie?"

Gansevoort threw out a fog of nautical language—he'd "discovered a sail three fourths of a point on the larboard bow, standing to the southward and westward; the *Somers* was steering N. 65° W on the morning of the 28th, civil time, between 4 and 8 o'clock, when the sail was seen . . ."—before admitting, "I don't know any attempt was made to overhaul her." Then he drew back still further, saying, "I don't recollect to have heard of that sail."

That closed the proceedings for February 13; the next day Norris did not return to the potentially helpful vessel, but to the Greek paper.

"When you found Mr. Wales's name on the list found in Mr. Spencer's locker, did you conclude it was put there without Mr. Wales's authority . . . after the conversation on the booms?"

Gansevoort said he had.

Then, "If it was put there after the conversation on the booms, what was there in the paper to excite alarm? Were not only four names down as certain?"

". . . My alarm was not excited by the paper, but from the manner of those that were on that paper. . . ."

"Seeing this paper then . . . did you believe Mr. Spencer had any matured plot with twenty men of the crew of the *Somers*?"

"Yes, sir; I did believe so, from the conversation which Mr. Wales had repeated, and from the appearance of the crew."

"Does Cromwell's name appear on that list?"

"It does not; there was a name which I think represented him." That would have been the intangible "E. Andrews."

Did the council of officers discuss "whether the vessel should be taken to St. Thomas, or any nearer port?"

"Yes, sir; I think it was mentioned."

"What do you mean by 'mentioned'?"

"I think the question was asked by some of the officers . . . and we came to the unanimous conclusion that the vessel could not be taken in to port, and that the immediate execution was necessary."

Norris asked almost the same question again: "Was this mutiny spoken of as having been designed certainly to break out before the arrival at St. Thomas?"

"I don't recollect." But he believed the opinion was in the air: "I think it was spoken of—I am not positive as to the officers; I think Mr. Rogers and Mr. Perry, as well as others, whose names I do not recollect at this time, expressed that belief."

"Did they give you their reasons for this belief?"

"They may have done so, but I don't recollect at this time."

Norris shifted his questions from the officers to the prisoners: Had they been told what the officers were discussing? "Not that I know of," said Gansevoort.

"From the time of his arrest to the time of his execution, did any officer apply to the commander or yourself for permission to explain to Mr. Spencer his situation, and what was contemplated in respect to him, that he might afford him any friendly services to take care of his rights?"

"I don't know that anything of that sort was done."

How about Cromwell and Small—had they been told they were on trial for their lives?

"Not that I know of." No officer had questioned any of them, and none had been called before the council.

Lieutenant Gansevoort finally finished his testimony on February 16, doubtless deeply relieved to be done with it; he had been on the stand for six days.

ACTING MASTER MATTHEW PERRY took his place. He was twenty-one years old, and third-in-command on the brig. To Mackenzie's questions he spoke of the ominous behavior of the crew—he'd seen "Wilson rubbing his battle-axe with a file, between two of the larboard side guns of the deck; on examining it I found it very sharp"—and of the "unusually exhausting" duties of the officers once Spencer had been ironed: "The officer of the decks had to wear two pistols, and the officer of the forecastle one, and to take charge of a cutlass . . . and while it was their watch below, to keep continually moving about the vessel. After Cromwell's and Small's arrest, the officers had to wear two pistols, a cutlass, and cartridge-box continually during the night; before the execution they were in two watches, watch and watch, and generally throughout the day continually on deck."

"How long," Mackenzie asked, "could the officers have continued to perform the duties imposed upon them?"

"I don't think they could have held out a day and a half longer."

Mackenzie took up the rush aft: the fallen topmast, the snarled tackle, the turmoil on deck. What if someone had gone overboard then? "Would it have produced confusion in the vessel, and withdrawn the officers and the most zealous of the crew from watching over the prisoners and disaffected, to the care of the vessel?"

"Yes, sir, it would."

Norris's turn: "Did you think at the time that the mast was carried away by design to afford an outbreak to the mutiny, or to rescue Mr. Spencer?"

"I did, sir."

"Were you on deck at the time of the occurrence to the mast?"

"I was not."

"How soon after did you come up, and how long did you stay up on deck?"

"I was on deck immediately, and went below after half an hour and stayed a few minutes, and remained on deck, with the exception of a few minutes, until sail was set on the new mast."

"Why did you go below?"

"The first time, I didn't remember why; the second time, for my meal."

Norris had done his homework: "Did you not swear before the court of inquiry that you went below because you found nothing to do?"

A faltering response: Perry "might have," and went on to say that, once he'd had a chance to take a look at "the records of the court of inquiry, I do recollect having sworn so."

He must have anticipated the next question: If the midshipman believed his ship was about to be seized and its officers murdered, "would it not have been your duty to remain on deck?"

It hadn't gotten dark yet, Perry said, and he thought there'd be no trouble until then.

Norris asked what happened when he went below.

Lieutenant Gansevoort "came down and gave me a pistol and cutlass, and told me to go on deck."

"If you feared a rescue while first on deck, why did you not arm yourself? Were there not battle-axes on the ship's bulwarks?" (How this Baltimore lawyer came to know so much about the smaller details of a warship's weaponry is lost along with almost every other aspect of his identity.)

Perry said, yes, there were battle-axes at hand, but "I did not think of it at the time."

Norris spent the next half hour asking about the council. He kept pushing to establish that the decision to execute the prisoners had been made before it convened.

"How was it that on the 28th of November . . . you told Mr. Gansevoort that Mr. Spencer, Cromwell, and Small, should be put to death, when you now state that you did not think the execution necessary until the day before the council of officers was held?"

"I said I think it was the day before," Perry said. "I am not positive; I do not mean to be positive about dates. . . ."

"When did you first hear that the mutiny was to break out before the arrival of the *Somers* at St. Thomas, and from whom?"

"From Mr. Wales, I think it was, during the evening of the arrest of Mr. Spencer."

The purser's steward had not mentioned St. Thomas until long after Spencer was dead, and Norris pressed Perry: "Did you hear Wales testify before the council?"

"I did, sir."

"Did you or not hear Wales testify that Mr. Spencer had told him that the mutiny was to break out before the arrival at St. Thomas?"

Perry answered, stiffly and unhappily, "By a reference to the record of the council of officers I see no mention made of such fact, therefore I conclude it was not made."

"Was it discussed in the council of officers as to whether the vessel could be carried into St. Thomas or any nearer port? Was the chart examined, and the distance of the vessel from neighboring islands calculated?"

Perry grew passionate. "It was discussed as to whether she could be taken into St. Thomas, and I, in answer, said I would rather go overboard than go into St. Thomas for protection—that I would never agree to a thing of that kind."

Why? Norris asked. The part of the ocean they'd been sailing at the time was studded with islands.

"Because I thought it would be a disgrace to the United States, the navy, and particularly to the officers of the brig; my reasons were that if an American man-of-war could not protect herself, no use in having any."

Captain Mackenzie enlarged on this a couple of days later, when, at the opening of the proceedings on February 20, he submitted a paper to be read to the assembly.

"To save the time of the court, and spare the judge advocate the trouble of a laborious investigation on which he proposes to enter, as to the distance of the *Somers* from various West India islands,"

Mackenzie said that he would never dream of seeking "protection against his crew in any foreign port, from any foreign power whatever, or from any foreign ship in port, or at sea, or anywhere, save in a port of the United States or under the guns of an American man-of-war."

Better, then, to kill a few shipmates than to risk ridicule from the Danes, or worse, the British.

NORRIS KEPT FEELING FOR CRACKS in the nearly uniform testimony. Despite his arid answers a few days earlier, the foretopman William Neville was recalled to the stand. The subject was the Greek letter, and Norris was hard on him.

"What time of the day was it you saw Mr. Spencer and Cromwell in conversation—at the time Mr. Spencer was showing Cromwell the paper?"

"I think it was in the afternoon; I can't say what time."

"How long did you observe them in conversation with the paper out?"

"About two minutes."

"Were you not within a few feet of them?"

"Within about two feet as I passed by."

"Was Cromwell's face or back to you when you first saw them?"

"His back was to me."

"Was Spencer's face toward you?"

"No, sir."

"When you last saw them there, did you still see the paper?"

"Yes, sir; he had the paper in his hand."

"Was Mr. Spencer holding the paper immediately in front of Cromwell?"

"No, sir; he was not holding it directly in front."

"Take a piece of paper, and show the court how the parties were standing, and how Mr. Spencer was holding it."

From what follows, it sounds as though Neville had been handed the Greek list itself, or a facsimile. He held it up for the court to see. "He was standing this way."

"How then did you see the back of the paper?"

"Part of it was turned over this way."

"Did you show that it was doubled at first? And why did you not?"

"Because I understood you to ask me to show you their position; I did not understand you to ask if the paper was doubled up."

"Look at that paper, and see if the part having the geometrical figures on it were doubled over, whether it would not have been in Mr. Spencer's hand upside down where the writing was?"

"I could not say it would have been upside down; I saw geometrical figures."

"Is not the lower half of the paper without geometrical figures on it?"

"No, sir; not a half—about a quarter."

"If as much as half had been doubled over, could any of the writing be seen?"

"No, sir."

"How much of the paper was doubled over?"

"I can't say how much—there did not appear to be much."

"If there was not much doubled over, and there are no geometrical figures on a quarter of the lower part, how did you see the geometrical figures."

"I saw it, sir," said Neville miserably. "I can not tell you how I saw it; I saw it."

By now February had dwindled into March. On the ninth, another Perry took the stand: "My name, Oliver H. Perry, my age seventeen; I was on board the *Somers* in her last cruise, as commander's clerk."

Norris asked him about Spencer's last hours.

"Do you know whether Mr. Spencer wrote home to his friends?"

The frequent midshipman response: "No, sir."

"Do you know whether, at his request, any one else wrote for him?"

"No, sir."

"Did you not say, in the presence of the secretary of the navy, and other gentlemen, that you were of the impression that Mr. Spencer did send a written message home?"

Perry folded immediately. "At the time of the execution it was my impression he did send a message home; the captain was copying something."

"How near were you to the commander when he was writing?"

"I was standing between the binnacles, about four or five feet off."

"State the conversation that then passed between the commander and Mr. Spencer."

"I did not hear any of it; I thought he was writing a letter home to his parents, and did not try to hear it. . . ."

"Did you see the commander order Dunn [James Dunn, the captain's African American steward] to bring him paper and ink?"

"Yes, sir."

"Did you hear Mr. Spencer say he could not write with his irons on?"

"No, sir."

"Did Mr. Spencer take the pen, and try to write?"

"I did not see him."

"Did you hear the commander tell him he would write for him?"

"No, sir."

With that answer, Captain Mackenzie rose to his feet and—for the only time throughout the trial—walked over to Norris and spoke to him directly. He was angry.

"Why do you ask him this question about Mr. Spencer's not being able to write in irons? He declined to write."

The judge advocate was civil but firm. "Yes, sir," he said, "but I am told he afterward dictated to you what to write."

"He said he did not wish to write."

"Yes, sir," again, and again: "but I am told he afterward dictated to you what to write."

Mackenzie changed his story as quickly as young Perry had. "Yes, he did."

"Then he did dictate to you what to write?"

"Yes, he did, and the substance of it is in my official report."

THE NEXT MORNING Mackenzie appeared with a statement that he wished added to the record of the previous day's hearing. It said that "not having for some time read his official report" he "may have been mistaken in admitting that Mr. Spencer declined to write, that he said he did not wish to write."

Norris wrote a colleague, with grim satisfaction, "I wish the world *could have seen the shaking agony, and the craft with which he admitted it.*"

According to Mackenzie, Spencer would have refused to write at all save for the captain's humane urging. "It was only after earnest solicitations from Commander Mackenzie that he consented to send any message whatever." And once his captain had coaxed it out of him, "the message of Mr. Spencer to his friends was communicated to the Secretary of the Navy, as the least painful mode that occurred to Commander Mackenzie of making it known to them."

But what had happened to the message? Spencer's friends and family had yet to receive it.

It wasn't mentioned in the next day's proceedings (there was instead another rehash of the fallen mast from Oliver Perry), but the day after that Daniel McKinley gave Norris a full account of Spencer's final interview. "The commander asked him if he wished to write; Mr. Spencer said that he did; the commander ordered Mr. Dunn to fetch paper and a camp-stool out of the cabin; Spencer took the pen in his hand—he said, 'I can not write.' The commander spoke to him in a low tone; I do not know what he then said; I saw the commander writing; whether Mr. Spencer asked him to write for him or not, I can't say. The commander told Mr. Thompson, before he began to write, to tell him when the time was up; he did so when the time was up, but the commander kept on writing."

Kept on for close to an hour.

A new witness took the stand: "My name is Egbert Thompson, my age twenty-one; I was on board the *Somers* in her last cruise as midshipman."

Norris asked him if he'd seen the commander talking with Spencer. "Yes, sir. . . . The commander spoke to him; what he said I did not hear; he afterward ordered up a camp-stool by Dunn, and some paper; sat down by the arm-chest and wrote."

"Was Mr. Spencer's face then toward you?"

"I could see his face."

"Seeing his face, what did you judge was passing between him and the commander?"

"The commander was writing some of the time, and conversing with Mr. Spencer some of the time."

Norris asked, "Did the commander address to you any observation when he commenced to write?"

"Not that I recollect. Ah, yes; after he had spoken to the others, he told Mr. O. H. Perry, I think, to note the time; Mr. Perry and myself both noted it."

"Did you report the end of the time?"

"I think I did. It is so long since these things occurred, that it is impossible to remember these trivial things. . . ."

During the wearing days before, Norris had increasingly come to believe that the officers had concocted a story that was fundamentally untrue. He was sick of all of them, and he snapped at Thompson.

"Do you regard it as a trivial thing to report the expiration of ten minutes, which were the limits of Mr. Spencer's life?"

Thompson bridled at the question. "I did not say it was a trivial thing; my remark referred to some trivial questions you have put to me; my answer is by no means."

Norris's blood was up. "Have you a bad memory?"

"I can't say I have a good one."

Mackenzie took over the questioning; he extracted more examples of Cromwell's insubordination ("His manner was not insolent, but disrespectful; he did not touch his hat, to my knowledge") and asked the midshipman if he thought the *Somers* could have made port without the hangings. Thompson was firm: "No, sir; she could not."

"The Court," says the record, "then adjourned until to-morrow (Tuesday), March 14, at 10 o'clock, A.M."

AND SO IT DID, but tomorrow brought a message:

U.S. NAVY YARD,
BROOKLYN, MARCH 14, 1843

The Court met this day . . .

Present—[were the captains and commanders and] W. H. Norris, Esq., of Baltimore, Judge Advocate.

Commander Alexander Slidell Mackenzie sent the following certificate, which was read by the judge advocate—

"SIR: I do hereby certify that Commander Mackenzie, in consequence of serious indisposition, will be unable to attend the court this day.

"Very respectfully,

"R. W. Leecock,
"Asst Surg . . ."

So that was that for March 14. Nor did the commander show up on the fifteenth. On the sixteenth all the gold braid and epaulets were back in the navy yard chapel, and again their wearers heard that Leecock, now joined by "John Haslet, *Surgeon of the Yard*" had certified Mackenzie too sick to attend.

He did not reappear until Friday, March 17. The trial recommenced with Midshipman Oliver Perry back on the stand, and Norris again taking up Spencer's last words with his captain. At first, like so many of the other witnesses, Perry professed not to remember much of anything. Having pushed him to admit that he did, after all, recall Spencer being on the campstool, Norris wanted to know why the midshipman hadn't said so earlier.

"I referred to the mutiny," said Perry, "not to Mr. Spencer's particular actions and gestures."

Norris, whose attitude had not been sweetened by Mackenzie's lengthy absence, asked, "Did you not consider the messages of dying men, and the form they chose to give them, an important concern as respects the mutiny, and not mere gestures and actions?"

This drew an objection from the defense, which was upheld.

The acrid exchange between midshipman and judge advocate might have continued had not Mackenzie usurped the proceedings by announcing that he now had the letter Spencer had dictated to him, and would like to share it with the court.

"May it please the court," he wrote, as always in the third person, ". . . the judge advocate has already occupied much time in endeavoring to ascertain whether a letter or a mere message was dictated by Mr. Spencer, and has at length declared a belief that a letter was written by Commander Mackenzie, for Mr. Spencer, which has never been delivered—a letter, too, containing protestations of innocence! Commander Mackenzie, for the purpose of completely refuting his gratuitous and offensive assumption, and to put an end, if possible, to the interminable consumption of time, desires to submit to the court the paper hereto annexed . . . as the identical memorandum taken down by him during his last conversation with Mr. Spencer."

The "memorandum" is extraordinary—a pell-mell chowder of broken sentences, shifting tenses, and frayed ends of half-formed thoughts. "Identical" does not mean the same thing as "original"; and although Mackenzie had submitted the document swearing it was "the one made by him, and the only one, on the day of the execution," Norris came to believe the commander had written it during an illness feigned to give him time to fabricate Spencer's last words. If this is Mackenzie's own work, it suggests a mind close to disintegrating under pressure. When it was published, it came accompanied by the trial transcript's only footnote: "The above paper of Commander Mackenzie is so illegible, as not to be correctly written.—ED."

Yet, more than any of the court testimony, it conveys an immediate sense of what was going on when it was supposedly set down: Spencer on his campstool speaking in the shadow of the yardarm that is about to extinguish his life, Mackenzie standing over him on the spar deck scribbling across three wind-teased pages amid the cowed and puzzled crew and the miasma of hysteria that has seeped throughout the trim brig.

Here it is:

When asked if he had any message to send. None that they would wish to receive. Afterwards that you die wishing them every blessing and happiness. You deserved death for this and other sins. That you felt sincerely penitent and only fear of death was that your repentance might be too late. Many that he had wronged but did not know how reparation could be made to them. Your parents most wronged. Excused [crossed out and illegible word or words written above it] himself by saying that he had entertained same idea in John Adams *and* Potomac. *But had not ripened it into. Do you not think that a mania which should. Certainly. Objected to manner of death. Requested to be shot. Could not make any distinction between him and those whom he had seduced. Justifiable desire at first to save others. Cromwell. The. Last words he had to say and hoped they would be believed that Cromwell was innocent. Admitted it was just that no distinction should be made. Asked that his face might be covered. Granted. When he feared that his repentance might not be in season, I referred him to the story of Penitent thief. Tried to find it could not. Read the bible. The Prayer book. Did not know what would have become of him if succeeded. Makes no objection to death but objects to time. Reasons. God would consider shortness of time. Offences. Pictured to him a [illegible]. Many sins. Dies praying God to bless and preserve. I am afraid this may injure my Father. God who was all merciful as well as all wise could not only extricate the difficulty growing out of shortness of time and from the abundance of his mercy forgive. Be the death of my poor Mother. Do you not think she would have felt worse if instead of dying you had succeeded in undertaking. Horrors here others in course of piracy. Cut off by Cromwell. Passing to gallows. Met at pump well. Asked for Mr. Wales. Mr. Wales I beg you to forgive me for having tampered with your fidelity. Mr. Wales much affected. Are you not going too far? are you not going too fast Sir. I think sir you [blank space] The best service he could render his Father was to die. Small said Shipmates "give me quick and easy death." Knot, toggle, shift knot, asked leave to give word. Granted. Took station on trunk to see all parts. Waited. Waited. Prayer. "Shall I die?" Browning of opinion only then began to think he really was going to die. He kept such good heart. Small up. Suffocated. Told him in scarcely audible whisper to tell Commander he must give the word himself. Preparations live coal match—keep passing them up so as to have [illegible] perpetually there. Cromwell and Spencer meeting. No Notice of each other. Spencer as calm as at any moment of life. Wales. Small. Asked forgiveness no by God Mr Spencer can't forgive you. You betrayed me [these three words crossed out]. Consulted him Mr Wales so both together. Forgive me Small for leading you into this trouble—We shall soon be in the face of God Almighty then see. You must forgive me Small. I told him to be more generous. He softened.*

I do forgive you Mr. spencer. Shook hands. May God Almighty forgive you also. Small on hammocks asked leave to address the ship's company. Now boys &c Now Brother Topmates give me a quick death. Run me up smartly. Do not let there be any interval between word & firing. Asked 1. Lieut. If firing with lock. match. Open arm chest & get wafers. Ordered live coals to be passed up from galley. "Stand by" "fire!" instantaneous. Shotted gun. Arrangements. Conversation about coffin. Beating to call. Gan't asked about covering face. No hangmen. You others [?] nothing to do with requirements [?] of business and as done in secure seamanlike manner. The starboard rope string stitched to the [illegible] of [illegible]. [illegible] a strain, hooks moved. Tail chocks well secured. Roll. S. Small stept up. Cromwell overboard. Rose dripping to yard arm."

Some of this welter has to be Philip Spencer speaking ("Cromwell was innocent"); some of it is Mackenzie answering him ("Could not make any distinction between him and those whom he seduced"), and some a frenetic record of what was going on that had nothing to do with Spencer (Small's farewell to his shipmates).

Broken and chaotic though it is, little in this testament is wholly incomprehensible. And the last two sentences are perfectly clear. And disturbing: "Cromwell overboard. Rose dripping to yardarm."

Gansevoort had said that Cromwell's final handclasp had been so powerful that he briefly feared the boatswain's mate would try to leap into the ocean and take the lieutenant with him. Had Cromwell, in his fury and desperation, actually managed to fling himself over the rail? And then been retrieved? That would not have been easy or quick: at least one boat lowered from its davits, a struggle to pull Cromwell into it, several sailors battering him upward back onto the deck, and then forcing him into the noose and hoisting him to the yardarm with the seawater rilling from his clothes.

Such a spectacular failure in managing the execution would have been a severe embarrassment to Mackenzie. But however thoroughly he and Lieutenant Gansevoort might have managed to conceal such an incident from the hearing and the court-martial, would a hundred harrowed witnesses have kept it a secret, not just from the officers aboard the *North Carolina*, but from the avid press, and then . . . forever? But the court did not question the six-word statement.

The scattered, confounding testament was read that Friday, and the court reconvened on Saturday to hear Mackenzie's official account—the one that had so disgusted Philip Hone—which consumed the entire day.

The next few sessions brought more midshipmen, more apprentices, more on the fallen topmast, more on the execution. But the trial was winding down.

Philip Hone wrote in his diary, "The court-martial at Brooklyn, on the 'Somers' case, drags along its tedious length so slowly, and there is such an everlasting sameness in the examination, that the public here appears to have lost all interest in the matter, and you scarcely hear an inquiry made to its progress, or the probability of its termination." (Britain, however, was still having a fine time with it, to Hone's wrath: "I am indignant that this 'scum of Britons' should avail themselves of this distressing occurrence to cast the contents of their 'stink pots' upon my country." And the *Herald* was reporting their calumnies. Imagine "that a wretch should be found among us base enough to ladle them out to the last loathsome drop. But above all, I am humiliated that my fellow-citizens should give to this infamous journal a circulation greater (if the mendacious sheet may in any sort to be believed) than that of any other daily newspaper in the country.")

Norris would have agreed with Hone about the trial having become boring, although he said the tedium had been forced on him by the utter lack of help he'd had at the outset: "Had these officers allowed a private examination at the start, much of the prolixity and toil of cross-examination would have been avoided." But "as it is, a bunch of keys has been thrown at the judge advocate; one word would have told the one fitted to each door, but [I have] been compelled at every lock to try the whole bunch."

Mackenzie was on trial for murder, but there wasn't any doubt about his being the perpetrator. Norris had set out to prove that there was no mutiny, and that the killings were gratuitous. Trying all those locks, the judge advocate had opened doors on many contradictions, evasions, and more than a few outright lies.

On March 21 he told the court, "The judge advocate does not wish to protract this examination further, or he would call every unexamined member of the *Somers*, even, to prove that no plan of mutiny was known to any but Wales, before the arrest; and that no proposal of rescue was talked of afterward; if any witness can be named to prove the contrary, he offers to call him. . . ."

He must have known that was a sterile challenge.

THE NEXT DAY, the defense made its case. Hone may have been weary of the trial, but he was there in the courtroom, along with his daughters—and much else of New York. The chapel was packed, and "never was an audience more attentive." It was not listening to John Duer; he had worn himself out fending off Norris and John Spencer and Margaret Cromwell, and had been replaced by George Griffin.

Born in Connecticut, educated at Yale, and eventually moving to New York, Griffin had been a member of the bar for more than forty years, and was very good at what he did.

He started out by saying: "In judging of the necessity of the execution, it is of vital importance to ascertain, primarily, whether a mutinous conspiracy in fact existed on board of the *Somers*. . . ."

No question about it: "That such a conspiracy existed; that it had for its object the conversion of the brig into a piratical cruiser; that such an object was to be effected by the murder of the officers and faithful of the crew; and that Mr. Spencer and Small were not only parties but ringleaders in the conspiracy—appears from their own repeated and solemn declarations and from unequivocal documentary evidence."

Griffin first went over Wales's story of his talk with Spencer on the booms. He moved on to the "guilt of Cromwell" being clear from "the badness of his general character and conduct," and "the exhibition of the [Greek] paper by Mr. Spencer to Cromwell." (Norris had been at pains to cast doubt on that in his cross-examination of Midshipman Neville.)

Griffin gave Cromwell near-Satanic powers: "He was not only the officer of the deck, where the main struggle was expected, but was to act throughout as the master spirit of tumult and death; and, clothed with a sort of evil ubiquity, was to interpose his malign counsel and grant strength wherever they should most be needed." His very claim of innocence "only proves he was a more hardened offender than either Mr. Spencer or Small."

The brig itself was in league with Cromwell, he said, given how easy it would be to take, how difficult to defend. So was the crew of apprentices: "The season of youth, especially of untutored youth, is proverbially exposed to temptations. How impressive, then, must have been the mutinous appeals to the crew of the *Somers.* . . ."

"Between the arrest of Mr. Spencer and the execution, the mutinous indications were unceasing." But what about there having been no overt act? Those mutinous indications "were deep rather than loud. The fire beneath the surface which causes the earthquake, reserves for the explosion its more palpable and awful demonstrations." What about Mackenzie's trial of the three seamen being illegal under Navy rules? "He had with him a volume of nature's laws, written by the finger of God on the human heart."

Griffin was—or says he was—persuaded not only by Gansevoort's account of the terrible look Spencer gave him, but also by "the dark and portentous looks of the crew, which, like a lowering sky presaging a tornado, a seaman's eye could detect and appreciate, but which a seaman's tongue could not adequately describe."

Then on to the grandeur of the Republic. "A nation's honor was now at stake. A vessel which had been born into our naval family, and consecrated as a defender of her country's glory, and one of the protectors of the great commonwealth of civilized man, was about to be torn from her sphere, and let loose a lawless wanderer upon the deep, carrying along in her devious course, like a comet loosened from its orbit, devastation, and terror, and death. . . ."

"Suppose," Griffin asked the court, "that the *Somers*, now turned pirate, while cruising off our coast, had been permitted by Heaven, in an evil hour, to capture a vessel plying between this and Europe, freighted with the talent and beauty of the land. The men are all murdered, and the females, including perhaps the new-made wife, and maidens just blooming into womanhood, are forced to become the *brides of pirates*. . . . And where then could the commander of the *Somers* have hidden his head, branded, as it would have been, by a mark of infamy as indelible as that stamped on the forehead of Cain!"

Griffin spoke for an hour and a half, so impressing Hone that he transcribed the peroration in his diary: "The case of the *Somers* may form an epoch in our naval history. Should the course of the commander be approved by his country, mutinies will probably hereafter be of rare occurrence." A safe enough prediction, as they had been nonexistent before.

"But should this court, or the high tribunal of public opinion, pronounce sentence of condemnation on the course he felt himself bound to pursue, it is respectfully yet solemnly submitted that the sentence will be the signal for the general prevalence of insubordination in our navy. The means and subjects of mutinous excitement are always at hand, filled with men of mixed national character, crowded with spirits as turbulent as the element on which they dwell, the ship's berth deck ever abounds in materials of combustion, which a single spark may ignite. The commander must quench the flame, even if it is sometimes done by the sacrifice of life. . . .

"Discipline is the first and second and third virtue in the naval code. It was discipline, perhaps more than even courage, which during our last war with England enabled our little navy to work its miracles on the lakes and upon the ocean. . . . Let discipline for ever be regarded as its sheet-anchor; and let it never be forgotten that subordination is the life, and mutiny the death, of discipline. In this view of the subject . . . the American nation rears its august form, entreating that her youngest, her favorite, offspring, may be saved from its worst enemy—that it may be saved from the demoralizing, destructive principle of insubordination."

The audience—greatly stirred, according to Hone—began to disperse and, the transcript says, "the court was then cleared, and reading of the testimony commenced."

That took five days, and must have tried the patience of the officers, who had heard about the rush aft and Spencer on the booms for many long weeks, and now had to sit through it all over again.

ON MONDAY, MARCH 27, "the judge advocate then read the accompanying paper."

This paper was Norris's presentation of the prosecution's case. He didn't get to deliver it in front of a rapt crowd as Griffin had, but perhaps he took some satisfaction in having the last word.

He began, for the only time in the trial, by speaking of himself in the first person:

"I have an official duty to discharge, and I trust I shall be excused, in a case of such exciting interest and importance, in giving permanent form to the opinions I am thus called upon to give . . . and securing them from forgetfulness—I owe that much to myself. In discharging this task, I shall observe as much brevity as the comprehensive nature of the subject will admit. . . ."

Which might not have chimed with the court's idea of brevity, as more than ten thousand words lay ahead. The kernel of his argument, though, is simply stated: there had been no proven mutiny.

What he calls "marine police law" is at its most severe on a naval vessel, and has to be. But when it comes to executing a crew member, "the difference between public and private vessels [men of war and merchant ships] ceases in time of peace, save in one particular." In both, a death sentence must be the last resort.

The laws that govern the crew are different from any civilian ones. "The agents of a factory, the slaves on a plantation, may conspire against authority" and not meet the hangman; "but if the authority and property be national, and military or naval, the dread enforcement of implicit obedience attaches."

This means that those enforcing naval law must be more rather than less cautious in weighing a capital crime. There are exceptions: "In the case of a wreck, and two persons have hold of a plank which is sufficient to buoy only one, the right to force off the other into the sea has been allowed by law, by virtue of [the] privilege of self-preservation. It can, from necessity, consign even innocence to death."

However, "the necessity must be extreme, absolute, and impending." A naval officer "may have been separated from his consorts by stress of weather or cruising orders; no matter how innocently he is removed from the resource of a court, he cannot become a judge to try or execute an unallowed sentence. . . ."

The crewmen of a United States warship "are not the serfs of an irresponsible power. They are shielded by guaranteed privileges; guilt is not to be branded on them by imputation." The law "tells of a legally constituted court, of the right of challenging the judges, of examination and confrontment of witnesses. . . . These safeguards are covenants" in every officer's commission, "solemnly entered into by the government, and the fulfillment of which is required by the constitution."

Speaking directly to the situation on the *Somers*, he continued, "If it could be proved that a proposition in terms mutinous was a premeditated jest or amusement, no one would contend that the crime was established, though believed by its hearer."

Norris went on to cite many judicial precedents; his was a drier speech than Griffin's spread-eagle performance, except toward its end: "Arms and public ships are creatures of the law, and meant to sustain, and not to overstretch it. In no portion of the nautical population is the law so systematically inculcated as in that of the national marine. Its officers are sworn to sustain the constitution. . . . The flag of the navy a higher power than that of the constitution!!! That flag had better be lowered forever than permitted to float from so lofty a peak!"

14 **Verdicts**

On March 28, "the court met this day in pursuance of adjournment. . . . And the court being cleared, the court proceeded to consider the charges and specifications, and to make their finding thereon."

The commanders and captains had a week to reach their verdict. On Saturday, April 1, they delivered it:

> The court having heard and duly considered the evidence and testimony offered under said charges and specifications, do find—
>> That the first specification under first charge is not proved;
>> That the second specification under first charge is not proved;
>> That the third specification under first charge is not proved. . . .

So it went until all the charges were enumerated.

For all of them, "Not proved."

> The court, therefore, do acquit Commander Alexander Slidell Mackenzie of the charges and specifications preferred by the secretary of the navy against him.

*   *   *

A FEW DAYS EARLIER, Philip Hone had written, "I am not as clear as I could wish to be in my opinion of the absolute necessity of the dreadful act of discipline resorted to by Mackenzie, and for his sake, as well as for the sake of national justice, I sometimes think I should like to have evidence of some clearly overt act of mutiny."

The verdict did away with his hesitations: "The agitation of the public mind in relation to the trial of Commander Mackenzie is put to rest by the promulgation of the decision of the court-martial. The character of the navy is sustained and the majesty of the laws vindicated by the full and honorable acquittal of the accused from all the charges brought against him."

The picture wasn't quite so sunny for Mackenzie as Hone believed. Upshur made clear that "not proven" is not the same as "full and honorable" when he circulated "a copy of the official announcement of the finding of the court-martial trial in the case of Commander Mackenzie." It had appeared in the *Madisonian*, the paper that had ignited so much early debate by publishing John Spencer's "S" letter, and it ends with: "The finding, therefore, is simply *confirmed*, and carried into effect without any expression of approbation or disapprobation on the part of the President; no such expression being necessary."

In a naval court-martial, the verdict had to be approved by the navy secretary and the president. Tyler, who had no familial connections with the Navy, might have been an ideal juror on the civil trial Spencer wanted. His approval of the court's findings was about as chilly as it could be.

The trial had put Upshur in an unhappy position. Initially, the *Somers* had been a source of pride for him. When he became navy secretary, he had cast a sharp, knowledgeable eye on shipbuilding costs. The *Dolphin*, a brig launched by the Brooklyn Navy Yard a few years

before he took office, had cost $82 per ton to build; under Upshur, the *Somers*, built in the same yard, came in at just $46 per ton.

Now she was a misery to him. When Tyler's cabinet met in Washington on March 29 to discuss the *Somers* verdict, its members had asked John Canfield Spencer to recuse himself. Intransigent in most things, he was immovable on this most personal one.

Upshur, having gone through the court-martial transcripts, initially recommended approving the verdict with an "honorable acquittal." Infuriated, Spencer demanded—as he had from the start—that Mackenzie be tried for murder. The president had the legal power to reduce a court-martial sentence, and even to dismiss a guilty verdict altogether. But he was not able to put any citizen into double jeopardy.

Spencer, one of the best legal minds of his era, knew this perfectly well—and he didn't like having Tyler explain to him in the meeting "that when a man had once been fairly tried, he should not be tried again on the same charges and evidence."

Sound though Tyler's position was, his heart probably wasn't in the argument, as he too had read the transcripts, and thought Mackenzie should have been found guilty. Later he said he believed Philip Spencer had done wrong only in his "great imprudence of speech," but because his captain had been acquitted by "an able and dignified court-martial," Tyler had no choice about confirming its verdict. Then the president added, "As long as my power should last Mackenzie should never be entrusted with another command." Nor would he have "interposed an objection had Mackenzie been ordered shot."

A week later the *Madisonian* ran a brief article on the meeting: "A most absurd and ridiculous report is going the rounds of the newspapers that a personal conflict took place at a recent Cabinet meeting between Secretaries Spencer and Upshur. We assure the public that there is not the slightest foundation for such a report. There was neither a fight nor even an angry or unpleasant word between the Secretaries on that or any other occasion. The whole story is a naked fabrication."

236 | **SAILING THE GRAVEYARD SEA**

Anyone over the age of twelve who read this would immediately assume there *had* been a fight.

There had, and the newspapers were unlikely to overlook such a tangy incident. The *Lynchburg Virginian* reported that Upshur, goaded into a "glorious rage" by Spencer, had thrown a punch at him and they got into a fistfight. Perhaps the least likely account, in Philadelphia's *United States Gazette*, explained that Spencer had been taking a few moments to exercise his arms and Upshur had misunderstood this wholesome pastime as a threat. The two do seem to have been so hotly engaged that President Tyler had to jump from his chair to break up their scuffle.

What may have been the liveliest cabinet meeting in American history ended with Mackenzie losing the "honorable" from his acquittal.

For his part, Upshur was credulous enough about young Philip Spencer's claims to send a warship to investigate them. Senator Thomas Hart Benton of Missouri, one of those who believed the hangings were outright murder, wrote, "The Secretary despatched a man-of-war immediately on the return of Mackenzie to the Isle of Pines, to capture the confederate pirates (according to Wales's testimony), who were waiting there for young Spencer and the *Somers*. A bootless errand. The island was found and the pines; but no pirates! Nor news of any for nearly twenty years!"

If that mission's failure, and the dropping of "honorable," hurt the commander, there was much to draw the sting.

Some four hundred of "the most eminent citizens of Boston," said a local newspaper, marked "their approval of his noble and heroic conduct" with a laudatory letter "handsomely written on parchment" which "was transmitted to Commander Mackenzie in an elegant silver case, with an envelope of morocco."

Richard Henry Dana, loyal from the start, wrote from Boston, "I wish that, while subjected to the varying and unsatisfactory exhibitions in New York, you could have refreshed your spirit with a little of the more wholesome public breath of our peninsular city. . . . Among the educated people, in the professions, and in what we call in America the upper classes, you were (you must excuse me in the indelicacy of a direct compliment to a stranger) a hero, and not a hero of the sword, but the hero of a moral conflict."

The *Baltimore Clipper* praised citizens of that city for sending him "a pair of gold epaulettes, as a tribute of respect for his firmness and ability as an officer, and his character as a man."

The *New-York Weekly Tribune* reported that "a subscription list has been opened at the Exchange, for the purpose of raising funds to present a sword to this gallant officer. In order that it may be a general matter the subscription price is limited to $1 each." (Mackenzie would have found less gratifying the response of a *Boston Courier* reader, who wrote that although the story had described the hilt of the sword very well, there was no word about the blade: "Whether *this* weapon has a blade of steel, or of tin, or of lath, or, none at all, is left in painful doubt. Since some of our navy officers have acquired so much glory in conquering with *halters* . . . the blade might, with propriety . . . be made of *hemp*.")

Philip Hone happily told his diary that "three hundred merchants and others of our most respectable citizens . . . have raised a sum of money by subscription to pay the lawyers' fees and other charges attending the trial; but this fact is delicately kept out of view in the correspondence."

Despite Hone's griping about the British response to the mutiny, the *Boston Post* ran a letter from a Royal Navy officer on the West India station that ended: "The firmness and decision of Captain Mackenzie . . . has been much commented upon in our squadron, and we think the officer who dares to step beyond the letter of the law when circumstances require it deserves well of his country."

Henry Wadsworth Longfellow, whom Mackenzie had met through Washington Irving in Spain—and who found him "a very good fellow, with very sound sense and great love of literature"—wrote from

Cambridge, "The voice of all upright men—the common consent of all the good—is with you." In return, Mackenzie suggested that the poet consider composing an epic about the *Somers* mutiny.

A TRAGICALLY DIFFERENT RESPONSE came from Richard Lee-cock. On the evening of March 31—hours before the verdict was announced—the ship's surgeon went into the wardroom of the *Somers* and, alone there, put a pistol to his forehead above his right eye and shot himself. The *Tribune* said his suicide was the result of "a settled melancholy and a partial derangement induced by a long and severe attack of the yellow fever, which he contracted on a former voyage to the Coast of Africa in the U.S. schooner *Shark*." It is difficult to believe that was the only cause.

THROUGHOUT THE COURT-MARTIAL, the final harvest of *Somers* prisoners remained confined aboard the *North Carolina*. At first Mac-kenzie had wanted them all put on trial, but the Navy had had enough mutiny publicity for one year. Moreover, charges had yet to be brought against any of them, and one by one they went free. George Warner came from a family with some clout—his father was collector of cus-toms for the city of New York—and he was soon sprung with a writ of habeas corpus. He never went to sea again.

Nor did many of the apprentices, who, having spent months with the cat and the colt and perpetual crowded discomfort, deserted. Thirty-five of them ran off.

In the end, their captain seemed to lose interest in any further prosecutions. He left Brooklyn before the court-martial issued its verdict. His wife wrote, "My husband was allowed to return to his home after nearly four months spent in New York in scenes of daily trial such as few have known." He had done "the most painful and

stern duty . . . at the price of a personal suffering such a few could know because few have the capacity so keenly to feel."

William Norris returned to Baltimore and obscurity, leaving behind his summation of the trial: a "clear case of *fraud, management, and virtual conspiracy*."

A balladeer named Horser Clenling, "Quarter Master U. States Service," agreed, and published in the *New York Herald* a poem, forty-three quatrains long, called "The *Somers*," which reads in (very) small part:

> Come listen landsmen, one and all,
>   Come listen unto me,
> I'll make you bless your lucky stars
>   You've never gone to sea. . . .

> But what's the cause, and what's the crime,
>   That thus, in manhood's bloom,
> And without form of law, three men,
>   To such a death can doom.

> Alas! Suspicion, hate and fear,
>   And vanity, are rife;
> And a poor pride, that will not count
>   The worth of human life. . . .

> The whips are manned with pistol raised
>   The first Luff [lieutenant] bravely stands
> To guard that on the murd'rous ropes
>   Are laid unwilling hands. . . .

> The deed is done! that cruel deed—
>   "Three cheers" the captain cries,

"Three cheers" for that dark blood striped flag
That o'er us mocking flies.

A better-known voice than Quartermaster Clenling's was about to take up a similar refrain.

After he began to follow the hearing, James Fenimore Cooper had written his wife, "Mackenzie's affair looks bad enough. The report he sent to Washington is considered to be the work of a man scarcely compos mentis. I never read a more miserable thing in my life." The court martial did not change his opinion. "That the [Navy] Department has favored Mackenzie I take to be indisputable. Why was he left in command of the brig, containing all the witnesses? Every officer should have been taken out of her the instant she arrived, or the men transferred beyond their influence. The world cannot show a parallel to such stupidity, or such corruption."

Cooper knew who Mackenzie was. In 1839 he had published a history of the United States Navy in which the Battle of Lake Erie got a good deal of space (it was, after all, the only time Britain surrendered an entire fleet—and one commanded by a Trafalgar veteran). Mackenzie admired the book, but took exception to Cooper's treatment of Oliver Hazard Perry's second-in-command, Jesse Duncan Elliott: Mackenzie believed he had failed to support the commodore properly; Cooper leaned toward Elliott's side—or, at least, failed to condemn him.

This led to a quarrel between the two writers. Cooper was a great one for getting into such fights, and when he began working on an account of the *Somers* mutiny, many expected him to be as intemperate in his view as he had been in his earlier remarks.

He wasn't: one of his biographers rightly calls his "Review of the Proceedings of the Naval Court Martial" a "masterpiece of calm sanity." It was not to be a hidden masterpiece. John Spencer's son-in-law had urged Cooper to take up the mutiny as a subject, and Cooper's commentary was published with the transcript of the trial: customers couldn't get one without taking the other.

Most important among the points Cooper raised was that Norris had believed the judge advocate's case depended on his establishing "that a mutiny actually existed; second, that the parties executed were connected with it; third, that the executions were indispensable to the safety of the brig; and in the last place that every opportunity . . . was given to the men hanged to vindicate themselves. . . ."

Cooper thought this was not the "true issue. . . . The reader will see that our issue does not turn on the literal facts of the case but on the manner in which these facts, real or supposed, were presented to Captain Mackenzie."

First, though, Cooper examined several ancillary issues. He spoke of the claims that the *Somers* was too small for her officers to defend. He found them absurd:

"We see nothing to have prevented Captain Mackenzie from sending all but his officers below, of securing the gratings, and of carrying the brig across the ocean, if needed, with the quarter-deck alone." But that wouldn't have been necessary: "Captain Mackenzie was not reduced so low. All the best of his crew, the petty officers, and a seaman or two, to the number of nine, had so much of his confidence as to be armed at the crisis of the execution. . . . A rope might have been stretched across the deck, and an order given for no man to pass it unless called by name, on the pain of death. This would have prevented everything like a surprise of the quarter-deck; did that fail, Mr. Spencer's own alleged expedient, that of two of the quarter-deck guns pointed forward, loaded with canister [in effect, a bucket of musket balls that turned the cannon into a giant shotgun], would have rendered the quarter-deck of so *small* a craft, as inviolable as a sanctuary."

The Greek list only confirmed the frailty of Spencer's plan. "Taking the paper as a guide, the conspiracy is reduced, as to any serious danger, to three individuals, Spencer, Andrews, and M'Kinley. Admitting the most, or that the four who it was thought would be *induced . . . had* been so induced, the serious danger was then confined to seven! This, even admitting it to be true, does not strike us as a conspiracy to derange the propriety of a man-of-war's quarter-deck, with the ringleaders in irons and all the details in the captain's own hands!"

Cooper believed that in seizing Spencer, Mackenzie "did no more than his duty, though the *manner* of the arrest was a little too melodramatic." Too public, too showy, "and then to place him on the quarterdeck, in full view of the crew." No doubt "that much the greater portion of the ominous conversations, groupings, shakings of the head, and strange looks, which seem to have awakened so much distrust aft, had their origin in the natural wonder of the crew, at seeing an officer in this novel situation; and he, too, not only a favorite forward but one known to be the son of a minister of state."

Cooper is also scornful of Mackenzie's account of the muster where he studied Cromwell and Small and found both suspicious: "In his report Captain Mackenzie gives this extraordinary specimen of his own reasoning powers." The two men showed their guilt "by directly contrary deportment. In order to escape his distrust, a man must be neither firm nor irresolute; look frightened, nor look determined; hold his battle-axe quiet, nor pass it from hand to hand; stand erect with his muscles immovable, nor shift his weight from leg to leg; look steadily, but indifferently, across the deck, nor let his eyes wander, without looking, however, at mine!"

And the "affair of the mast." The captain "attributes the loss of his main-royal-mast to the fact that Small gave the brace a sudden jerk." Mackenzie says, "To my astonishment . . . all those *who were most conspicuously named in the programme of Mr. Spencer . . .* , no matter in what part of the vessel they might be stationed, mustered at the main-top-mast-head. . . . THE COINCIDENCE CONFIRMED THE EXISTENCE OF A DANGEROUS CONSPIRACY."

How?

Notes Cooper, "Cromwell was acting boatswain, and there is nothing surprising that he should go aloft. . . . Had he remained below, no doubt it would have been deemed a *confirmation* that he stayed on deck to profit by circumstances by seizing the vessel. . . . As for Small, he was captain of the main-top, and if any one was to go aloft, *he* clearly ought to have been there."

At this crisis, Mackenzie noticed that "'the eye of Mr. Spencer travelled perpetually to the mast-head, and cast thither many of those *strange* and *stealthy* glances which I had heretofore noticed.' . . . Can anything be more violent than the inference as to Mr. Spencer's motive? He was at sea, seated on an arm-chest, in irons, with nothing to do, and nothing but the vacant ocean to gaze at outward. . . . A mast is carried away in full view of him, and it is thought extraordinary that he sought the very natural relief of gazing at what was going on!"

As for the council of officers, and their unanimous conclusion that the three men be hanged: "Under ordinary circumstances, there would be great force in the argument." Not in this case. "The *Somers* was sent to sea with too much the character of a family yacht." The purser and the surgeon "would be men of unusually decided characters to venture opinions opposed to those of the sea-officers," and four of those five officers "were just of an age to render them active assistants in quelling a physical attempt to seize a vessel, but to render them questionable counsellors."

Moreover, "it is in proof that three members of this council were of opinion of the necessity of the execution as early as the 28th." They would surely have tried to persuade the others "of what they already believed, as to obtaining the truth. When this bias was left to act on a tribunal before which *the accused had not even a hearing*, it is easy to imagine its effect. . . ."

He derides the "exhaustion of the officers, as a reason for the necessity of the execution." What was there to get so exhausted about? "These gentlemen were in watch and watch; so too are thousands of others daily. We have ourselves, at a tender age too, been watch and watch for weeks and weeks, and had our rest broken night after night" and didn't hang anybody.

Cooper goes on, pointing out many flaws and contradictions in the testimony, but his judgment on the actions of Gansevoort and Mackenzie is less harsh than his preceding observations might suggest.

The rush aft and the rest of it "might justify Mr. Gansevoort in believing a crisis had come, *under his previous impressions*, though we think the impressions themselves to have been insufficiently sustained. The conduct of Mr. Gansevoort, *always allowing for his impressions*, was spirited and good."

Clearly Cooper felt more warmly toward the first lieutenant than he did toward the captain, whose "mental obliquity, so very obvious throughout the whole affair, renders an ordinary analysis of human motives exceedingly precarious." Yet Mackenzie had acted on his beliefs; he did not have to prove that a mutiny existed, only to "show that such a case was presented to him, as JUSTIFIED him in BELIEVING in all the facts." Cooper feels this may lift from him the stigma of murder. But not by much. "God alone can say how far any selfish feeling was mixed up with the mistakes of this terrible transaction. The act was, unquestionably, one of high moral courage, one of the basest coward-ice, one of deep guilt, or one of lamentable deficiency of judgment."

WHILE HE WAS PONDERING his "Review," Cooper wrote, "I regard the affair of the *Somers* as one of the darkest spots on the national escutcheon." He might have held a still harsher opinion had he lived to be ninety-four and then (which is less likely) read the autobiography of Thurlow Weed, published in 1883.

In it, Weed tells of learning something about the council of offi-cers aboard the *Somers* that came out in neither the inquiry nor the court-martial.

A few days after the *Somers* docked in Brooklyn, he stayed over at Philadelphia on his way back from New York to Washington. There he met Hunn Gansevoort, Guert's cousin who had just been turned away when he tried to visit the brig. "Both of these officers were from Albany, where I had known them in their boyhood. Of course the *Somers* affair formed the staple of our conversation."

Hunn told Weed he'd spent the previous evening with his cousin. The two had a long talk, "and at a late hour, and after much hesitation," Guert had "made a revelation" to Hunn "which he thought proper to make to me as a friend of them and their families. That revelation, as literally as I can remember it, was as follows:—"

After the council had finished with its last witness, said Guert, "I went on deck and informed Captain Mackenzie that the testimony was not as strong as had been represented to him, and that I thought from the indications the court did not attach much importance to it. Captain Mackenzie replied that the witnesses had not been thoroughly examined, and directed me to recall them, and put certain interrogations to them, a copy of which he handed to me."

Gansevoort took the list to the wardroom and presented the new questions. They "elicited nothing more specific than the first examination had brought out. Some general conversation after the conclusion of the testimony satisfied me that the court was not prepared to convict the accused."

Gansevoort went back up on deck "and expressed my opinion to Captain Mackenzie, who replied that it was evident these young men had wholly misapprehended the nature of the evidence, if they had not also misapprehended the aggravated character of the offense, and that there would be no security for the lives of officers or protection to commerce if an example was not made in a case so flagrant as this. It was my duty, he urged, to impress these views upon the court. I returned and did, by impressing these considerations, obtain a reluctant conviction of the accused."

The day after confiding this news to Weed, Hunn Gansevoort set sail aboard the 10-gun schooner USS *Grampus*, and died that March when the ship went down with all hands in a gale off Charleston.

He had left behind an anxious Weed when the two parted. "I was greatly disturbed as to the course I ought to pursue in reference to this painful revelation. The father of Midshipman Spencer, Hon. J. C. Spencer, was then Secretary of War. We had been for several years intimately associated in public life, and were warm personal friends. I was to meet him in Washington, and the question with me was whether the above statement ought or ought not to be laid before him."

Weed still hadn't made up his mind when he called at Spencer's home. He turned out not to have to, as "the servant, who took my card, returned saying Mr. Spencer was engaged." Friends or not, Washington was Washington, and politics stood in the way of the visit. The servant's message could not have been a complete surprise to Weed; he said that recently a colleague had written him warning he had "become so obnoxious to the President that my appearance in Washington would seriously embarrass him (Spencer) and to request me not to come there." So Spencer "declined to see me, thus depriving himself of the opportunity of proving at the court of inquiry, subsequently held on Captain Mackenzie, that his son had been unjustly executed."

The next summer found Weed in Boston where, visiting the receiving ship *Ohio*, he ran into Guert, and asked him to dinner. In the mellow gaslight of the Tremont House the two shared a bottle of champagne, and "the sad fate of his kinsman was spoken of." Weed "remarked that I had passed the evening with him previous to sailing from Philadelphia, adding that we sat gossiping over our hot whiskey punch into the small hours. The lieutenant, with evident surprise, asked with emphasis, 'Did he tell you that I passed the previous night with him?' I answered in the affirmative. He said, 'What else did he tell you?' I replied, with equal emphasis, 'He told me all that you said to him about the trial of Spencer.' Whereupon he looked thoughtfully a moment, then drank off his champagne, seized or raised the bottle, again filled his glass and emptied it, and, without further remark, left the table."

Weed finished his champagne alone and did not see Gansevoort again for seven years—"seven years which had told fearfully on his heath and habits. In the last years of his life he was stationed at the Brooklyn Navy Yard, then a sad wreck of his former self, he came frequently to see me, but was always moody, taciturn, and restless."

That may overstate the case. Gansevoort did spend the rest of his career in the Navy. He served with distinction at the siege of Veracruz during the war with Mexico, and in 1856, commanding the sloop-of-war *Decatur,* helped hold Seattle against a Native American force two thousand strong. Yet that same year, at Mare Island, California, no less a figure than David Glasgow Farragut suspended him for being drunk at eleven o'clock in the morning.

The next year he asked the secretary of the navy for "the Command of any sea going ship," but instead was posted to the Brooklyn Navy Yard. Early in the Civil War he performed the valuable service of plucking from the gunboat *Dacotah* two big Dahlgren cannon and putting them in the inaugural Union ironclad *Monitor.* Shortly after, he got command of the steam sloop-of-war *Adirondack.* He ran her aground on a rocky shore; nobody died but the sloop was destroyed. A court of inquiry acquitted him; the secretary of the navy rejected the finding. The subsequent court-martial found the specification "not proved."

But he never held another seagoing command before he died in 1868. Weed wrote of Gansevoort and the *Somers* mutiny, "In my conversations with him I never again referred to this affair, nor do I know that he ever spoke of it to others. But I do know that a bright, intelligent, high principled, and sensitive gentleman, and a most promising officer of the navy, spent the best part of his life a prey to unavailing remorse for an act the responsibility of which belonged to a superior officer."

As for that officer, Weed absolved him of one failing and replaced it with something worse. "I never coincided in the opinion which attributed the execution to cowardice on the part of Captain Mackenzie. I could not then and cannot now resist the belief that he was influenced by ambition for the *éclat* which would follow the hanging of a son of the Secretary of War as a pirate."

Like his first lieutenant, Commander (his rank for the rest of his days) Mackenzie had trouble getting back to sea. Despite being acquitted by his court-martial, he was soon relieved of command of the *Somers*. Back in Tarrytown, he revised a popular biography he had written of Oliver Hazard Perry, and wrote one about Stephen Decatur. He began a book about his travels in Ireland, but never finished it.

The Mexican War again brought him, briefly, a command of his own: the steam frigate *Mississippi*—the vessel that would later carry his brother-in-law to Japan.

In 1848 the war was over, and Mackenzie returned to Tarrytown, where he wrote in the mornings and liked to go riding in the afternoons. On September 13, when he rode back to his front door, a stable hand came to take the horse and discovered the commander still upright in the saddle but dead of a heart attack. He was forty-five years old.

ALEXANDER SLIDELL MACKENZIE had survived the *Somers* by a year and a half.

In the winter of 1846, the brig was patrolling the Mexican coast off Veracruz under the command of Raphael Semmes. She was still capable of all the speed that had recommended her to Philip Spencer as a pirate, and so, Semmes wrote, was "a very efficient blockader. . . . As the season of northers had now arrived, it was our practice to get under-way every morning at daylight, stand 'off and on' in front of the city during the day, and toward sunset, run in to anchorage again."

The *Somers* had been following this routine for forty-five days when, shortly after sunrise on the eighth of December, with the barometer sharply falling, Semmes made for the harbor. The brig had nearly reached her anchorage when the lookout shouted, "Sail-ho!" Semmes put his glass to his eye and saw what he was sure (he turned out to be right) was a blockade runner.

"I immediately abandoned my intention of anchoring, as the gale had not yet set in, and hauling on a wind, under topsails and courses, commenced beating up the passage, a second time. . . ."

The storm came on. "Lieutenant Parker took the mainsail off her, and had got the spanker about half brailed up, when the squall struck us. It did not appear to be very violent, nor was its approach accompanied by any foaming of the water, or other indications which usually mark the approach of heavy squalls. But the brig being flying-light, having scarcely any water or provisions, and but six tons of ballast on board, she was thrown over almost instantly."

Semmes ordered the helm put over, but "the brig was on her beam-ends and the water pouring into every hatch and scuttle." With the masts lying horizontal on the sea, Semmes ordered them cut away.

There was no time. "A few moments more, and I was convinced, in spite of all our exertions, the brig must inevitably go down. . . . I gave the order, 'Every man save himself who can!' whereupon there was a simultaneous plunge into the sea of about sixty officers and men, each striving to secure some frail object that had drifted from the wreck. . . . Some reached a grating, some an oar, some a boat's mast, some a hen-coop . . . but many poor fellows sprang into the sea, to perish in a few minutes. . . ."

Thirty-six of the *Somers*'s eighty-man crew went down with the vessel; two had been aboard her under Captain Mackenzie. Semmes, a strong swimmer, made it to the buoyant grating of an arms chest. That was good luck for him, but not for what was then his navy. In the years to come, he would command the fearsomely successful Confederate commerce raider *Alabama*, taking sixty-five ships valued at $6 million—$104 million in today's money.

When George Templeton Strong learned of the sinking, he wrote in his diary on December 30, 1846, "The *Somers* capsized in a squall and sunk—many lives lost." Then, looking back across four years, Strong added, "I always predicted that brig would come to no good end."

AFTER THE COURT-MARTIAL ENDED, and reporters had begun seeking other objects of fascination to pester, few of Mackenzie's fellow officers would speak of the *Somers*. Acquittal or not, the hangings sent a current of shame through the Navy for more than a generation.

The apprentice system the brig had sought to establish was quickly and quietly abandoned.

So is there anything hopeful to be taken away from this doleful story? Any brightwork clinging to the drowned timbers of the *Somers*?

Perhaps.

That the mutiny was considered a forbidden topic in naval circles did not mean it was forgotten, or that nobody tried to find lessons in it.

Some in the service had been calling for an academy since as early as 1814. In 1845 the Navy got a new secretary. George Bancroft was a scholar, a historian, and a fervent nationalist. He knew all about the cruise of the *Somers*, and as soon as he took up his post he managed to talk the secretary of war into letting him have Fort Severn in Maryland, which, built to defend the river of the same name during the War of 1812, had been decaying ever since.

Fort Severn was in a town called Annapolis. By the end of the year Bancroft had seven teachers instructing fifty-six midshipmen inside the abandoned works, which now housed the United States Naval Academy.

In almost exactly a century this long-opposed institution would prove itself the seedbed of the mightiest navy the world has ever known.

Epilogue

THE HISTORIAN FREDRIC SMOLER, who has made a study of mutinies in the British navy, writes, "In both the Royal and American
navies mutiny was a very loosely defined capital crime. Any resistance
to authority—indeed, any show or even shadow of resistance—was
prohibited, and in theory punishable by death. This meant that here
was no clear and indisputable line between mutiny, insubordination or
even silent insolence, since a man could in theory be guilty of 'dumb
mutiny,' and hang for it. The world the crime of mutiny implied was
impossible, and the problem of sanely policing departures from an
impossible world called for excellent judgment and profound sanity.
A remarkable number of naval officers possessed these qualities—but
not all of them did."

For all his copious explanations of why he had to hang three
men, Commander Mackenzie's behavior remains a mystery. Many
who knew the man described him as "tenderhearted," and yet the
record of floggings during his school cruise—while not violating
naval law—appalled several more senior officers even in that harsher
world. As captain, Mackenzie's vigilance against disorder—from drink

("more dreadful than malaria") to spitting on the deck—could be backed up by a then-customary violence that seems barbarous to twenty-first-century eyes.

The execution tourism of his Spanish days, although presented in the best possible light (since he was doing the presenting), feels stranger. And his account of the *Somers* executions carries a scent of the same enthusiasm, of a liking for theatrical death.

There may have been another element in what happened on that mortal cruise. Thurlow Weed ended the account of his talk with Guert Gansevoort in the Tremont House by giving his own theory of the hangings. It is unique.

Some believed the executions raw murder, and some saw them as a heroic stroke. History has yet to reconcile these views, but with the single, surprising word *éclat* Weed proposed that Commander Mackenzie had another motive: he was showing off.

Here was a man of such ironclad vanity that, even while embroiled in a court-martial, he could write the secretary of the navy instructing him about what to do, going on not only to remind Upshur of the honor Mackenzie had bestowed on his brother with his book dedication but declaring that the honor had been undeserved. He never doubted his own righteousness.

Mackenzie held the Navy in near-religious regard—remember his rapturous description of seeing that US ship of the line—and spent his life surrounded by naval heroes. He lived in a thicket of Perrys.

And he had found himself running a school ship at a time when all the Atlantic world was at suffocating peace. Never mind that his well-received travel book sailed aboard every American warship, or that he had a genuine interest in naval education—true achievement could come only from getting alongside a British frigate and hammering it out muzzle to muzzle.

With his great coup on Lake Erie, Mackenzie's brother-in-law Oliver Hazard Perry had instantly won lasting fame. But how to equal that when the British frigate is your ally? When your main duty is to keep adolescents from drowning? When your only waterborne foe is a squalid, fleeing slave-ship?

You would need to strike a blow impressive enough to echo across all the drearily quiescent seas. Well, putting down a mutiny would have a good deal of shine to it—especially for someone with the serene confidence that nothing *he* did could ever justify any shipboard discontent—and this one had been instigated by the son of one of the highest counsels in the land.

Dispensing with such a well-connected malcontent (who had also called him "a damned old granny") would surely reflect the audacity of a Decatur, a John Paul Jones. Boldness, determination, initiative, reverence for the service—all these would be revealed by such an audacious act.

If any of that went into his calculations, it paid off. He returned home to celebrity.

Only for a little while, though. In the few years left to him after the cruise of the *Somers*, Mackenzie found himself living in a navy where his most notable deed was a matter of embarrassment: not discussed, seldom even mentioned. And after he'd replied to the many well-wishers who congratulated him on the outcome of the court-martial, he rarely brought it up either, and he never wrote about it.

The military laurels that had eluded him went to one of his three sons. The two younger spent their lives in the Navy, both rising to a higher rank than their father had reached. But the eldest, Ranald Slidell Mackenzie, joined the engineering corps and made such a success of himself during the Civil War that Ulysses Grant called him "the most promising young officer in the Union Army."

He had a hard war. He was there for most of the eastern battles, and got wounded six times—a Rebel bullet took away two of his fingers at Petersburg—and was cited seven times for gallantry.

After Appomattox, he went west, where he served with General Philip Sheridan fighting Indians, who came to call him "Bad Hand," both for the missing fingers and for his skill as a warrior. He defeated the Comanche in Texas in 1872 and, a year later during the Red River War, beat the Comanche, Kiowa, and Cheyenne at the battle of Palo Duro Canyon.

Sent to avenge George Armstrong Custer after Little Big Horn, he captured the famous Sioux chief Red Cloud, and went on to put down the Utes and the Arizona Apaches. At twenty-four he had been the youngest brevet brigadier general in Grant's army; at forty-two he became the youngest brigadier in the Regular Army.

His troops didn't warm to him; they called him (and perhaps we see a trace of his father here) the "Perpetual Punisher." All his superiors, however, liked the results he got in the field, and he surely would have kept rising in his service. But his many wounds had told on him, and there was worse: the awful effects of tertiary syphilis robbed him first of his reason, and then, in 1889, of his life.

John Canfield Spencer, having triggered the reaction against Mackenzie with his "S" letter, seems to have kept his own counsel throughout all that followed. For such an influential backstage figure during the *Somers* hearings, he is bafflingly aloof.

No later remarks of his on the death of his son have come to light, but his anger at President Tyler for not somehow forcing another trial seems to have festered. He had other quarrels with the president. Tyler had moved him over to the secretaryship of the Treasury when, in 1843, the *New York Evening Post* reported that a final split with the administration had come from "Mr. Spencer's declining to deposit $100,000 as secret service money with a confidential agent in New York, for the purpose of fitting out a naval expedition against Mexico."

Spencer twice refused. A Northerner in an increasingly Southern-leaning government, he was dead set against his country's seizing Texas, and resigned over it.

He went home to New York and practiced law until his death in 1855.

*   *   *

DURING THE YEARS AHEAD, the *Somers* story, like the planks of long-sunken wrecks that sometimes swim briefly to the surface, kept returning to visibility.

In 1889, Gail Hamilton (the pseudonym of the popular writer Mary Abigail Dodge) published in the long-lived *Cosmopolitan* magazine a three-part article under the forthright title "The Murder of Philip Spencer."

She was tougher on Commander Mackenzie than even Cooper had been. The senior Spencer has a hero's role in the article: "The horrible news broke upon him and upon all the world at once. It was only on Saturday that the messenger brought it. There were no telegrams, no premonitory, preparatory hints. His boy was hanged—had been a fortnight dead. That was the first hint as well as the first announcement. Under the shadow of this ghastly fact, the father examined the papers presented by the man who had hung him. His iron nerves did not fail. His clear mind caught the case instantly.

"By Tuesday he had mastered the legal points leading up to the execution at sea; he had discerned the carefully laid machinery to justify that execution . . . ; and he was ready to speak, and did speak, for his lost son.

"Nor did he forget that son's humble companions. With a calmness which, under the circumstances, was marvelous; with a trust in his country's sense of right which, considering the issue is most pathetic; with a self command which cannot be too much commended,—he sought not to pervert or to prejudice the truth, but to stem the current of falsehood; not to prevent a severe, but to stay a hasty judgment; not to avert but to secure justice."

Hamilton calls his appeal "vain," and goes on to brush against Weed's *éclat* theory: "Was it that there was something so captivating to the American people in the idea of hanging the son of a Cabinet officer, that they utterly refused to be balked by so unimportant a question as whether he deserved hanging?"

Nowhere in Hamilton's long and thorough article does she doubt Mackenzie's culpability, as "his unvarying habit was to assume a theory of the mutiny, and then to swear it before the court as if it were a fact. He had a theory in his own mind that these boys were planning murder, and on oath before the court he speaks exactly as if the plan of murder were proven. . . ."

She begins with a rallying cry: "In the name of truth, which is eternal; of justice to the dead, which is the highest duty that can devolve upon the living; the verdict of history should be reversed, and everywhere it should be told and known that Philip Spencer and his two companions were illegally and unjustifiably put to death, absolutely innocent of the crimes wherewith they were charged." She fiercely and eloquently defends this rhetorical promontory throughout all three installments. It is an impressive performance.

Strangely—the story having lain fallow for so long—another popular monthly, the *American Magazine*, had, exactly a year before, published an article called "The Mutiny on the *Somers*," by a Lieutenant H. D. Smith. Like Hamilton, Smith did his research, but he came to a completely different conclusion: "Commander Mackenzie was not a man to flinch in the hour of danger or emergency. He had carefully studied the situation, and he adopted what appeared to him the best and most politic course . . . the safety of the vessel requiring . . . immediate execution." Smith was hoping to efface what he saw as James Fenimore Cooper's scurrilous assessment of the mutiny, in which "with his fertile brain and biting sarcasm [he] wrote a scathing article and review of the case, handling Mackenzie in an exasperating manner."

Wrote Charles Roberts Anderson in 1940: "It seems more than probable that [Herman] Melville read these accounts of a sea-tragedy in which his intimate kinsman Guert Gansevoort had played a leading and somewhat ambiguous role, and that he found in them at least the germ of his novelette *Billy Budd*." Anderson was one of the first movers of the Melville revival that began in the early 1920s and is still going strong.

Some of those early Melville scholars thought the *Somers* was the primary source for *Billy Budd*; he had been working on it when the two articles appeared. This conviction has waned in recent years: the book takes place aboard not an American brig but a British ship of the line; Billy Budd hangs for actually—if inadvertently—killing the evil master-at-arms Claggart; and there is little in Billy's sweet nature to suggest Philip Spencer's moody, contrary one.

But Melville did know a lot about the *Somers* business. It was a family matter, after all. In *White-Jacket*, during his denunciation of the Articles of War, he writes that "these bloodthirsty laws" are enforced even in time of peace, and asks, "What happened to . . . those three sailors, even as you, who once were alive, but are now dead? 'Shall suffer death!' those were the three words that hung those three sailors."

In the next chapter, he returns to the *Somers*. The "well-known case of a United States brig" is "a memorable example, which at any moment may be repeated. Three men, in a time of peace, were then hung at the yard-arm, merely because, in the captain's judgment, it became necessary to hang them."

Nearly half a century after writing those lines, Melville mentioned the *Somers* directly in *Billy Budd*. "Not unlikely," he says, that the men who hanged Billy "were brought to something more or less akin to that harassed frame of mind which in the year 1842 actuated the commander of the U.S. brig-of-war *Somers* to resolve, under the so-called Articles of war, Articles modeled upon the English Mutiny act, to resolve upon the execution at sea of a midshipman and two sailors as mutineers designing the seizure of the brig. Which resolution was carried out though in a time of peace and within not many days' sail of home. An act vindicated by a naval court of inquiry subsequently convened ashore. History, and here cited without comment."

That lack of comment feels much like the one President Tyler seems to have forced on Navy Secretary Upshur.

Melville was also thinking of the *Somers* in a book of poems he published in 1888, *John Marr and Other Sailors*. In it he writes of "Tom Tight," by which he means "tight-lipped." Tom is his cousin Guert, the lieutenant who would never talk about what had happened aboard his ship:

> *Tom was lieutenant in the brig-o'war famed*
> *When an officer was hung for an arch-mutineer,*
> *But a mystery cleaved, and the captain was blamed,*
> *And a rumpus too raised, though his honour it was clear.*
> *And Tom he would say, then the mousers would try him,*
> *And with cup after cup o' Burgundy ply him,*
> *"Gentlemen, in vain your wassail you beset,*
> *For the more I tipple, the tighter I do get,"*
> *No blabber, no, not even with the can [of drink]—*
> *True to himself and loyal to his clan.*

Ninety years after Tom Tight made his appearance, Samuel Eliot Morison, in *Old Bruin*, his fine 1967 biography of Commodore Matthew Perry, devoted a good deal of space to the *Somers*.

He has no doubt whatever of the justice meted out by the council of officers and the captain who convened it. He says the fallen mainmast could not have been an accident: "Every yachtsman knows that if you tauten a vang and let out the mainsheet you risk breaking the gaff, and that shrouds too taut may break a wooden mast. It is inconceivable that an old seaman like Small could have hauled in and belayed the weather brace accidentally, especially when ordered to do the contrary, and when the ship was rolling leeward."

This is a point that few land-bound writers would be eager to argue with Rear Admiral Morison. But the mast did go up again and resume its work, and after its collapse and the rush aft, nobody raised a hand against the ship or its officers.

Morison holds that those who criticize Mackenzie are "the malignant and the sentimental." To him, Cooper was both: "In his 81-page *Review of the Proceedings of the Naval Court Martial* . . . he used every argument good or bad to prove Mackenzie to be a jittery, incompetent martinet. He sneered that *Somers* was more of a 'family yacht' than a man-of-war, and boasted how he himself could have handled the situation better. Cooper flattered himself that his tract would 'finish' Mackenzie as a naval officer, which it certainly did not. It should have finished Cooper as a competent authority on naval affairs." And as for Philip Spencer, "he was a prototype of what nowadays is called a 'young punk.'"

Morison believed the *Somers* controversy returns to public attention "every few years," with those promoting Cooper's view using "arguments and innuendoes of the sort which have become familiar in discussions of Pearl Harbor and the assassination of President Kennedy." That is, conspiracy theory peddlers.

So the *Somers* sails on through the squalls of an argument that cannot be settled.

Herman Melville gave his book *White-Jacket* the subtitle *The World in a Man-of-War*. He meant just that: a ship is its own world, carrying with it always the idiosyncrasies and unknowable corners and reckless passions of the world itself.

"Outwardly regarded," he writes, "our craft is a lie; for all that is outwardly seen of it is the clean-swept deck, and oft-painted planks comprised above the waterline; whereas, the vast mass of our fabric, with all its store-rooms of secrets, forever slides along far under the surface."

Acknowledgments

THE SOLITARY WRITER is as much a myth as Paul Bunyan. It would be hard (and, for me, impossible) to write anything without being supported by extensive underpinnings: the goodwill of friends who collude with me in believing that writing a book is actually legitimate *work*, and the enthusiastic—and, when it matters, tactful—support of my wife, Carol, who until recently ran the division of the Hearst Corporation that included the magazines *Esquire*, *Town and Country*, *Elle*, and *Harper's Bazaar*. This calling not only had the advantage of allowing her to dress like a movie star; it also kept me in undeserved comfort while I soldiered my way through the tiny, eye-scarring print of 150-year-old trial transcripts. I am fortunate, too, in my agent, Farley Chase, who, when I wrote a long bleat about my favorite Greenwich Village restaurant closing, in a dazzling coup found the piece a home in something like four hours.

And of course there is the publisher. I was wonderfully lucky to have washed up on the shores of Scribner, in large ways and small (I am the only writer I know who has never had occasion to complain about his dust jacket design). Its peerless copy department has once more gently saved me from many humiliating gaffes: Mark LaFlaur, for instance, showed saintly patience as I repeatedly spelled Churchill C. Cambreleng's name in many different ways, but never the right one.

My editor, Colin Harrison, is simply the very best I've ever had the privilege of working with; and so it's no surprise that his lieutenant, Emily Polson, is swift, smart, efficient, and always responds to my e-mails in a matter of minutes.

I must make one more acknowledgment. Not long after I submitted this manuscript to Colin, I read *Stolen Words*, Thomas Mallon's 1989 study of plagiarism, which is both fascinating and very funny. (Of a nineteenth-century scholar praising the British novelist and dramatist—and plagiarist—Charles Reade, Mallon writes, ". . . the professor, in a ghastly foreshadowing of the language of his present-day successors in academe, urged readers to 'bear in mind . . . Mr. Reade's allotropic modification of the story.'") *Stolen Words* is also scary, at least for writers.

Mallon quotes Thomas Pynchon as saying that this specialized thievery is "a fascinating topic. . . . As in the penal code, there are degrees. These range from plagiarism down to only being derivative, but all are forms of wrong procedure." This set off an uneasy stirring in my mind about the present book's title.

I had originally been planning to call it *A Rough Passage*, but everyone at Scribner thought that was pretty drab, and so it became *Sailing the Graveyard Sea*. And what was worrying me were those last two words. I used them in the text thinking, if I thought about it at all, that "graveyard sea" was a nineteenth-century phrase. But now, having had Pynchon brought to mind, I remembered his first novel, *V*, which came out in 1963, when I was sixteen. I had read it with great admiration, if far from complete comprehension, and part of the book seemed to have stayed with me in some barnacle-encrusted depth of my consciousness. This was a song that begins:

The eyes of a New York woman
Are the twilit side of the moon,
Nobody knows what goes on back there
Where it's always late afternoon.

And ends:

Dead as the leaves in Union Square,
Dead as the graveyard sea,
The eyes of a New York woman
Are never going to cry for me.

I went to the internet and tried to find other examples of that phrase. There are none (save, oddly enough, in a video game). Paul Valéry wrote a poem called "The Graveyard by the Sea" (*Le Cimetière marin*), but of course that isn't the same thing at all. As far as I can tell, "graveyard sea" is Pynchon's and Pynchon's alone.

So, I want to thank Mr. Pynchon for my title.

Bibliography

Anderson, Charles Roberts. "The Genesis of Billy Budd." *American Literature*, November 1940.

Beach, Edward L. *The United States Navy: 200 Years*. Henry Holt, 1986.

Benton, Thomas Hart. *Thirty Years View: or, A History of the Working of the American Government for Thirty Years, from 1820 to 1850*. D. Appleton, 1883.

Berube, Claude. *On Wide Seas: The U.S. Navy in the Jacksonian Era*. University of Alabama Press, 2021.

Brown, David S. *The First Populist: The Defiant Life of Andrew Jackson*. Scribner, 2022.

Caldwell, Mark. *New York Night: The Mystique and Its History*. Scribner, 2005.

Chapelle, Howard I. *The History of the American Sailing Navy: The Ships and Their Development*. W. W. Norton, 1949.

Cordingly, David. *Under the Black Flag: The Romance and Reality of Life among the Pirates*. Random House, 1996.

Dana, Richard Henry, Jr. *The Journal of Richard Henry Dana, Jr.* Edited by Robert F. Lind. 3 vols. Harvard University Press, 1968.

Delgado, James P. "Rediscovering the *Somers*." *Naval History*, March/April 1994.

Dolin, Eric Jay. *Black Flags, Blue Waters: The Epic History of America's Most Notorious Pirates*. Liveright, 2018.

Duban, James. *Melville's Major Fiction: Politics, Theology, and Imagination*. Aquiline, 2017.

Egan, Hugh. "The Mackenzie Court-Martial Trial: Cooper's Secret Correspondence with William H. Norris." *Studies in the American Renaissance*, 1990.

Ellms, Charles. *The Pirates Own Book, or Authentic Narratives of the Lives, Exploits, and Executions of the Most Celebrated Sea Robbers*. Marine Research Society, 1924.

Feuer, A. B. "A Question of Mutiny." *Naval History*, March/April 1994.

Franklin, Wayne. *James Fenimore Cooper: The Early Years*. Yale University Press, 2007.

———. *James Fenimore Cooper: The Later Years*. Yale University Press, 2017.

Gilje, Paul A. *To Swear Like a Sailor: Maritime Culture in America, 1750–1850*. Cambridge University Press, 2016.

Glenn, Myra C. *Jack Tar's Story: The Autobiographies and Memoirs of Sailors in Antebellum America*. Cambridge University Press, 2010.

Goldberg, Angus Ephraim. "The *Somers* Mutiny of 1842." PhD thesis, University of St Andrews, Edinburgh, 2000.

Gouverneur, Marian. *As I Remember: Recollections of American Society during the Nineteenth Century*. D. Appleton, 1911.

Guttridge, Leonard F. *Mutiny: A History of Naval Insurrection*. Naval Institute Press, 1993.

Hall, Claude H. *Abel Parker Upshur: Conservative Virginian, 1790–1844*. State Historical Society of Wisconsin, 1964.

Hamilton, Gail. "The Murder of Philip Spencer." *Cosmopolitan*, June, July, and August, 1889.

Harland, John. *Seamanship in the Age of Sail: An Account of Shiphandling of the Sailing Man-o'-War, 1600–1860*. Naval Institute Press, 2016.

Hayford, Harrison. *The* Somers *Mutiny Affair*. Prentice-Hall, 1959.

Hone, Philip. *The Diary of Philip Hone, 1828–1851*. Dodd, Mead, 1927.

Howe, David. "Essay on the Legal Aspects of *Somers* Affair." Naval History and Heritage Command (website), 2020.

King, Dean, with John B. Hattendorf and J. Worth Estes. *A Sea of Words*. Henry Holt, 2002.

Langley, Harold D. *Social Reform in the United States Navy, 1798–1862*. University of Illinois Press, 1967.

Leyda, Jay. *The Melville Log: A Documentary Life of Herman Melville, 1819–1891*. 2 vols. Harcourt Brace, 1951.

Mackenzie, Alexander Slidell. *The American in England by the Author of "A Year in Spain."* Richard Bentley, 1836.

———. *Spain Revisited*. 2 vols. Richard Bentley, 1836.

———. *A Year in Spain by a Young American*. 3rd ed. 3 vols. Harper and Brothers, 1836.

McFarland, Philip. *Sea Dangers: The Affair of the* Somers. Schocken, 1985.

Melton, Buckner F., Jr. *A Hanging Offense: The Strange Affair of the Warship* Somers. Free Press, 2003.

Melville, Herman. *Billy Budd, Sailor (An Inside Narrative)*. Edited by Harrison Hayford and Merton M. Sealts, Jr. University of Chicago Press, 1962.

———. *Redburn: His First Voyage*. Edited by Raymond M. Weaver. Albert & Charles Boni, 1924.

———. *White-Jacket, or The World in a Man-of-War*. Modern Library, 2002.

Mercier, Henry James. *Life in a Man-of-War, or Scenes in "Old Ironsides" during her Cruise in the Pacific. By a Fore-Top-Man*. Lydia R. Bailey, 1841.

Minnigerode, Meade. *The Fabulous Forties, 1840–1850*. G. P. Putnam's Sons, 1924.

Morison, Samuel Eliot. *"Old Bruin": Commodore Matthew C. Perry, 1794–1858*. Little, Brown, 1967.

Nordhoff, Charles. *Man-of-War Life*. Seaforth, 2013.

Parker, Hershel. *Herman Melville: A Biography, Volume I, 1819–1851*. Johns Hopkins University Press, 1996.

———. *Herman Melville: A Biography, Volume II, 1851–1891*. Johns Hopkins University Press, 2002.

Parker, William Harwar. *Recollections of a Naval Officer, 1841–1865*. Charles Scribner's Sons, 1883.

Pope, Dudley. *The Black Ship*. J. B. Lippincott Co., 1964.

Proceedings of the Court of Inquiry Appointed to Inquire into the Intended Mutiny on Board the United States Brig of War Somers, *on the High Seas; Held on Board the United States Ship* North Carolina *Lying at the Navy Yard, New-York; with a Full Account of the Execution of Spencer, Cromwell and Small, on Board Said Vessel; Reported for "The New-York Tribune."* Greeley & McElrath, 1843.

Proceedings of the Naval Court Martial in the Case of Alexander Slidell Mackenzie, a Commander in the Navy of the United States, &c Including the Charges and Specifications of Charges Prepared against Him by the Secretary of the Navy. To Which Is Annexed, an Elaborate Review by James Fennimore [sic] Cooper. Henry G. Langley, 1844.

"Recollections of an Old Stager: The *Somers* Tragedy." *Harper's New Monthly*, April 1873.

Rogers, Robert C. "Reminiscences of Philip Spencer and the Brig *Somers*." *United Service*, July 1890.

Semmes, Raphael. *Service Afloat and Ashore during the Mexican War.* Wm. H. Moore, 1851.

Slifer, H. Seger, and Hiram L. Kennicott, eds. *Centennial History and Biographical Directory of the Chi Psi Fraternity.* Chi Psi Fraternity, 1941.

———. *The Chi Psi Story.* Chi Psi Fraternity, 1951.

Springer, Haskell, ed. *America and the Sea: A Literary History.* University of Georgia Press, 1995.

Strong, George Templeton. *The Diary of George Templeton Strong: Young Man in New York, 1835–1849.* Edited by Allan Nevins and Milton Halsey Thomas. Macmillan, 1952.

Tucker, Spencer. *Arming the Fleet: U.S. Navy Ordnance in the Muzzle-Loading Era.* Naval Institute Press, 1989.

Valle, James E. *Rocks and Shoals: Order and Discipline in the Old Navy, 1800–1861.* Naval Institute Press, 1980.

Van de Water, Frederic F. *The Captain Called It Mutiny.* Ives Washburn, 1954.

Weed, Thurlow. *Autobiography of Thurlow Weed.* Houghton Mifflin, 1883.

White, Andrew Dickson. *The Autobiography of Andrew Dickson White.* 2 vols. Century, 1905.

Index